Beginning Nokia Apps Development

Qt and HTML5 for Symbian and MeeGo

Ray Rischpater
Daniel Zucker

Apress®

Beginning Nokia Apps Development: Qt and HTML5 for Symbian and MeeGo

ISBN-13 (pbk): 978-1-4302-3177-6

ISBN-13 (electronic): 978-1-4302-3179-0

Printed and bound in the United States of America (POD)

President and Publisher: Paul Manning
Lead Editor: Steve Anglin
Technical Reviewers: Nicholas Foo, Balagopal K.S., Daniel Rocha, Jakl Andreas, Petro Soininen and Wai M. Seto
Editorial Board: Steve Anglin, Mark Beckner, Ewan Buckingham, Gary Cornell, Jonathan Gennick, Jonathan Hassell, Michelle Lowman, Matthew Moodie, Duncan Parkes, Jeffrey Pepper, Frank Pohlmann, Douglas Pundick, Ben Renow-Clarke, Dominic Shakeshaft, Matt Wade, Tom Welsh
Coordinating Editor: Adam Heath
Copy Editor: Mark Watanabe
Compositor: MacPS, LLC
Indexer: BIM Indexing & Proofreading Services
Artist: April Milne
Cover Designer: Anna Ishchenko

Distributed to the book trade worldwide by Springer Science+Business Media, LLC., 233 Spring Street, 6th Floor, New York, NY 10013. Phone 1-800-SPRINGER, fax (201) 348-4505, e-mail orders-ny@springer-sbm.com, or visit www.springeronline.com.

For information on translations, please e-mail rights@apress.com, or visit www.apress.com.

Apress and friends of ED books may be purchased in bulk for academic, corporate, or promotional use. eBook versions and licenses are also available for most titles. For more information, reference our Special Bulk Sales–eBook Licensing web page at www.apress.com/info/bulksales.

The source code for this book is available to readers at www.apress.com.

This book is dedicated to my children, Eli and Annie; my parents, Donald and Dorothy; and my wonderful wife, MB; without any one of whom this book would not be possible.

—Dan

There is an irony in dedicating any book to my family, when time after time they patiently wait for me to put down the laptop and put away the manuscript, but there it is: this book is for Meg and Jarod.

—Ray

Contents at a Glance

Contents

Foreword

Developers have been a key component of Nokia's ecosystem since the first Symbian product launched nearly a decade ago. In the time since then, Symbian has risen to power the majority of the world's smartphones, in no part due to the creativity and resourcefulness of you, the developers of mobile applications.

Here at Forum Nokia, our goal has been and remains to empower you to create compelling and original applications for Nokia's mobile telephones and computers. In the last decade we've offered developer solutions to you for Symbian, Series 40 in Java, Series 60, Maemo (now MeeGo) and Qt. Along the way, as we supported freedom of choice, we've occasionally inadvertently added to the number of platforms you must manage when developing for the diverse array of mobile devices on the market today.

All of that has changed now with Qt. With Qt, Nokia promises that you need to write your application once, using Qt—Qt's libraries, C++, and Qt Meta-object Language (QML) if you choose—and target your application to all of Nokia's smartphones and mobile computers running Symbian or MeeGo. Understanding that many of you have existing or new applications written using HTML5, we also support an HTML5-compliant mobile browser to support the latest web applications running within the browser, giving you another path to your customers.

When Daniel and Ray approached Forum Nokia about a book on cross-platform software development for Nokia products, I knew immediately that the project would be a success, because the book was to meet your needs by sharing Nokia's developer story with you. Their past experience with Nokia's platforms—"eating our own dog food" as they developed solutions internally using the same tools you use—guarantees that they can answer your questions about the challenges you face in bringing your application ideas to reality on Nokia's platforms.

I can't wait to see what you create using Qt and HTML5.

Purnima Kochikar
Vice President, Forum Nokia & Developer Community

About the Authors

Ray Rischpater is an engineer and author with more than 15 years of experience writing about and developing for mobile computing platforms. During this time, Ray has participated in the development of Internet technologies for Java ME, Qualcomm BREW, Palm OS, Newton, and Magic Cap, as well as several proprietary platforms. Ray is currently employed as a senior research engineer at Nokia's Palo Alto Research Center. When not writing for or about mobile platforms, Ray enjoys hiking with his family and public service through amateur radio in and around the San Lorenzo Valley in northern California. Ray holds a bachelor's degree in pure mathematics from the University of California, Santa Cruz, and is a member of the IEEE, ACM, and ARRL. Previous books by Ray include *Software Development for the Qualcomm BREW Platform* (Apress, 2003), *Wireless Web Development, 2nd Edition* (Apress, 2002), *eBay Application Development* (Apress, 2004), and *Beginning Java ME Platform: from Novice to Professional* (Apress 2008).

Daniel Zucker currently works in Nokia's Palo Alto Research Center heading a research team focused on User Experience innovations. He has more than 20 years of experience in Silicon Valley, with 14 of those years in mobile. He has held a variety of industry positions, including CTO of ePocrates, the leader in handheld medical applications; Senior Director of Technology at ACCESS, maker of the market-leading Netfront mobile web browser; and Vice President of Engineering at Mobilearia, innovator in bringing mobile computing to the car. He holds bachelor's, master's, and Ph.D. degrees in electrical engineering from Stanford University. Daniel has written more than 20 professional publications and presentations. When not writing for or about mobile platforms, Daniel manages development of software for mobile platforms—and sometimes finds time to spend with his wife and children.

About the Technical Reviewers

Nicholas Foo
Title: Manager, APAC Technical Support and Consultancy
Nokia

Balagopal K.S.
Title: Technology Expert
Nokia

Daniel Rocha
Title: Solutions Consultant
Nokia

Jakl Andreas
Title: Senior Technical Consultant
Nokia

Petro Soininen
Title: Chief Engineer, Web Technologies
Nokia

Wai Seto
Title: Technical Marketing Manager
Nokia

Acknowledgments

It seems unfair that two of our names are on the cover, when so many have contributed to this book. First and foremost, we must thank our families, who provided support and encouragment throughout the project. Thanks especially to Annie, Eli, and Jarod, all of whom showed patience beyond their years as their fathers spent mornings, nights, and weekends poking away at their keyboards. Thanks also to our wives, MB and Meg, who both put up with the distraction and shouldered extra work when there was "just another chapter due" or "a quick e-mail from Apress that needed a response."

We owe a large debt to the staff at Apress itself, not least Adam Heath, Steve Anglin, Jeff Pepper, Brian MacDonald, and all the others who contributed to this book. Apress was exceedingly flexible as we adjusted the manuscript to best tell the story of Nokia's developer platform and tools, with several members of the project working nights and weekends to accommodate our need for changes and the publication schedule at the same time. Thank you all for your efforts.

We would also like to thank Wai Seto, Purnima Kochikar, Leslie Nakajima, and the others at Forum Nokia for their support. While right from the start this was a project for us outside our daily responsibilities at Nokia, their encouragement, review, and support has been instrumental, especially in ensuring alignment between our experience working with Nokia's tools and the information you need to develop your applications with those tools. (Of course, any errors that might remain are our responsibility, and we'll address them going forward on the Apress web site.)

From NRC, we 'd like to thank Kari Pulli for his helpful input and reviews, and especially thank John Shen, whose great support and encouragement came at a time when it was really needed.

Finally, we'd like to thank our fellow staff members so far left unmentioned, both in Nokia's Smartphones division and in the Nokia Research Center in Palo Alto. In our work with these folks, we learned much about Qt that we might not have learned alone; discussing our experiences with others greatly informed the process of writing this book. A special thanks to our peers at Nokia Research Center, who tolerated our frequent distractions in the last weeks of the effort, as work on the book bled into our office time.

Ray Rischpater and Daniel Zucker

Introduction

Popular acceptance of the smartphone has brought technology once only previously imagined in science fiction to today's reality. You can now use the small electronic device that used to be a simple cell phone to manage your calendar, listen to music, take pictures, provide maps and navigation, and browse the Internet—and still make a phone call. The technology that links you to the vast information store on the Internet any time and anywhere is perhaps the greatest revolution in information access the world has seen. Not only available to the developed nations where we expect to see high-end smartphones, these devices are also widely available in developing nations, where they are often the primary device people use to access the Internet.

The convergence of low-cost high performance processors, cheap memory, and wireless networking is only some of the technology that make the smartphone possible. The widespread use of open mobile computing platforms is the key to the smartphone's success. These platforms have opened the door for third parties (that's you!) to write software applications for these mobile computing platforms quickly and inexpensively.

Applications are no longer the exclusive domain of the device manufacturer. Now, anyone can imagine an application and implement it. These applications are with you everywhere that you carry your cell phone, and can take advantage of positioning information and wireless connectivity provided by the phone. It is this ability for anyone to create an application that has made the cell phone the truly wonderful device of tomorrow.

Why Should You Read This Book?

Even after nearly 40 years between us developing applications for mobile computing, we remain excited seeing what people have realized and looking at what the future holds. Mobile applications continue to influence the way people work and play in a way that very few market segments do. Whether you're just starting to develop mobile software, or if you've already been part of that revolution, this book is for you.

When first talking about this project, we agreed immediately that providing a technical foray of all the current mobile platforms today was simply too large a project. We also noticed the relative paucity of books that discuss Nokia's open platforms, a sad gulf given Nokia's worldwide market penetration. Through Nokia's contributions to the open platforms maintained by the Symbian Foundation and MeeGo, Nokia and other manufacturers using these platforms in their products make up more than 40% of the smartphone market worldwide, and show no signs of slowing. It was immediately obvious that what we needed to bring these platforms to your attention.

Once we realized this, choosing what to share was easy. A key strategy at Nokia is to leverage open platforms for their software developers across the entire smartphone product line, whether the underlying operating system is Symbian or MeeGo (a Linux derivative). To do this, Nokia provides both a web-based programming approach that lets you write local or networked applications using HyperText Markup Language (HTML)-JavaScript-Cascading Style Sheet (CSS), with access to native platform services such as messaging and geolocation, as well as more traditional application development stack based on Qt and C++ atop Symbian and MeeGo. As you read this book, you learn about both the web-based and Qt-based cross-platform approaches, and are equipped to select which makes the most sense for you in your endeavors.

In our writing, we assume that you're new to Nokia's open platforms, but not new to software development itself. We assume that you have some experience in software development. As we show you examples of both of HTML-JavaScript-CSS and C++ based development, you should have at least a nodding acquaintance with the technologies that lie beneath the web stack as well as C++. Rest assured, though, that we're careful to document anything tricky we've done that you might encounter along the way.

How Should You Read This Book?

Think of this book as a technical survey of what's available in the Nokia ecosystem for you. We understand that most of you don't read a technical book from cover-to-cover at first, but tend to dip in and out of chapters as their titles and your curiosity resonate. Although we understand that you're likely to do exactly that, we urge you to give a cursory reading of each chapter as you go along. Because much of the material we cover is loosely coupled (for example, you don't need to understand how a web application is deployed in order to begin using Qt), you can certainly open to any chapter and give it a go. Despite that, though, there's a coherent story throughout the book, and one of the things we aim to show you is how to pick which of Nokia's open platforms is best for your application.

This book has nine chapters, covering both the fundamentals of Qt using C++, as well as web technologies such as HTML5.

- In Chapter 1, we survey the Nokia ecosystem, starting with a brief history of Nokia's contribution to the mobile computing arena and looking ahead at the opportunities to come. You'll learn about Nokia's cross-platform strategy and how it fits together from the first line of portable code that you write to packaging and delivering your application through Nokia's Ovi platform.

- In Chapter 2, we discuss the all-important yet neglected topic of designing applications for today's mobile devices, looking at how people interact with their phones and what they expect from today's mobile applications.

- In Chapter 3, we provide a detailed tutorial of how to use the Nokia Qt Software Development Kit (SDK), a cross-platform environment for designing, implementing, building, and packaging Qt applications for both Symbian and MeeGo devices.

- In Chapter 4, we show you the fundamental concepts you need to understand when writing Qt applications. You learn about Qt's object model, how Qt uses signals and slots to communicate between objects, and aspects of Qt's cross-platform porting layer, as well as how to design and build applications using the model-view-controller paradigm in Qt.

- In Chapter 5, we continue your Qt education, moving on to more advanced topics, including how to integrate Qt-based C++ applications with web content, how to create your own widgets, and how to abstract user actions in your user interface.

- In Chapter 6, we explore QML, the Qt Meta-Object Language, and how you can create dynamic user interfaces using QML and JavaScript that bind back to C++ for high performance when you really need it.

- In Chapter 7, we shift gears and look closely at writing applications using HTML, JavaScript, and CSS for Nokia's WebKit-based web browser.

- In Chapter 8, we discuss how to prepare your application for deployment, looking at how Nokia's tools support your cross-platform integration and testing efforts.
- In Chapter 9, we discuss application deployment itself, looking at the options available to Nokia developers as they publish and market their applications through Nokia's Ovi Store.

Throughout the book, we use various implementations of a simple application, "Shake" which harvests information about recent earthquakes and displays the data using lists, detail views, and maps. This sample application—written in different implementations using both C++ using Qt and the Web—demonstrates many of the key concepts you need to understand, including model-view-controller design, XML parsing, and network access. Of course, these samples are all available electronically at the Apress web site, http://www.apress.com/.

A Word on Conventions We Use in This Book

As with other technical books, it helps to make a distinction between what's meant for you to read and what's meant for your computer to read.
Whole listings of code are set in the code style, like this:

```
typedef struct _Node
{
    /// Next node
    struct _Node *mpNext;
    /// Pointer to data for this node
    void *mpData;
    /// Pointer to any additional data for this node.
    void *mpMetaData;
} Node;
```

As with many coauthored works, we present our opinions and views in the first person using the collective pronouns "we" and "us" to refer to both of us. On occasion, where we want to emphasize an experience that belongs solely to one of us, we use singular pronouns, identifying the author after the first use of the singular pronoun.

Part I

Design

Introducing Nokia's Software Platform

One of the world's largest providers of smartphones, Nokia is at the heart of a global ecosystem of devices, services, and applications. With this success comes diversity. A handset that sells successfully in the United States or Europe may be too expensive to sell in developing markets, and a phone inexpensive enough in developing markets may seem primitive by the standards in Europe or the United States. This diversity can lead to fragmentation; fortunately, Nokia is well aware of this and responds to the threat of fragmentation with software development platforms that span product lines.

In this chapter, we take a brief look at Nokia's hardware and software platforms. Once you understand the platforms that Nokia offers, we discuss application distribution options when targeting Nokia products. After reading this chapter, you should be able to select the appropriate Nokia platform for your application and understand how you will deliver your application to others.

Why Nokia?

As we write this (early spring, 2010), Nokia's global device market share rests at 38%[*], consisting of 126.9 million phones for the fourth quarter of 2009. These devices run one of three platforms (more about Nokia's phone platforms in the section "Introducing Nokia's Phone Platforms" later in this chapter), letting Nokia dominate segments ranging from the emerging market, where price can remain a major concern, to markets in Europe and elsewhere demanding high-end, versatile computing devices.

Today, Nokia's portfolio includes not just mobile communications devices ranging from feature phone to mobile computers, but services under the Ovi brand, including

---

[*] Statistics taken from Nokia's press release at
www.nokia.com/results/Nokia_results2009Q4e.pdf.

messaging, contact management, mapping, photo sharing, and an application store. In addition to the Ovi brand, Nokia has launched several services to specific markets, such as Nokia Life Tools (providing agricultural and educational services to emerging markets) and Nokia Money, a mobile banking service built with Obopay.

Introducing Nokia's Hardware Platforms

To deliver compelling products to such a wide range of markets, Nokia must produce devices at a wide range of prices that reflect manufacturing and software development costs. With device costs tightly coupled to component costs, the key to producing inexpensive devices is to manage expenses on components. This in turn affects the software the product is able to run. To support this, Nokia divides its software portfolio into three software platforms: Series 40, Symbian, and MeeGo.

Series 40

The Series 40 platform is among the world's most widely used mobile device platforms. A low-cost platform requiring little by way of hardware, it was introduced in 2002 and remains a key platform for Nokia and its customers around the world.

Series 40 is a closed platform. No native SDK is available for you to write your own applications using the S40 native platform. Instead, Nokia provides support for both Java Mobile Edition (Java ME) and Adobe Flash Lite applications, and its browser permits the development of traditional server-side web applications as well. Because of this, we don't say much about Series 40 throughout this book.

Symbian

Symbian has a long history in the mobile marketplace, having originally been built as an integration of software contributed by Nokia, NTT DoCoMo, Sony Ericsson, and Symbian Ltd in 1998. Ten years to the day of Symbian Ltd's inception, Nokia announced its intent to acquire all Symbian Ltd shares and create the Symbian Foundation. Today, the nonprofit Symbian Foundation oversees the development and growth of the open source Symbian platform, working with contributions from companies and individuals around the world.

Nokia remains one of the major contributors to the Symbian source code base, even as Symbian remains the platform of choice for smartphones built by members of the Symbian Foundation and others. As component costs have dropped and contributors continue to optimize the software, Symbian is now able to run on lower-cost devices. This enables Nokia and others to produce an increasing number of Symbian devices for cost-conscious markets. as well as for more demanding users.

Symbian developers have a broad array of software platforms available, including:

- Qt, a C++ based cross-platform development environment.

- A web-based platform using HTML5, JavaScript, and CSS.

- Java ME, a dialect of the Java language and APIs suited for mobile devices.

- Adobe Flash, generally Flash Lite, a dialect of Flash suitable for mobile devices.

We discuss each of those platforms in the next section, "Choosing a Development Platform."

MeeGo

MeeGo is a Linux-based fusion of Nokia's Maemo and Intel's Moblin projects. Both Maemo and Moblin have strong Linux roots. Moreover, past Maemo releases have shipped to consumers on Nokia's family of Internet Tablets, the Nokia N770, N800, N810, as well as the N900 mobile computer. As we write this, MeeGo remains a platform for higher-end devices. That may change: MeeGo isn't just a phone platform, but a general Linux-based platform for phones, web-enabled tablets, set-top boxes, and other networked computing devices.

Because MeeGo is powered by Linux, developers can use either C++ with Qt or web standards to create applications for MeeGo. As with Symbian, we discuss developing for MeeGo throughout this book.

Choosing a Development Platform

Platform fragmentation is a serious challenge for mobile software developers. Already, developers are often asked to support multiple platforms—the market is the mobile market, not just users of a specific smartphone. Thus, many developers are tasked with writing an application not just for an iPhone, Android, or Nokia, but they also write for all three. Seemingly worse is that it appears Nokia isn't just one platform, but several.

To address this challenge, Nokia products support a number of development platforms across product lines. Key platforms include:

- Qt with C++

- Browser-based applications leveraging HTML5, JavaScript, and CSS

- Java ME

- Flash

Table 1–1 shows Nokia's phone platforms and the development options available for each. To summarize, Nokia provides Qt as the definitive platform for smartphone development, spanning both Symbian and MeeGo. For developers with legacy web applications or who have other strong reasons to use web standards (such as portability across multiple platforms), the Web, with support for advanced standards such as HTML5, is also an option. Java ME remains an option when you want to target the very low-cost Series 40 devices, and Flash remains available on Symbian and MeeGo.

> **NOTE:** Throughout the book, we focus on mobile-device software development for Qt and HTML5, as considerable documentation is already available that describes Java ME and Flash. If you're looking for resources for either of those platforms, consider *Beginning Java™ ME Platform* or *AdvancED Flash on Devices: Mobile Development with Flash Lite and Flash 10*, both available from Apress.

Table 1–1. *Open Software Technologies Across Nokia's Product Line*

Platform	Qt	HTML5	Java ME	Flash
Series 40				✓
Symbian	✓	✓	✓	✓
MeeGo	✓	✓		✓

Qt

Although you may not know it, many well regarded applications use Qt, an open cross-platform framework acquired by Nokia through its acquisition of Trolltech in 2008; Google Earth, KDE, Opera, and Skype all use Qt to ease porting between multiple platforms. Qt as a framework for portable computing devices is not new either, having been used in mobile computing, running Linux and Window Mobile devices for several years.

As you learn in Chapters 4, 5 and 6, Qt provides a broad set of abstractions above native hardware, including:

- Help with memory management in C++ through its use of smart pointers, owned objects, and shared data between objects with copy-on-write.

- A lightweight meta-object framework implemented using the C preprocessor and C++ to permit run-time type detection and message dispatching.

- Not one, but *two* graphics frameworks, one based on widget hierarchies and the other on scene-based rendering and transformation of viewable items.

- Cross-platform wrappers for network, file system, and other operating system services.

- Access to hardware capabilities using either Qt Mobility or access to native Symbian APIs to use the camera, location services, access contact records, and other native operations.

- QtWebKit, a wrapper for WebKit to permit Qt applications to load and render Web content.

Qt is available on both Symbian and MeeGo products and is a good choice for your application if:

- You have existing C, C++, or Qt code from another platform that you want to bring to Nokia products.

- Your application needs to squeeze out every bit of performance from the platform.

- You intend to port your application to other platforms in the future.

On the other hand, if one or more of the following are true, you should take a good look at the Web:

- Your application's content is primarily web-centric.

- You are providing a thin shell application that uses Representational State Transfer (REST) or similar web-based interfaces to provide a mobile client for a server-side application.

- You are targeting your application for other web-based environments, such as desktop widgets.

Now and in the future, Qt is the primary platform when developing software for Nokia's smartphones. Engineered to provide high performance across Nokia's products, it offers a highly portable environment that lets you target multiple devices through a single SDK, requiring only recompilation when moving your application between Symbian and MeeGo.

HTML5

Nokia has been a strong supporter of WebKit, the popular layout engine behind most of today's mobile web browsers. WebKit fully supports HTML, JavaScript, and CSS, giving you a state-of-the-art web-rendering stack for your web-based applications. Nokia remains committed to supporting open web standards, including HTML5 in the built-in browser used to access the Web. You should consider using web technologies when:

- You are porting a browser-based web application (perhaps written to support other devices as well) from a server to run locally on a device.

- Your application sources content from a web server using either HTML or XML

- You are fluent in HTML, CSS, and JavaScript and do not have the luxury of learning another development platform, such as Qt.

On the other hand, if one or more of the following is true, you may want to use Qt instead:

- Your application must meet tight performance constraints, such as a graphics-intensive game.

- You're porting parts of an existing C or C++ application from other platforms.

- You also want to deploy your application on other vendors' hardware platforms that provide Qt.

The Web remains a crucial component people use to access information using mobile devices, and Nokia is fully committed to supporting it through a high-end mobile browser that supports existing and the emerging HTML 5 standard.

Hybrid Applications

Before we move on, it's worth pointing out that you can wrap your web content within a Qt application, too. You can do this because Qt supports HTML, JavaScript, and CSS through its inclusion of QtWebKit, a port of the popular WebKit web environment to Qt. You should consider this approach when:

- You want to provide the user with the experience of downloading and installing an application, but your content is largely written using web technologies.

- Your application has key dynamic content available via the Web that should be presented to the user.

Distributing Your Application

Picking a software platform and writing your application is only the start. Once the application is written, there's the question of distribution: how do you get your application into the hands of prospective users, and how do you monetize those transactions? Nokia platforms give you a variety of options, not least being the Ovi Store, available on all new devices and a surprising number of existing ones.

Distributing applications to smartphone users is nothing new; both Symbian and Maemo devices for several years have enabled you to install applications from other sources, including the Web. This is an example of *off-deck* distribution—that is, distribution from a source other than the network operator.

Off-deck can sound simple—you may now be thinking, "Oh, I'll just put an installer for my application on our web site"—but it can quickly grow out of hand from the business perspective. Application purchases and subsequent registration may need special handling, and you may not even be equipped to process payments within your web site. Moreover, several companies are available to carry and sell your application off-deck, and to maximize your reach in the market you may choose to contract with one or more of those companies for distribution as well. While web and SMS delivery of your application is possible with these companies, you usually will need to execute separate agreements with each off-deck distributor you choose.

On-deck, as opposed to off-deck, is listing your application with the network operators within their application distribution platforms. Nearly every operator now has either a web site or native application that lets consumers browse and purchase applications; this is the "deck." Landing your application in an operator's store takes an agreement with the carrier, which generally takes a percentage of application sales from its site or store application. Carriers typically pay you for your content and regularly provide details about application sales. Some carriers can give you near real-time sell-through statistics, letting you measure the results of advertising campaigns or other marketing efforts.

Participating in the carrier's distribution can be helpful if your application is well placed on the deck and well promoted. As with off-deck, you can usually distribute your application through more than one carrier, although then you need to have business relationships with more than one carrier. If you're seeking to launch an application with global presence, acquiring these relationships can be both challenging and time-consuming.

An ideal way to cover multiple markets is to list your application with Nokia in its Ovi Store. The store is an application and media store that supports more than a hundred devices with listings in 30 languages as I write this. To facilitate monetization of your application, the store itself is integrated with 66 different operators in 19 different countries, permitting integrated mobile billing; in areas without this integration, your customers can remit payment to Nokia via their credit card. The Ovi Store complements application promotion, such as from your web site, too; you can use Ovi Store's marketing tools to create banners that deep-link to your content in the Ovi store.

We discuss the process of preparing your application for deployment and making money from sales of your application in Chapter 9.

Wrapping Up

Nokia's product portfolio spans the gamut of prices, with sales numbers in the tens to hundreds of millions each quarter. Nokia's broad and deep reach around the world drives a software market for almost any mobile application developer.

To address the myriad markets where Nokia sells handsets, Nokia groups devices into three platforms: Series 40, Symbian, and MeeGo. One platform, Qt running on Symbian, lets you target mid-range and premium (Symbian and MeeGo) devices using C++ and a robust porting layer. Nokia's support for HTML5 and other web standards leverages your knowledge of HTML, JavaScript, and CSS to develop hybrid and web-based environments using the latest web technologies. Most applications can be easily constructed using tools from either platform, letting you choose the platform that most closely meets your skills and prior projects. Using Qt requires skills in C++, but provides the highest possible performance, while the web route provides more-than-adequate performance with the added benefit that since it's based on W3C standards, porting from other platform's web-based applications isn't difficult.

In the next chapter, we look at what you need to know to get started designing your application for Qt and HTML5 on Symbian and MeeGo. Chapter 2 is preliminary information for all developers new to mobile software; if you're ready to dive in and begin developing your application, skip ahead to Chapter 3, where we introduce the various tools at your disposal.

Designing Your Application

Design, followed by develop and distribute, is the first of three steps you must go through to create your Nokia application. In this section we talk about design. This chapter covers the theory and practice of designing your mobile application. We discuss how designing for mobile is different from the desktop, present the steps in the design process, and then go into some practical details for designing your application.

This chapter cannot even come close to covering design for mobile completely—not even a full book dedicated to the topic would suffice. To comprehensively cover design in detail, a university level master's course might begin to do the topic some justice.

Our goal for this chapter is to give you, the application developer, enough of an overview of design so that you can write your first application well. After that this material can serve as a framework upon which to continue your study.

In the next chapter of this book, we do some hands-on exploration of the tools you will use to actually design and later develop your application.

Now, let's get started.

Designing for Mobile

Designing a mobile application is different from designing a desktop application. Yes, both applications run on computers and both are built using technologies such as the Web or C++. Even the underlying platforms are remarkably similar: the mobile device of today has virtually the same amount of volatile memory, non-volatile storage, network bandwidth, and processing power as the desktop of only a few years ago. Yet mobile is different. The user expects different things from an application on his mobile device as from his desktop. To understand this better, we need to think about *User Context*.

User Context

What is the user doing when he is running an application? How is the mobile device used differently from the desktop computer? What special scenarios arising from mobile must you consider different from the desktop? These are all questions considered in User Context.

User Context is consideration for what the user is doing and where he is when he is using your application. The mobile device is different because it is mobile. It can be used in noisy, crowded environments. It may be used in bright environments. The user may be in a situation where he has time to interact with his device only for a small amount of time and only with partial attention and not the long interaction timeframe typical with a desktop.

Mobile applications, therefore, are typically designed to do one task or activity well. The user may be doing something else while using your application. Consider this when designing.

Mobile Interaction Considerations

What else do you need to keep in mind when designing your mobile application? Obviously, the mobile device has a much smaller display than a desktop device. How do you need to change your application layout and interaction paradigms to accommodate this difference in user interaction? Input methods are usually different for a mobile device. How will this impact your application design?

How does the environment affect how the user interacts with his device? Is this application intended to be used when one-handed operation is critical? Are you expecting the user to quickly check for a particular piece of information, or will the user be engaged in a protracted interaction?

Furthermore, the device is always on and always connected. Your application can be designed to send notifications to the user at odd times. Because the device is with the user all the time, he will get the notification at any time. The device demands instant interaction, so long wait times are not acceptable.

The application needs a consistent style when interacting with the user. It can't force the user to do extra thinking or remember additional things. The mobile device should be an easy-to-use extension of daily life—not a mandate to memorize different interaction methods.

Finally, the device is extremely personal. A smartphone is typically used by a single individual and not shared. It should, therefore, be easy to customize and personalize. The mobile device can quickly become an extension of the user; an integral fashion accessory, it is now an inseparable element critical to his daily routine.

Technical Considerations

There are technical considerations for mobile design as well. Though mobile devices are similar in specifications to the desktops of yesterday, they are still not as powerful as today's desktops. You must therefore keep an eye toward the limited resources available for mobile. Memory, both dynamic and non-volatile (analogous to a PC's hard drive) are limited. The CPU is also typically less powerful than that available on a desktop.

When designing your application, you must take these limited resources into account. In choosing algorithms, try to select those that require less memory. When designing data structures, avoid wasted memory. It is critical to spend the extra time upfront to ensure your memory allocation is as efficient as possible.

You also need to design your application so that it can handle situations when such device resources as memory are low or exhausted. Typically this is implemented by handling a signal or message from the system telling you that the system is out of resources. When this happens, your application should make an attempt to free up resources by cleaning up any unnecessary memory usage. You also need to handle the case where a forced application shutdown is imminent. In this case, the application should save state if necessary and prepare to exit immediately.

Bandwidth is also limited on a mobile device. When designing your application, be efficient about how data is requested over the network. Request only the data you really need. Can you prefetch data so that when the user accesses it, the download appears much faster than it actually is?

Additionally, you must code for corner cases not always present in the desktop world. On a mobile device network, coverage is frequently lost and regained. You need to ensure your application gracefully accommodates an unexpected switch into offline mode.

Another common case is low battery. Your application can query battery status and take appropriate action when the level is too low. You can send a message to the user, for example, or switch the application to a mode where less power is consumed. This is not always possible but, depending on the application, it may be possible to trade performance for less battery usage, such as reducing the framerate of video playback application. Below is some example code using Qt (from the Qt Mobility Project) where battery status is monitored and an appropriate message is sent to the user.

```
void Dialog::displayBatteryStatus(QSystemDeviceInfo::BatteryStatus status)
{
    QString msg;
        switch(status) {
        case QSystemDeviceInfo::BatteryCritical:
            {
                msg = " Battery is Critical (4% or less), please plug in the charger.";
                QMessageBox::critical(this,"QSystemInfo",msg);
            }
            break;
        case QSystemDeviceInfo::BatteryVeryLow:
            {
```

```
        msg = "Battery is Very Low (10%), please plug in the charger soon";
        QMessageBox::warning(this,"QSystemInfo",msg);
    }
    break;
case QSystemDeviceInfo::BatteryLow:
    {
        msg = "Battery is Low (40% or less)";
        QMessageBox::information(this,"QSystemInfo",msg);
    }
    break;
case QSystemDeviceInfo::BatteryNormal:
    {
        msg = "Battery is Normal (greater than 40%)";
        QMessageBox::information(this,"QSystemInfo",msg);
    }
    break;
    };
}
```

So you see, in designing mobile applications, you need to consider a range of factors. The device is physically different, both in terms of physical characteristics, such as display size or input methods, and the components of the device, such as memory and processor. Furthermore, the environment in which the user interacts with it is different. These are all factors that must be considered when designing your application.

Cultural Considerations

Consider designing for different cultures when planning your application. Obvious cultural factors include different languages and different methods for text entry. But different cultures also can have significantly different design aesthetics. Remember this when designing your application.

Even the use of color can have cultural significance. In Western cultures, white commonly connotes freshness and purity; in Eastern cultures, white can be a symbol for death. Fundamental symbolism can be radically different across cultures. Testing with real users is the best way to avoid these pitfalls.

Forum Nokia describes characteristics for four of the major mobile markets—China, Europe, India, and the US.

China is a market composed of heavy mobile users. There is more emphasis on leisure time use of the mobile, and user interfaces tend to be more busy and crowded. Chinese users also are typically heavy users of the mobile internet.

Europe is a more mature market for mobile. The market is composed of many different countries, ethnicities, and languages so there can be much variation. Generally the design aesthetic in Europe calls for simplicity, clarity, and a logical flow.

India is a diverse marketplace with huge potential. It is the largest market for entry-level devices. Therefore, there is a preference for applications with lightweight technical requirements. The mobile phone can be the user's first real contact with technology. Like China, the "more is more" principle applies.

The US is a massive mobile market recently caught up with the rest of the world in terms of mobile data and mobile application usage. American pop culture spreads rapidly around the world, making the US an epicenter of new ideas and styles. Americans appreciate ease of use, so that a long list of features sometimes is less important. Americans also appreciate a good visual and tactile experience.

More detailed analysis of these regions can be found in a series of four Design Update articles from Forum Nokia at:

`http://library.forum.nokia.com/topic/Design_and_User_Experience_Library/GUID-25ACF758-7658-4A84-9300-93EAD530D33D.html`

The Design Process

Now let's talk about how to actually design the application. It is a big project, so how do we get started? In this section, we discuss a formal set of steps that you can go through to design your application. This section is based on information presented by Forum Nokia. More complete information can be obtained from the web site:

`www.forum.nokia.com/Design/Design_process/`

When designing your application, you do not need to follow every one of these steps, but it is still useful to understand the full range of tools at your disposal when designing your application.

Forum Nokia presents a process with these key steps:

- Getting started
- Design research
- Conceptual design
- Interaction design and prototyping
- Visual and information design
- Testing and evaluation

Getting Started

Why are you building the product? In this phase you outline the basics to understand what you want to do and why you are doing it. Did you identify a market need that is not currently being met, or are you planning to improve a product that already exists.

This is also a good time to start choosing your technology approach. Will you use a native SDK like Qt, or will you use HTML5? Is there a new technology that now makes things possible that weren't before?

At this early stage, you should understand what you are trying to accomplish, as well as the constraints you are under—both business and technical—in order to get it done.

You should understand your target user and the marketplace you are aiming for. You should also learn about competitors and why your product is better than theirs.

In the next section we talk about research, which will help you better understand the information you need to move forward.

Design Research

Why do research? It can help you generate or evaluate ideas, clarify your product's strengths or potential, understand strengths and weaknesses of competing products, and understand how your user will use your product.

There are two main types of design research: quantitative and qualitative. Quantitative research focuses on gathering and analyzing numerical data. The output is usually in the form of charts, tables, or graphs. An example of quantitative research data collection is counting the number of times a user does a particular task during the day, such as checking his calendar appointments.

Qualitative research attempts to cast a wider net and gain a more holistic understanding of how your product will be used. Some techniques commonly used in performing qualitative research are observation, interviews, and photographic studies.

Observation, as the name sounds, means to observe someone doing something. This can be as simple as sitting on a park bench watching how people interact with their mobile devices. Or it can be more structured observation, such as giving the user a particular task assignment and seeing how he accomplishes it. For example, you might ask, "How would you view the vacation photos you took last summer?" Structured observation can involve shadowing, following behind someone in their day-to-day activities, or undercover study. In an undercover study, you pretend to be someone for the sake of observation—a bank customer, for example, to better understand the process of creating a new account.

Interviewing means talking to people and asking about how they perform a task or use a product. When interviewing, remember that what people say and what they do can be very different. Some useful techniques for interviewing are story telling or desk tours. In story telling, you ask the participant to walk you through some of his activities as though he is telling you a story. In a desk tour you examine part of the participant's life much as you might the contents of his office desk. You walk through each part in detail to try to gain an insight into the overall desk situation.

Photographic studies mean taking pictures of people, places, and things you are interested in. Afterwards you can group the photos to make observations and draw conclusions.

It is also possible to gain much information by researching on the Internet or reading documentation. This is especially useful for gathering market data and understanding competitor's products. Remember, though, that reading information is no replacement for getting out and talking to real people.

Remember to document your findings. Also, it is good practice to involve the project stakeholders in the research process as much as possible from the very beginning.

Conceptual Design

Now that we've completed our research, let's start designing our app. Conceptual design is the stage where you start thinking about your application's main features and flows.

Brainstorming is one technique that can be a good place to start. It also gives you a chance to involve your entire team in the creative process. To brainstorm, gather all team members and give them 10 to 15 minutes to design on their own. Then members share their ideas. In brainstorming, it is important to make everyone feel comfortable to share ideas no matter how crazy. It is also a good way to generate new ideas and can foster a sense of ownership and buy-in from the team.

Sketching is a useful technique for communicating ideas. Pick some of the top ideas from brainstorming and develop those further using sketching. Sketches are quick drawings that begin to bring the product to life in a visual sense. They can also describe technical aspects, such as flows or diagrams.

The next step is to define scenarios, also called use cases. Scenarios tell a story of how your product will be used. A scenario for an e-mail application, for example, might be "create a new e-mail and send it to someone in my contacts list." These are very useful in understanding how all the parts fit together to allow the user to accomplish a particular task. They are also useful to help team members understand how the product will really be used. This will help the developer make better decisions when designing and building the product.

The goal of conceptual design is to synthesize business goals, initial ideas, and research into a product idea. If you have a good idea of what the product is and how it fits into the marketplace, then it is time to move to the next step in the process, interaction design and prototyping.

Interaction Design and Prototyping

Interaction design is the next step, a point at which your product or application is designed in greater detail. Ideally interaction design should be coupled with prototyping. A prototype is an early implementation of your product or application, one that can begin to allow real interactions. Prototyping allows you to validate, test, and then evolve your design based on real feedback.

Interaction design is the act of defining the touch points, behaviors, and interactions involved with a product. It can include specification of hardware and software controls and affordances; system logic, including background processes and states; and system feedback, such as notifications and alerts. It can also include manipulation models, such as touch or gestures, animations, sounds, and vibrations.

Good interaction design encompasses these elements:

- Consistency
- Trustworthiness
- Cleverness
- Responsiveness
- Playfulness and pleasure

Consistency is important to ease the user's cognitive load. Inconsistencies force the user to think and remember more than necessary, contributing to a more painful user experience. It is important to build a level of trust with users. Otherwise, they will not trust your company or brand for future iterations.

Your product should be clever. How do you define a clever product? That's a good question with a difficult answer. How does one define a beautiful painting or a fragrant flower? This gets to the essence of design—yes, design has core elements that need to be taught and studied, but truly great design is like great art. Throughout this chapter we give rules and guidelines for building great products, but I can give step-by-step guidance for creating a clever product only as easily as I could give step-by-step guidance for creating a great painting or sculpture.

Lack of responsiveness can cause the user to wonder if the application is broken. Most times the perception of responsiveness is as important as the application's actual responsiveness. So even if your application takes some time to perform a task such as accessing the network or doing a long calculation, it is important to give the user an indication that the application is doing something and still able to take user input. And lastly, playfulness is important even for adults. Remember that a mobile device is very personal and usually carried 24 hours a day. All work and no play does indeed make Jack a dull boy.

Documentation

Documentation is very important in interaction design. It is useful to communicate your product vision and helpful to clarify your thoughts when the ideas are being formed. Documentation specifies how your application should work. It should include descriptions of application architecture, flows, states, views, data structures and bindings, components, and content, such as strings, tool tips, and alert text.

Documentation is useful only if people read and understand it, so it should be concise and should communicate ideas you are trying to express. Remember that a picture is worth a thousand words, so that it is often better to communicate your ideas with pictures or diagrams, rather than only text. Some useful types of documentation are navigation maps, task flow diagrams, wireframes, and prototypes.

Navigation maps are one useful form of navigation, like the one seen in Figure 2–1. Navigation maps show the hierarchical structure of your application and document the interconnections between views.

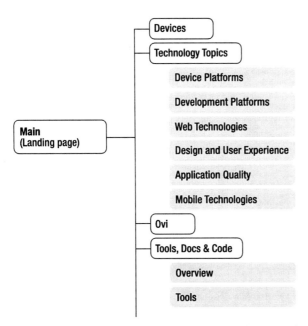

Figure 2–1. *An example navigation map (courtesy Forum Nokia)*

Task flow diagrams (shown in Figure 2–2) are another type of diagram used to document applications. These diagrams document the flow a user can go through to achieve a certain task. This drawing usually includes decision points where the flow can change based on system state or the user's input.

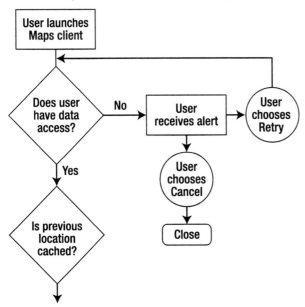

Figure 2–2. *An example task flow diagram (courtesy Forum Nokia)*

Wireframes (shown in Figure 2–3) present a visual representation for how the application will look without specifying the visual or industrial design. Wireframes show placement of functional and structural visual elements, such as buttons, check boxes, input fields, scroll bars, and so on. Wireframes show the different application views and also how the views are related to each other.

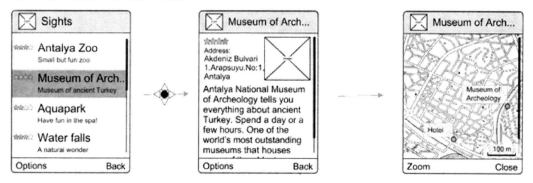

Figure 2–3. *An example wireframe diagram (courtesy Forum Nokia)*

Flowella

Prototypes are perhaps the most useful method to document your interaction design. They can be used to document your current design and as a means to iterate and expand the design for the future. Prototypes should be quick to build and quick to modify, so that new ideas can be evaluated in a timely manner. A complex prototype can quickly become useless if the design has evolved rapidly beyond what the prototype can show.

Instead of one large all-encompassing prototype, it may be more efficient to make multiple smaller prototypes that focus on a single feature or experience of the application. Furthermore, prototypes do not need to be actual working code. Some application behavior can be represented and explored using a static visual representation, such as PowerPoint or even drawings on pieces of paper.

Flowella is an interaction design and prototyping tool available from Forum Nokia. It is meant for designers and other nonprogrammers to quickly prototype and interact with UIs during the design and development process. The tool allows you to quickly and easily add navigation and flow information to visual assets, then play with the resulting prototype on a desktop simulator or on an actual mobile device using Flash, web widgets, or even QML. The graphical assets can be anything from simple sketches or wireframes to production-ready artwork. Flowella allows an easy creation of device-ready prototypes, so it is a cool way to quickly generate lots of real-world interaction data.

Let's take a more detailed look at Flowella by walking through an example. Let's imagine we want to design an application to look at data of recent earthquakes. We probably want to see all the recent quakes displayed in a list. When you touch a single quake, we want to go to a details screen that shows more information about that particular event. Finally, it would be cool to display a map with the location and magnitude of all the quakes. Let's call the app Shake. We can get the data from USGS web feeds, but for now we're only worried about the UI We'll talk more about this application when we implement it using first the QtSDK and again using HTML5. In this section, let's focus on the visual and interaction design of Shake.

Installing Flowella

Let's get started by downloading and installing Flowella. You can get it from Forum Nokia here:

```
www.forum.nokia.com/info/sw.nokia.com/id/7557c13f-0b43-4805-85ce-
8414bfbade57/Flowella.html
```

Flowella is built using Adobe Air, so you need to make sure Air is installed as well. If you don't yet have it on your PC, download Air from here:

```
http://get.adobe.com/air/
```

Flowella includes the application, a short tutorial, and an example podcast application. Let's launch Flowella and take a quick look at the UI. The Flowella UI contains five work areas:

- Library
- Workspace
- Toolbox
- Top menu bar
- Preview window

Flowella is shown in Figure 2–4 below.

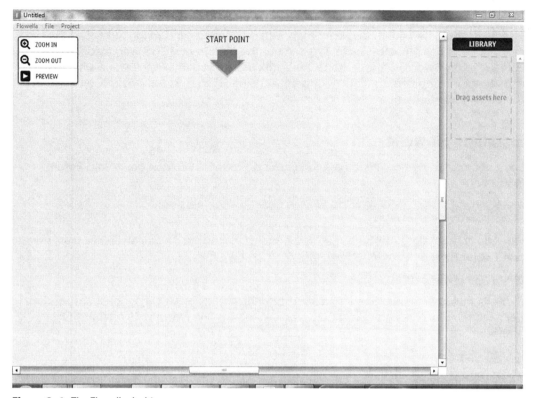

Figure 2–4. *The Flowella desktop.*

The library is displayed on the right side of the Flowella workspace. This contains the graphic images that you will drag

 into Flowella. These images are then dragged into the workspace to construct the flows. The workspace is the large area in the center of UI where you arrange and connect your views. The toolbox is a floating command box with buttons to zoom in, zoom out, and preview. The top menu bar gives you access to things like saving your project and adjusting project settings. Last, the preview window opens as a separate popup window when you launch a Flowella preview.

Now let's get started designing Shake.

Create Views

First we need to create our views. In Flowella each view is a graphical representation of the display. This can be production-ready art or a simple sketch that has been digitized with a scanner. Flowella applications do not contain any application logic; it is designed only to prototype user interactions. Flowella can understand images formats in png or jpg. For Shake, we have four views:

- List view

■ Selector view

■ Map view

■ Detail view

These four views are shown in Figure 2–5 below. You should save these images using an easy remember names such as List, Select, Map, and Details.

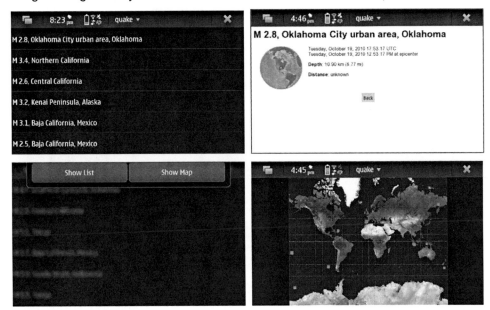

Figure 2–5. *The four views used in the Shake Flowella example.*

Create the Project

Let's now create a new project. Select File ➤ New from the top menu. Now, using the file explorer, drag the images representing the application views that we created above and drop them into the Flowella library. Do this for all four images.

Next, drag the images from the library to the Flowella workspace. Let's start by dragging only the list view. When you define a Flowella project, you need to tell Flowella which view to launch when the app is started. You do this by dragging the Start Point in the Flowella workspace (the Start Point is visible in Figure 2–4 previously) to the view where you would like the app to launch from. For this example, drag the Start Point to the list view. Finally, drag the details view to the workspace. Now we are ready to connect the two views together.

Create the Connections

The next step is to connect the views together. This is done by defining hotspots for each image. A hotspot is an area that when pressed by the user causes another view to open. To create a hotspot, first click the view where you would like to create your hotspot. This should cause the view to become much larger so you can see the detail more easily. Next, use the mouse to click-and-drag to define a rectangular hotspot area. Let's do this by creating a hotspot around the first list item in the list view. This is the item labeled Oklahoma City Urban Area. After the hotspot is created, it should look something like Figure 2–6.

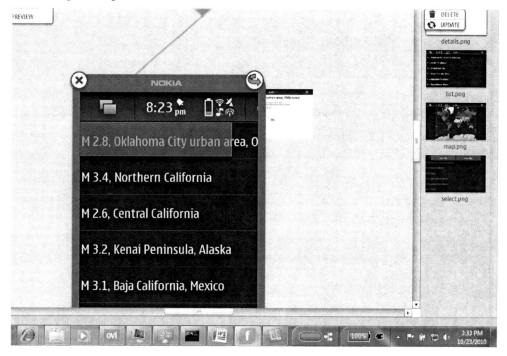

Figure 2–6. *Creating a hotspot around the Oklahoma City Urban Area list item*

After the hotspot is created, mouse over the hotspot to make the controls visible. The hotspot has three main controls: a button to delete the hotspot, seven resize handles that can be dragged to resize the hotspot, and a connector. The connector is the dot with an arrow in the center of the hotspot. This is what you use to assign an action to the hotspot. These controls are shown in Figure 2–7.

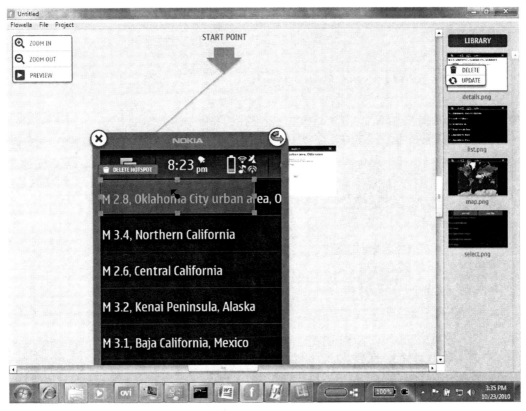

Figure 2–7. *Hotspot controls.*

To tell Flowella which view to go to when the hotspot is touched, click on the connector dot and drag the area to the view that you would like to be activated when the touch spot is touched. For our example, drag the touch spot for the Oklahoma City quake to the details view.

> **TIP:** When the view is enlarged, it sometimes will cover the view you would like to indicate as the target. When this happen simply grab the enlarged view by its gray border and drag it out of the way to expose the intended target.

Note that because Flowella does not allow any kind of application logic or data processing, we must manually link one particular item to a static image of details for that item. This is because Flowella is targeted at prototyping visual interactions and navigation flow, not full application functionality.

We have created one connection: from a list item to the details view. Now let's complete the application flow by creating the following additional connections:

- Connect the title bar of the list view to the selector view.
- Connect the title bar of the details view to the selector view.

- Connect the back button of the details view to the list view.

- Connect the map and list buttons of the selector view to the map and list view, respectively.

- Create a hotspot on the map over Oklahoma City. Connect this to the details view.

Your completed flow should look as shown in Figure 2–8.

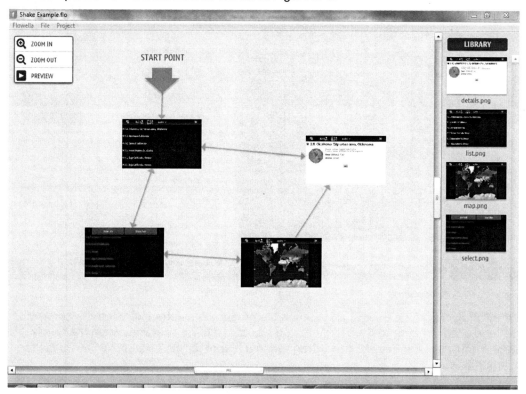

Figure 2–8. *The completed Shake prototype in Flowella.*

Now click on the Preview button in the Toolbox. The preview popup window should open and let you try your application interaction. Try it out. What do you think? Is this the type of interaction you would like to see for Shake?

Export and Interact

One of the coolest things about Flowella is that it is so easy to preview your application on a real device. To do this, you need to export your prototype to a format that can be installed on a device. The supported formats are Flash, QML, and web widget.

Exporting your prototype is quite simple. Go to the top menu and select File ➤ Export. Here, select the file type you would like to export to: Flash, WRT (the Symbian web runtime widget format), or QML (also known as Qt Quick and discussed later in this book). Select a location and save the files on your PC. That's it. Copy the files to your device and you're ready to go.

> **TIP:** When exporting to Flash, make sure to copy all the files to your device. There are a number of files created, including images, XML files, and a SWF file. Make sure to copy all of these to your device. Just click to run.

> **TIP:** When exporting to WRT format, the files are saved as a .wgz formatted file. This file type can be run on Symbian, but not MeeGo devices.

Visual and Information Design

Visual and information design determines what your application looks like. It includes designing the layouts, copyrighting, colors, fonts, graphics, icons, animations, and transitions of your application. The visual aspect of your application is often the first thing the user notices, so it is important. Strong information design promotes strong usability of your application. It can highlight and prioritize critical elements, and help clarify the purpose of UI controls. A beautiful product can enhance your company's brand and image and will definitely help to market your product.

Detailed tips on visual design are presented below. This section is based on information presented by Forum Nokia. More complete information can be found on the Web here:

```
http://library.forum.nokia.com/topic/Design_and_User_Experience_Library/GUID-CB5D4F7A-
CA69-49E6-839D-2F7E30641498.html
```

Screen Size

When designing the visual appearance of your application, consider screen size. Depending on the device you are targeting, screen sizes can come in a wide variety of resolutions from 120 x 160 (or less) up to 360 x 640.

Furthermore the physical size of the display is also very important. Consider the three devices shown in Figure 2–9. All have the same resolution of 320px x 240px, but because of the difference in screen size, graphics displayed on one can look very different on another.

Figure 2–9. *These three devices have the same resolution, but different physical screen sizes (courtesy Forum Nokia)*

Consider all possible display resolutions and dimensions when designing the visuals for your application. Test on real devices as much as possible.

Scalable UI

Design your UI to be scalable. Strive to support different screen dimensions to support multiple current and future devices. Use platform components as much as possible. This not only helps ensure that your application will scale automatically, but also ensures that you are using the common design language expressed by the platform-common components.

Selecting the Correct Orientation

Your application can be designed to use either landscape or portrait orientation. This is an application specific decision for how best to present to the user. For example, a movie application is best shown in landscape, while an e-mail application is best used in portrait.

You can also support both orientations and let the user decide which view is best.

Full-Screen Usage

Use full-screen mode where appropriate for your application. Full-screen mode means your application takes up the entire screen and does not show any system chrome, such as battery-level or signal strength indicators or application title bars. In some cases, such as watching a movie or web browsing, it is desirable to use all available screen real estate.

There are three rules for full-screen usage:

1. Use full-screen mode when appropriate.

2. The UI can look different.

3. The visual look may vary, but the application behavior should remain the same.

Figure 2–10 below shows an example of the Symbian photo application. In this case the application designers felt it was important to use the entire screen area to display the photo. The UI does not look like the standard Symbian UI: there is no header and the controls do not look like standard Symbian buttons or menus. This is a good illustration where full-screen usage is desired to present great photo viewing to the user, yet the application functionality is not compromised.

Figure 2–10. *The Symbian photo application is an example of full-screen usage*

Fonts

Mobile devices typically have limited font support. There is usually one font installed on the device referred to as the native or device font. When using your browser to display information, consider that font styling may be limited to the basics of size, color, and mode (such as bold or italic). Availability of multiple fonts is becoming increasingly common, but should not be taken for granted.

Pay attention to font size when creating screen designs such as wireframes on your desktop. Incorrectly sized fonts can easily cause your layout to appear different from how it will appear on the device.

Colors

When selecting colors, consider that the mobile device may be used in bright light or viewed from different angles and orientations. In order to accommodate this, a good rule of thumb is to select colors emphasizing strong contrast. Another consideration is power consumption: on devices with Organic Light Emitting Diode (OLED) displays, brighter colors consume more power, and darker colors use less, so there's a tradeoff to be made in selecting colors for contrast.

Avoid using gradients for backgrounds since complex gradients may not appear as expected.

Color representation can vary across different mobile devices. In working with brand managers or marketing departments, set expectations that color accuracy may vary. It is difficult to match Pantone colors on a mobile display. As before, test on as many actual devices as possible.

Graphics

Levels of graphic format support can vary, so plan your implementation carefully. Think about image formats in the design phase. Use scalable image formats such as SVG-T where possible.

An informative presentation with tips on optimizing graphics for mobile can be found here:

```
http://sw.nokia.com/id/09102b7a-f5fb-4e1f-b3d0-
e813d6d7c54b/Graphic_Optimisation_v1_0_en.pdf
```

Animations

Animations can be useful to guide the user's eye and to help navigation, but they can also be distracting and slow the user from completing his objective. Be careful to use animations only when the net result is positive for the user's experience.

Additionally, be aware that animations can cause your application to perform poorly.

Testing and Evaluation

The last step in the design process is testing and evaluation. Until your product is tested with real users on real devices, you cannot know for certain whether it is successful. The mantra here is test early and test often. Test on real devices. Test with real users. Iterate until your product is perfect!

For more information on testing, we will return to this topic in more detail later in Chapter 8.

Additional Topics: Gestalt and Unity

Gestalt is a German word meaning shape or form. Within the context of design, gestalt refers to a design's wholeness, which is more than the sum of its parts. Gestalt emphasizes how the different parts of a design interrelate. Key principles of gestalt perceptual organization are:

- Similarity: refers to how objects look. Items that appear similar will be naturally grouped together.

- Proximity: refers to where objects are located. Items that appear near each other will be grouped together.

- Repetition: a repetition in positioning, size, color, or shape creates a natural unity

- Figure-to-ground relationship: discusses the relationship between the figure, or foreground, and the ground, or background. The eye naturally focuses on the figure, but it is important to keep the figure and ground balanced.

- Closure: the mind supplies the missing elements to naturally complete an image or grouping.

- Continuation: means that once you start looking in a particular direction you will continue looking in that direction until you see something significant.

We don't have space to cover the gestalt principles in detail in this book, but an excellent introductory article can be found at the Forum Nokia web site here:

http://library.forum.nokia.com/topic/Design_and_User_Experience_Library/GUID-CC587793-848B-4CA8-B43A-C58CC1D55A08.html

Unity is another important goal in design. Unity means the entire application fits together as one. To achieve unity, gestalt principles are applied to these design elements:

- Space: is limited on the mobile display, yet it is important to avoid a cluttered, overcrowded display.

- Visual flow: ensures the user is guided through your application in a natural flow. Do not force the user to move from group to group in an unnatural direction.

- Dominance: describes where one element visually dominates the others on the display. Use dominance to grab the user's attention such as the active icon in a menu.

- Hierarchy: establishing a strong visual hierarchy can be extremely useful in indicating relationships between elements and in guiding the user through the content in a consistent and predictable manner.

- Color: is extremely important for conveying information such as grouping or distinguishing between functional elements.   Ensure color is used judiciously so that it does not become a distraction.

- Images and graphics: are extremely important for concisely conveying information. But be focused on the information you are trying to convey. Avoid complex images on a small display.

- Animations and transitions: are very useful to help guide the eye or establish context within an application. However, when overused animation can distract and even slow the user from completing his desired task.

Again, for excellent coverage of Design Unity, please look at the Forum Nokia web site here:

```
http://library.forum.nokia.com/topic/Design_and_User_Experience_Library/GUID-EDA69912-
C994-4742-B936-AF5C3D855C41.html
```

We have presented a good, generic multistep framework for how to approach the product design phase of your application. Now let's jump into some specific tips guiding you toward good usability and visual design.

Usability Guidelines

The mobile device is used differently from a desktop device. In this section we present some design guidelines you should follow to make your application as usable as possible. This section is based largely on information from Forum Nokia. More complete information can be found here:

```
http://library.forum.nokia.com/topic/Design_and_User_Experience_Library/GUID-D35E7FD1-
F4DC-4AF1-A53D-DC6E42DE456C.html
```

Navigation

Navigation is the process by which the user travels through your application to get information or perform a task. Using a mobile device, we often have only the user's partial attention so navigation should be simple. Unlike a desktop, we cannot have multiple views at one time, so there is a temptation to lead the user through a long series of screens to get to where he wants to go. This should be avoided.

Don't force the user to configure things that can be configured automatically. A clever application can learn from the user's behavior, and additionally allows the user to manually change options that the system incorrectly assumed.

Plan for user customization.

Consider whether your target device is touch (the user can interact with the device by touching the display) or non-touch (the user must use hardware keys to interact with the device), or a hybrid combining both. This will fundamentally determine the navigation paradigm for your application. In recent times, touch UI has become preferred. A common case is to design for touch to be used for primary navigation, with hardware keys to be used as task accelerators. An example of this is the red end key. Typically, to exit an application, you choose the "exit" menu sub-option from the "options" menu. Pressing the red end key is a shortcut path to the same exit functionality.

When designing touch areas for your application, ensure the touch targets are large enough to be easily selected. Historically, the Symbian S60 UI style provides the following guidelines:

- 7 x 7 mm with 1 mm gaps for index finger usage.

- 8 x 8 mm with 2 mm gaps for thumb usage.

- List type of components should have minimum of 5 mm line spacing.

These guidelines still apply today with Qt on Symbian and MeeGo.

Entering Information

Entering information with a keypad is obviously more difficult than with a desktop keyboard. Keep in mind that the user has multiple avenues to enter information on the mobile. GPS sensors can be used to enter position information. The camera can be used to enter information such as by scanning a 2D barcode. The camera can also be used to enter information by taking a picture. Nokia's Point and Find, for example, takes input from the camera and returns new information about the photographed object. Motion sensors can be used as a method to input information by sensing gestures. When designing for keypad entry, consider that some devices will have a numeric keypad, while some will have a complete alphanumeric keypad. And, of course, consider that now touch is an extremely popular modality on today's modern mobile handsets. Depending on the target device, design for touch as a primary input, with keypad entry an optional accelerator.

To make it easier to enter information, you should try to automate data entry as much as possible. Try to automatically populate fields where appropriate. For example, the contact database can be queried to autocomplete entries or fill in additional fields.

Do not force the user to re-enter information after navigating back and returning to a data entry screen.

Finally, consider different languages and methods for input when designing your application. Chinese, for example, will have methods for information entry much different from Western languages.

Information Presentation

On a mobile device, space available to present information is limited, so you must carefully think through how information is presented to the user. Consider the overall function of your application and decide how best to organize and order the information so that it is convenient for the user.

Consistency is important. Use colors, graphics, and icons consistently. Use them in a way to support the user's ability to perform a task or extract some information. Avoid overuse of graphics that instead cause distraction. Do not use icons to replace essential information conveyed as text.

Consider whether to present your application in portrait or landscape—this will depend largely on the specifics of your application design. In a movie application, for example, it might make sense to force the user to use a landscape layout since this better fits the native aspect ratio of the movie. In many cases it may be better to support both portrait and landscape and let the user select either by physically rotating the device or using other methods.

Connectivity

Many useful applications will take advantage of connectivity to exchange information over the network. However, connectivity is a double-edged sword. The device can easily lose network coverage, and in some cases the user may be charged to access the network. Furthermore, connecting over the network can be slow.

So design your application to use network connections as efficiently as possible. Allow the user to manage the connections when appropriate. Ensure that sufficient status information is presented to the user about the connection state. Design your application to gracefully handle on and offline modes.

Usability for Enterprise Applications

Enterprise applications are typically administered by IT departments. Remember to build in features useful for administrators. This includes providing features that allow administrators to configure applications and installation packages, and features for remote administration. It is useful if the administrative interface can be integrated into existing administrative tools.

Usability and Security

Because the mobile device is so personal, sensitive information stored on the device must be treated with care. Use passwords and encryption where appropriate. Back up critical data if possible. Allow the user to delete all sensitive information when desired.

Advertising

Advertising is becoming increasingly popular in mobile applications. When placing advertising, consider that it should not be obtrusive to the user. Placing ads in natural application breaks or screen white space is a convenient way to insert it without affecting the application flow too much. Avoid using pop-ups and floating ads since these can be annoying to the user. Make sure the ads do not slow the user from accomplishing the application's primary task. Don't greet the user with an ad when the application first loads. It is better to draw the user into the application, then provide an advertisement within a relevant context. Be judicious with full-page advertisements.

Ads should clearly indicate that something is being advertised and be different from application content. Consider creating an easily recognizable look for advertising content. Take advantage of context to provide advertising content more meaningful to the user.

Platform Components

Use platform components whenever possible. These have been developed specifically to implement the design paradigms mandated for that platform. Using the platform components also gives you additional technological benefits, such as support for scalable UI and theming.

Information on platform components for Symbian is available here:

```
http://library.forum.nokia.com/topic/Design_and_User_Experience_Library/GUID-830CD3A9-
E6AC-40C2-9452-B3009D4F153F.html
```

And information for the MeeGo/Maemo platform is available here:

```
http://library.forum.nokia.com/topic/Design_and_User_Experience_Library/GUID-3A084AEA-
3683-45DD-AE8A-B67AF6F44FDB.html
```

Checklists

Is your usability design complete? The Forum Nokia web site has a comprehensive list of checklists you can use to evaluate the quality of your usability design. These lists are specifically designed to meet the quality requirements of different certification programs. The full set of checklists is available here:

```
http://library.forum.nokia.com/topic/Design_and_User_Experience_Library/GUID-3EE138E6-
1364-4293-9C3B-1B4BD62F176E.html
```

Summary

In this chapter, we presented a thorough overview for designing your application. We discussed how designing for mobile is different from designing for desktop applications. Next, we presented a series of steps you can follow in designing your application. Finally, we presented a series of concrete tips for good usability and visual design. You should use this chapter as a framework to build more information on good design.

In the next chapter we get our feet wet using actual tools for software design and development.

Part II

Developing Your Application

Chapter 3

Working with the Nokia Qt SDK

Just as desktop software development often uses an integrated development environment (IDE) with a compiler, linker, headers, and libraries, so does development for mobile terminals. Nokia provides such an IDE for performing Qt development. The Carbide.c++ IDE is still available for C++ development as well.

In this chapter we provide a tutorial that shows you how to get, install, and use the free IDE for Qt software development. After reading this chapter, you will be able to install the Nokia Qt software development kit (SDK) for your work, begin using the tools and designers available to create your application's user interface, and compile and load your application on to a Nokia device.

Choosing an IDE

While desktop and mobile platforms share the common need for a tool chain, including an editor, compiler, linker, headers, libraries, and debugger, there's a key difference: choice. Depending on the desktop platform you're familiar with, you may have a wide array of tool chains (think Qt Creator, GNU, Microsoft Visual Studio, and so on). This choice may have some benefits—one tool chain may provide a better debugger, for example, or a faster compiler—but forces you to actively choose (or simply accept the decision made by your peers or manager). By contrast, Nokia provides the equivalent of one-stop-shopping: the IDE you choose for developing on Nokia platforms depends solely on the technology your application will use. If you plan to use Qt to build your application, you will use the Nokia Qt SDK.

Introducing the Nokia Qt SDK

For some time, Qt has provided its own IDE, including an excellent source code editor, integration with existing compiler, debugger, and linker tools. Called Qt Creator, it is itself written in Qt, although it has some features that make using the environment quite comfortable for anyone familiar with Eclipse. More recently, Nokia began providing its own mobile-centric version of Qt Creator, called the Nokia Qt SDK. Available on Macintosh, Windows, and Linux, the Nokia SDK provides the standard suite of services for an IDE, as well as:

- A run-time simulator of the handset GUI, simulating display size, soft keys, GPS, and other device features.

- Cross-compiling to Symbian, Maemo, MeeGo, the Qt simulator, and Qt on the host platform (the Linux and Macintosh versions of the tool require remote compilation for Symbian, however).

- Source-level debugging on the Qt simulator, native Qt, and device.

- A visual GUI builder derived from Qt Creator.

- Usage of Qt's project files for meta-makefile management.

In practice, most IDEs today offer the same set of features, and learning to use an IDE is mostly a matter of figuring out which menu contains which commands, and learning (or rebinding) which function keys do what. The Nokia Qt SDK is no different; if you've used Eclipse or Visual Studio, you will feel right at home in a matter of hours.

The Nokia Qt SDK is truly cross-platform, running on Mac OS X 10.6 or later, Linux (Nokia recommends Ubuntu), or Windows (Windows XP Service Pack 2, Windows Vista, or Windows 7). The installation is not small. Expect it to consume about 4 GB of disk space, and it'll happily consume all the RAM and processor you can throw its way. There are some limitations on the Linux and Mac OS X version of the SDK, so be sure to check the documentation; these limitations center on the ability to cross-compile for Symbian and the SDK's use of a Nokia-hosted compilation cloud to enable cross-platform development to Symbian on these platforms. (One of us is happily running the Nokia Qt SDK in a virtualized Windows XP machine on his Mac OS X workstation, so virtualization is also an option.)

The Nokia Qt simulator is an essential part of the SDK that is written as a Qt runtime, emulating key device features. These include device status (such as battery, network access, and screen orientation) and device data (including device location and contacts data), as well as a device's specific Qt implementation of the screen and user interface. Not a device emulator and not a device skin, the simulator provides a fine balance between start-up and debugging performance with the ability to do things such as script device data with JavaScript to enable most debugging right on your development workstation. This eliminates much of the need for source-level debugging on your hardware target, which is still supported for the occasional pesky bug that materializes only on hardware.

Getting Started with the Nokia Qt SDK

If you've used Qt Creator in the past, you will find the Nokia Qt SDK very easy to work with. Folks familiar with other IDEs—say, Microsoft Visual Studio—may suffer moments of disorientation at first, but at its heart, the Nokia Qt SDK is simple enough that you can become proficient in a manner of hours. Here's a screen-by-screen walkthrough of the Nokia Qt SDK 1.0 to get you started.

Installing the Nokia Qt SDK

Nokia provides web-based and full installs of the Nokia Qt SDK at `/www.forum.nokia.com/Develop/Qt/Tools/`. (If it's not there, click the Develop tab, then the Qt item in the dropdown menu; once there, choose Tools, and follow the links to the Nokia Qt SDK's download page.) The online installers are pretty small (on the order of 20 megabytes or so), but what you save in the initial download you pay later when the installer downloads the half-gigabyte to gigabyte of tools, headers, and libraries you need for a full installation. The installer itself is easy to use, but budget ten or twenty minutes for the installation; as you might imagine, there are a *lot* of files and tools to install.

Once you complete the installation and run the Qt SDK for the first time, you see a screen that looks like Figure 3–1. Before you dive in and begin cutting code, however, let's take a few minutes and configure your test hardware. In the discussion that follows, we assume you're working with a PC running a variant of Microsoft Windows; Mac OS X and Linux instructions can be found with the Nokia Qt SDK for those platforms and are similar in substance:

- Install Ovi Suite so that your device and workstation can talk if necessary (not required for Mac OS X or Linux, or Maemo devices).
- Install Qt for Symbian on Symbian devices.
- Install a debugging shim on all devices.
- Enable the connection between your workstation and phone.

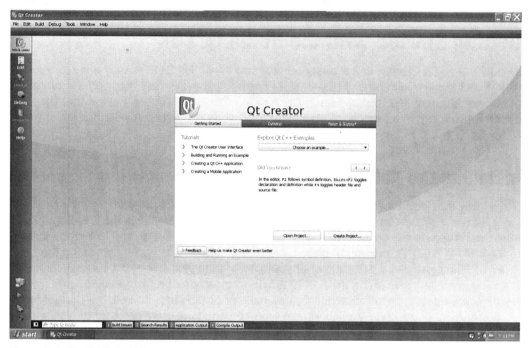

Figure 3–1. *The Nokia Qt SDK*

While the process sounds complicated, it takes only a few minutes.

Configuring a Symbian Device to Work with the Nokia Qt SDK

With your Symbian device should have come a copy of Ovi Suite, the software that enables a Symbian phone to communicate with your PC. Assuming you've installed it, you need only follow the links in the Nokia Qt SDK folder in your Start Menu to install SQLite, Qt for Symbian, and TRK, the Symbian debugger, and you're set (Figure 3-2). With the Nokia SDK installed, go to the Start menu and choose Start ➤Nokia Qt SDK ➤Symbian and select these packages.

As you do this, you should have about 20MB free on your Symbian device. As I write this, commercially available devices *don't* have Qt installed, so it's important that you install everything. By the time this book reaches you, newer devices will have Qt installed, and you need to install only TRK. If you're unsure, check Forum Nokia for specifics about the hardware that you have.

TRK is the debugging stub for Symbian development, and you'll need to have it running anytime you want to debug your application (including just downloading your app more quickly than packaging the application and installing via the application installer). Connect your device to your workstation using USB, and then launch TRK on the device. Choose "Settings," and then choose "USB."

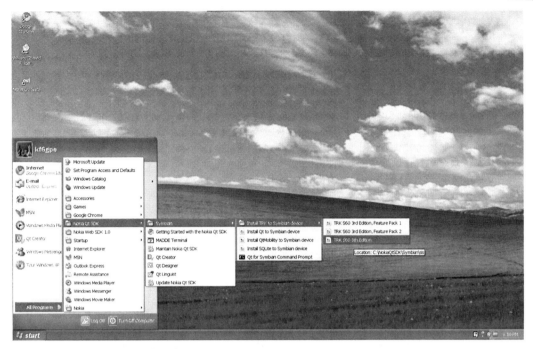

Figure 3-2. *Installing TRK on Symbian*

TIP: TRK also supports a Bluetooth connection, but the support may or may not be available with the version of the Nokia Qt SDK you have. It's worth checking into, although for long debugging sessions, we recommend that you stick with USB, which usually keeps your handset powered as well.

Configuring a MeeGo Device to Work with the Nokia Qt SDK

With MeeGo, the work is a little more involved, because you're going to use MeeGo's networking stack to connect via TCP/IP over USB or WiFi to your development workstation. Follow the steps included with the SDK, which should show you how to:

- Install the latest Ovi Suite or PC Connectivity Suite from Nokia for USB support on Microsoft Windows.

- On the MeeGo device, select the Application Manager, then Download, then Development, then find *Mad Developer* and install it. This client application lets you configure a network connection to your development workstation.

- Launch Mad Developer. You will see a screen similar to Figure 3-3.

■ To connect using WiFi, activate WiFi on your MeeGo device, and make sure you're connected to the same network as your development workstation. Note the IP address in the wlan0 row of Mad Developer.

■ To connect using USB, touch "Edit" on the USB row and confirm by touching "Configure." Note the IP address in the usb0 row.

You'll use Mad Developer any time you want to connect your device to the Qt Creator SDK. Later, in the section titled "Compiling and Running Your Code on a Device," we show you how to complete the workstation half of the connection in the Nokia Qt SDK. Figure 3–3 shows Mad Developer in action.

Figure 3–3. *Mad Developer*

TIP: Wireless debugging via WiFi is really cool, and works as long as you can ping between your development workstation and the device (that is, they need to be on the same logical network, but not necessarily the same physical network). However, USB is often a trifle faster, and connecting to USB usually powers your handset, too.

Finding Your Way around the Nokia Qt SDK

Returning to Figure 3–1 for a minute, let's get oriented with how the IDE is organized. When you first start the SDK, the large empty area with the Qt Creator box in the middle is a content area, where you spend most of your time editing visual layouts, source files, debugging, and so forth. Along the left hand side are selectors to different views the IDE can provide. (If you've used workspaces in Eclipse, the purpose is the same.) From top to bottom, the views are:

■ *Welcome* lets you pick a tutorial, a recent project with which you've worked, an example project, or create a project from scratch. This view actually has three panes: one for getting started, one to let you quickly load recent projects, and one that provides news and support from the Qt Labs blog. Forum Nokia. and other sources.

- *Edit* lets you do just that: edit the text of a file with a syntax-highlighting text editor.

- *Design* lets you create the visual layouts for your screens with a drag-and-drop editor that lets you build arbitrarily complex widget hierarchies. You do this using the Qt Designer, an integral part of the Nokia Qt SDK.

- *Debug* lets you start and debug your application in simulation or on a tethered device.

- *Projects* lets you work with the build configuration and other packaging for your application

- *Help* provides help not just for the IDE, but also for all of Qt, including Qt Mobility.

At the bottom of the left-hand side are progress annunciators for things like source code indexing, as well as four buttons:

- The target selector, which lets you choose the build target (device, simulator, and so on).

- The run button, which triggers a compilation if necessary and executes your application.

- The debug button, which triggers a compilation if necessary and executes your application in the source level debugger.

- The build button, which lets you trigger a compilation of your package.

Creating a Qt Application

Let's create our first Qt application—"Hello World," Qt style.

1. In the Welcome view, click "Create Project…"

2. In the dialog that appears (Figure 3–4), choose "Mobile Qt Application" and click "Choose…".

3. In the next dialog (the first of the creation wizard, Figure 3–4), name your project and choose a directory where it should be stored.

> **CAUTION:** Historically, some of these tools have not dealt well with spaces in paths. For best results, place your projects in directories with no spaces in the paths. Although it seems somewhat crude these days, one of us prefers just dropping new projects in a clean set of folders on the root of the boot or a secondary drive. It's easy to do, easy to find, and easy to back up or take with you if necessary, and it's guaranteed to work with just about any source-code control system you can find.

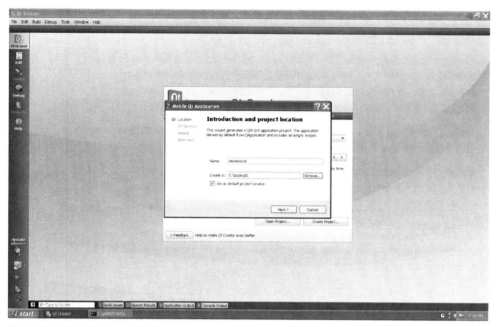

Figure 3–4. *Naming your project*

4. After naming your project, choose the targets for your application—
simulation, Symbian, and MeeGo—from the next panel

5. If you want, rename the main class and files, as we did (Figure 3–5).

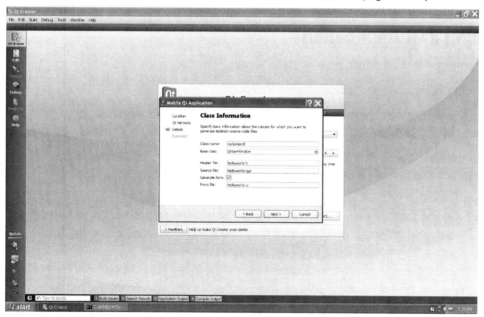

Figure 3–5. *Entering information about your main and class files*

6. Configure source-code control for your project if you want it, and click "Finish." You will see the Design view, as Figure 3–6 shows.

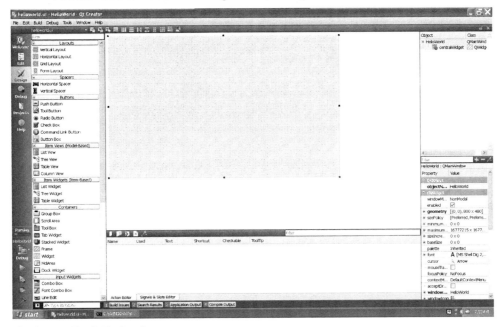

Figure 3–6. *The Qt Design view*

Let's add a label containing the text "Hello World" and a button, stacked vertically.

1. From the bottom of the palette on the left side of the window, drag a Label to the grey content window.

2. Right click the label, choose "Change plain text…" and type "Hello World".

3. Drag a push button from the middle of the palette on the left side of the window and drop it on the gray content window.

4. Right click the button, choose "Change text…" and type "Hello to you too!"

5. Right click the large gray rectangle on which you've been dropping controls and choose "Lay Out Vertically." You've just assigned a *layout manager* to the widget that the IDE provided when it created your window.

TIP: There's a big difference between having the layout assigned to the main window's widget and putting a layout manager (one of the layouts at the top of the palette on the left) on the widget! The former works wonders, generally doing what you'd expect. The latter doesn't, and leads to endless frustration when the layout doesn't appear to do what you want. Worse, the layout options in the right-click menu *only* appear once you've started putting child widgets in a widget, which is usually about the time you're getting very confused because the layout doesn't seem to be working. Don't panic, and remember the sequence: first, add child widgets, then right-click the containing widget. and choose the desired layout.

6. From the palette, drag a vertical spacer and drop it between the label and button.

You should now see something like the contents of Figure 3–7.

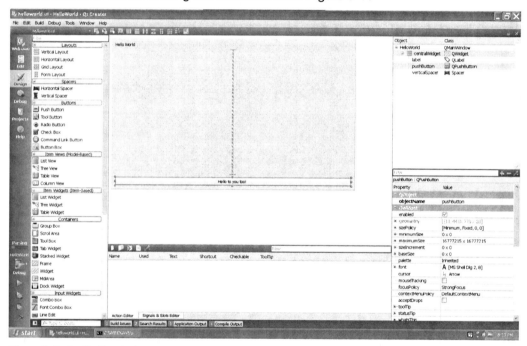

Figure 3–7. *Application design.*

Before continuing, let's see what the IDE has put together for us behind the scenes. Choose the edit view, and double-click "HelloWorld.pro" from the left hand column. You should see something like the contents of Listing 3–1.

Listing 3–1. *The application's project file*

```
#----------------------------------------------------
#
# Project created by QtCreator 2010-08-04T19:40:08
#
#----------------------------------------------------

QT       += core gui

TARGET = HelloWorld
TEMPLATE = app


SOURCES += main.cpp\
        helloworld.cpp

HEADERS  += helloworld.h

FORMS    += helloworld.ui

CONFIG += mobility
MOBILITY =

symbian {
    TARGET.UID3 = 0xec6083f7
    # TARGET.CAPABILITY +=
    TARGET.EPOCSTACKSIZE = 0x14000
    TARGET.EPOCHEAPSIZE = 0x020000 0x800000
}
```

This is your application's *project file* (also called a *pro* file, because its suffix is .pro), and defines the libraries your application links to, the source files that need to be compiled, and so forth. As we go along in the book, you'll learn to make small, targeted changes to this file (say, to add a library or an application icon), but in general, you probably won't need to edit it much, because the IDE does most of the heavy lifting. The project file is the input to qmake, Qt's metamake utility is responsible for analyzing project dependencies and coming up with a make file used by a specific platform's SDK, such as MinGW, the Symbian build chain, or the GNU cross-compilation tools for MeeGo. It's declarative in that you specify values for variables (such as SOURCES, a list of the source files from which your application builds), and qmake figures out the rest.

Next up is the "Forms" folder, which contains one file: the file you've been working on in the Qt Designer. The Qt Designer creates the XML you see in the form files that bear the .ui extension. The Qt Designer represents the interface as XML, so you shouldn't edit the XML directly. At compile time, these files get converted to C++ class declarations for your UI. That gives you the flexibility of a visual designer at development time and the performance of carefully tuned C++ at run time, so that there's no latency in setting up a complicated application UI.

> **TIP:** The IDE won't let you edit the XML directly, but of course with Emacs and caffeine, you can do whatever you want. We don't advise it.

The class header file "helloworld.h" defines a single QObject, extending Qt's QMainWindow class (Listing 3–2).

Listing 3–2. *The application's HelloWorld class.*

```
#ifndef HELLOWORLD_H
#define HELLOWORLD_H

#include <QMainWindow>

namespace Ui {
    class HelloWorld;
}

class HelloWorld : public QMainWindow
{
    Q_OBJECT

public:
    explicit HelloWorld(QWidget *parent = 0);
    ~HelloWorld();

private:
    Ui::HelloWorld *ui;
};

#endif // HELLOWORLD_H
```

The application's main window contains a central widget, which holds the controls for your application's user interface. (As you'll see in Chapter 6, you can actually swap in and out different collections of widgets, letting you show different screens in the same window.) The Qt Designer constructs this widget from the controls you've drawn out, using the XML and the automatically generated C++ we mentioned previously. This declaration of the user interface is done in your application's Ui namespace; as you see in Listing 3–3, you can access the compile-time-generated user interface components in that namespace.

Listing 3–3. *The implementation of the* helloworld *class*

```
#include "helloworld.h"
#include "ui_helloworld.h"

HelloWorld::HelloWorld(QWidget *parent) :
    QMainWindow(parent),
    ui(new Ui::HelloWorld)
{
    ui ->setupUi(this);
}

HelloWorld::~HelloWorld()
{
    delete ui;
}
```

There's a direct binding between the Designer's controls and your source code; if you return to the Designer, select a widget (say, the push button) and look at the right-hand side of the window (Figure 3–7). You'll see a list of properties for the widget you've selected, including the object's name. You can access the widgets in the Ui:HelloWorld class directly just by referencing their name, like this:

```
ui ->pushButton ->setText("Yo.");
```

Try this in helloworld.cpp, just after the call to ui ->setupUi(this). (You may need to compile your application first, if you're relying on name completion in the source editor.)

At this point, it's worth a quick compile-build cycle, just to see what you've created. Click the green Run button (the green arrow) at the bottom of the left-hand pane, and the IDE will compile your application and start it in the Qt simulator (Figure 3–8).

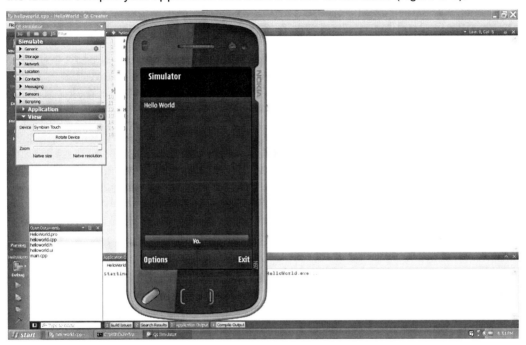

Figure 3–8. *Hello World, compiled and running in the Qt Simulator.*

Before you continue, we urge you to stop, put down the book, and spend an hour or so experimenting with Qt Designer and this sample application. Try:

- Adding more widgets to the main window.

- Adding an empty widget to the main window, and then dropping widgets on it.

- On the empty widget, set different layouts and see how things are positioned.

- Using the property inspector or source code completion in the editor, look at the properties different widgets bear. Try changing some of them. either at compile- or run-time.

▓   Place a breakpoint in HelloWorld's constructor by clicking next to the line numbers, and run the debugger by clicking the run arrow with the superimposed bug on the left.

▓   Anything else that comes to mind.

The Qt Creator is a powerful tool, and with it you can accomplish an awful lot right out of the box—without writing a line of code. Think of the time you spend playing with it now as a small investment that will reap rewards later when you sketch out or build your killer application's user interface.

Compiling and Running Your Code on a Device

Before we get to the nitty-gritty of running your code on a device, let's spend a couple more minutes looking at the Qt Simulator. The simulator has two windows—the window showing what your application will look like on the device, and a second window that lets you control the behavior of the simulator itself. This second view is divided into several auto-hiding panes; choose the View pane, open it, and try choosing a different device or adjusting the zoom level. As we write this, you can simulate Maemo, Symbian touch-enabled devices, and non-touch devices, which together span Nokia's platforms that support Qt. Other panes let you simulate various properties of the device, such as its battery level, position, network availability, contacts in the contacts database, and so forth. Much of this is important when testing applications that use Qt Mobility, which we discuss in Chapter 5.

Returning to the IDE, choose the Projects icon from the left-hand pane, and see the different build configurations for your project (shown in Figure 3–9).

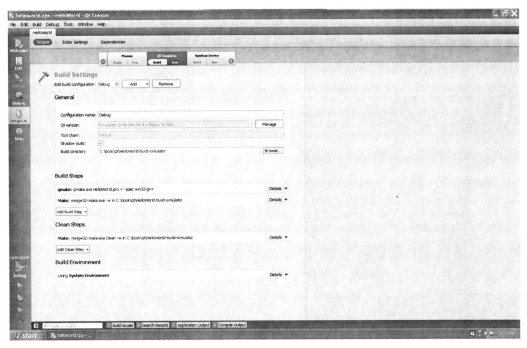

Figure 3–9. *Setting build configurations for your project*

You configure a specific build target here; for example, let's look at getting your code up and running on a MeeGo device. (First, be sure you've installed Mad Developer on your MeeGo device.)

1. In the Project view, choose "Maemo."[*] You can also choose this from the build target selector below the view buttons in the left-hand pane.

2. Start Mad Developer on your target device.

3. Press "Developer Password" in Mad Developer.

4. In the Nokia Qt SDK, go to the Tools menu and select Tools ➤Options… ➤Projects ➤Maemo Device Configurations ➤Maemo Emulator[†].

5. Click "Add," and name your configuration meaningfully (perhaps "WiFi").

6. Enter your device's IP address (from Mad Developer) in the Host Name field.

7. Enter the password shown in Mad Developer in the Password field.

---

[*] Newer versions of the Nokia Qt SDK may rename this tab "MeeGo."

[†] Again, this may be named "MeeGo."

8. Click "Test" to test the connection.

9. Click "OK" to save the settings.

10. Click the "Run" button.

After a short pause while the IDE rebuilds your application for MeeGo, you'll see the application running on the device.

The device's developer account and password work well if you're only going to do a quick test with a device, but for regular work, you're much better off creating a secure shell (SSH) key pair and installing the key on the device. To do this:

1. Return to the Tools menu's Maemo Emulator options.

2. Create a new configuration and ensure that the "Key" authentication type is selected.

3. Click "Generate SSH key… " and save the public and private keys somewhere. (You'll want to guard the private key, of course).

4. Choose "Deploy Public Key…" and choose the public key file you just created.

5. Change the configuration to use the one you just created.

Running your application on Symbian devices is even easier:

1. Choose "Symbian Device" in the Projects view or target selector.

2. Connect your device to your development workstation using a USB cable.

3. When the device prompts for USB mode, select "PC Suite" or "Ovi Suite" mode.

4. On the device, launch TRK. Ensure that the screen reads "Status: Connected" over USB.

5. Click the "Run" button.

The Qt IDE will recompile your application for Symbian, copy the application to the device, and start it.

Debugging Your Application

For developers today, support for debugging is as important as cross-compilation or any other aspect of the tool chain. While mobile developers have long used tricks such as logging to memory, reserving a few pixels on the display for status, or playing sounds at critical points in code to determine code flow, the Nokia Qt SDK relegates these tricks to the past with a state-of-the-art source-level debugger you've probably used in desktop development or on other mobile platforms. You can place breakpoints where execution stops, examine memory and variables, and step into or through routines, letting you inspect program state a source line at a time. Debugging works across all hardware targets; if you've configured the Nokia Qt SDK to download and launch your application on your target device (see the previous section), you've done the necessary work for on-device debugging.

To begin, you need to enter the Debug view in the Nokia Qt SDK by clicking the Debug icon on the left hand side of the display. You'll see the Debug view, as you see in Figure 3–10. In this view, the code editor shares space with debugging information. The two additional panes below the code editor display the stack trace and variable or memory information, breakpoints, or other information.

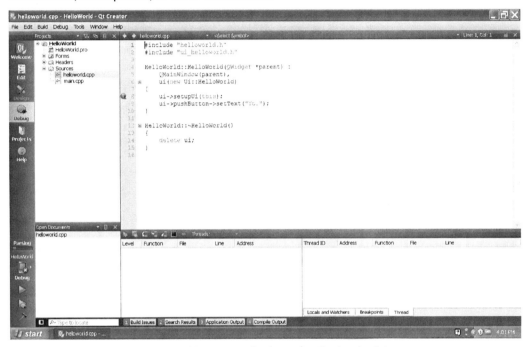

Figure 3–10. *The Debug view when writing your application and setting breakpoints*

To place a breakpoint, click the line of source code where you'd like to stop execution. Do this on the left side of the margin, just to the left of the source code line number. You'll see a red circle with an hourglass appear in that space; that is the breakpoint indicator. You can place as many breakpoints as you'd like; in Figure 3–10, we've placed one at line 8 of helloworld.cpp, in the constructor just before the user interface is set up.

To launch a debug session, click the run icon that has the bug overlaid at the bottom of the left pane, just above the hammer icon that represents the build operation. The SDK will build and start your application and the target (either the simulator or device) will execute your application until it reaches the first breakpoint, at which time execution stops.

With execution stopped you can do several things (Figure 3–11). Using the additional panes below your source code, you can:

- View the stack trace, seeing precisely where execution in your application has stopped (in the left hand pane).

- View variables in the current stack context, or add global watchers that show the values of global and static variables elsewhere in memory (in the right hand pane using the first tab) in the watch window.

- View a list of breakpoints (in the right hand pane using the second tab).

- View a list of running threads (in the right hand pane using the third tab).

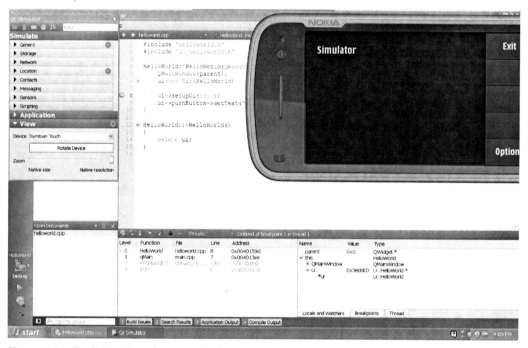

Figure 3–11. *The Debug View when execution has stopped*

You can add additional breakpoints by clicking additional lines of code, or add variables to the watch window by right-clicking the variable and choosing "Add to watch window". Using the row of small buttons above the left hand pane (the pane with the stack trace), you can:

- Continue execution from the current point by pressing the green continue button.

- Stop execution of a running application by pressing the stop button.

- Execute a single line, possibly executing a function in its entirety.

- Step into the next function call.

- Continue a function until it exits and returns to the caller, stopping execution immediately after the target executes the return.

- Switch from source-code debugging to viewing individual assembly-level instructions and stepping on an instruction-by-instruction level.

- Reverse execution flow to rerun a statement. (Of course, depending on application state, your application may not behave well after this operation!)

You can also right-click a source line in the editor and choose "Run to line" to continue execution and run to the specified line, a handy way to skip a bunch of code you know that works and stop at a potentially troublesome spot without placing another breakpoint. In the Locals and Watchers pane of the watch window you can also edit variable contents; this is handy if you see a variable is uninitialized and you want to fix it at once and continue without having to stop execution, edit your code, recompile, and debug until you get to the same point again. Double-click the corresponding value in the value column and enter a new value (string, hexadecimal, or text). Right-clicking a line in the watch window gives you additional ways to view a variable's contents, including:

- Opening a memory editor at a specified address, letting you view and edit individual words in memory.

- Add a permanent watch point to a variable or location in memory, so it's always visible in the watch window regardless of execution context.

- Change the display format of strings from ASCII to Unicode or other representations.

Wrapping Up

In this chapter, you've seen the Nokia Qt SDK, the tool chain Nokia provides for you to build Qt applications. You've used the Qt Designer capacity to draw full user interfaces, written and compiled a bit of code, and even built an application and ran it on the device. In the next chapter, we build on the experience you've gained in this chapter to see how to add that business logic that sets your application apart.

Chapter 4

Beginning Qt Development

As we write this chapter, Qt is about to enter its second decade as a cross-platform toolkit for software development. Given that Qt is used in applications from Autodesk Maya to the VLC Media Player, in applications both proprietary and open, Nokia's choice to provide it on Nokia smartphones and mobile computers is well justified. With support for graphics, multimedia, multithreading, and platform services such as network and file system access, along with a port of WebKit for application development, Qt offers a robust collection of APIs and elegant programming metaphor on top of C++.

In this chapter, we give you a whirlwind tour of Qt. While an introduction to Qt can fill an entire book (and does; see, for example, Johan Thelin's excellent *Foundations of Qt Development*, also available from Apress), one of Qt's strengths is that its basic principles are easy to understand and enable you to begin writing real code for real applications quickly. We begin by providing a high-level view of Qt's object model and the benefits it brings to you. Next, we show you Qt's solution to message passing between instances of classes, and we follow up with how it's used in both GUI and non-GUI development, such as access to the network. With these skills in hand, you're ready to learn about how Qt provides an elegant suite of classes to manage application interfaces using the popular model-view-controller (MVC) paradigm. Finally, we close the chapter with a concrete example that combines network access with an MVC user interface to display recent earthquakes from data provided by the United States Geological Service (USGS).

Understanding the Qt Object Model

While C++ provides a well-understood object model based on classes and inheritance, it's by no means perfect. Details including resource ownership, the static object system at runtime, competing graphical user interface standards, and so forth can make writing a complex GUI-based application in C++ alone a real headache. Qt begins with C++, and adds a robust object system that includes:

- A powerful inter-object communication system called *signals* and *slots.*

- A hierarchical object ownership system that reduces resource leaks.

- An interface to set and obtain object properties.

- Dynamic casting that works across object boundaries.

- Static resource management (for example, pictures, audio, XML, etc.) and contextual string translation.

- A template library for collections. These facilities are available to any class that implements the QObject object, the base class from which many Qt classes descend. Let's look at each of these facilities in a little more detail.

Understanding Signals and Slots

Signals and slots permit objects to communicate through a run-time conduit based on C++ method dispatch (ensuring that it's fast) while permitting the developer to provide the method without needing to subclass or implement an interface (so it's flexible). It's similar in principle to the callback technique used in C and C++, although considerably more flexible.

Any QObject descendant can emit a *signal* to indicate the occurrence of an event, such as a button being pressed, the movement of a slider, the completion of an HTTP transaction, or other events. Qt permits you to declare what signals a given object can emit, and lets you declare *slots* in QObject descendants that you can connect to appropriate signals.

> **NOTE:** Don't confuse "event" in the context of signals and slots with Qt's events, structures sent to specific methods of widgets, as they're not the same. It's easily to get confused at first, because some things Qt uses signals and slots for (such as a button press) are represented in other GUI frameworks as an event.

Signals and slots are type-safe, helping reduce potential programming errors. The coupling between signals and slots is loose, so that an object is free to emit signals as its state changes, even if no slots are connected to those signals. In the same way, slots need not be connected; they're just method declarations with a bit of extra glue in the class definition to indicate that you may be using the method as a slot, but you can still call them from your source code like any other method.

At runtime, you connect a signal to a slot using QObject's connect method, and disconnect using QObject's disconnect method. These connections are one-way, indicating that a signal should trigger a slot; the mechanism may be one-to-many, in which a single signal is connected to a number of slots, each through an invocation of

QObject's connect method. We show you a concrete example of how to do this later in the chapter in the section titled "Using Signals and Slots."

Making the Most of Hierarchical Ownership

C++, like C before it, relies on you, the developer, to keep track of when your application allocates memory and when it should release it for reuse. In small applications this isn't difficult, but as your application grows in complexity, it gets more difficult. Errors where you allocate memory and don't free it cause *memory leaks*; on constrained devices such as mobile phones, that can mean the difference between running and crashing as your application runs out of memory. Worse, large programs can see more insidious problems, such as using a region of memory after you've released it to the memory manager, which can cause crashes and other aberrant behavior in your application.

To help your application track when it needs to free allocated memory, Qt provides a hierarchy of memory ownership with most of its classes. When you create an object instance, you can designate another QObject as the owner (called the *parent*) of the object you're about to create. In turn, when the parent is released, any objects owned by the parent are also released. For example, to create a button to be released when the allocating object is deleted, we'd write:

```
QPushButton* button = new QPushButton(this);
```

In practice, it's generally best to use parented objects like this, rather than keeping a bunch of pointers and releasing them in the parent object's destructor.

As in other frameworks, it's common to use a null pointer (with the value 0) to indicate an object that has already been freed. To automate the process of setting a pointer to null when the pointer's memory is released, you can use the QPointer template, like this:

```
QPointer<QPushButton> button = new QPushButton(this);
```

For memory allocated in a function's scope, Qt provides the QScopedPointer, which automatically deletes the memory associated with the pointer when the scope ends, like this:

```
{
    QScopedPointer<QXmlStreamReader> xmlReader = new QXmlStreamReader();
    // ...parse the xml here...
} // xmlReader is deleted by the QScopedPointer
```

QScopedPointers are handy to have around in large functions with multiple exit points, where it's likely you'll forget to free an object. They're especially useful in doing device programming, where it's best to make light use of stack allocation, because the stack size on mobile devices is much smaller than what you're used to on desktop or server platforms.

Defining Object Properties

As we've already said, Qt object instances are just C++ instances with a bit of extra magic glue provided by Qt for things including the signal/slot mechanism and managing the memory used by parented objects. Another feature of Qt's objects that descend from QObject are *properties*, name-value pairs for attributes of the objects you define. As with other extensions to C++ that Qt provides, you can define properties in any class that inherits from QObject. Properties are especially important for things like integration with Qt Quick (see Chapter 7) and JavaScript in WebKit (see Chapter 8). To declare a property in an object, use the Q_PROPERTY macro inside the class definition, like this:

```
Q_PROPERTY(bool focus
           READ hasFocus)
Q_PROPERTY(bool enabled
           READ isEnabled
           WRITE setEnabled)
```

After specifying the property's type and name you can specify additional information in the form of functions that perform a specific action. All properties must have a READ directive that indicates the function the Qt meta-object system must invoke to obtain the value of the property. It's important to remember that *you* provide that function; all the Q_PROPERTY does is set things up with the meta-object system, rather than actually implementing functions like setters and getters.

In addition to READ, you can also provide several other directives defining the property, including:

- WRITE indicates the method to call to set the value.

- RESET indicates a function that returns the property to its default context-sensitive value.

- NOTIFY indicates a signal to emit whenever the property changes.

- DESIGNABLE is true or false and, when true, indicates that the property should be shown in the Qt Creator UI. You can also specify a member function that returns a bool for this directive. This value defaults to true.

- SCRIPTABLE is true or false and, when true, indicates that the property should be available to the scripting system in Qt Quick or JavaScript. You may also specify a member function that returns bool for this directive. This value defaults to true.

- STORED indicates whether the property is best thought of as an independent property rather than one computed from other values known to the object. Most properties are STORED true, and this is the default.

- USER indicates whether the property is designated as a user-editable property for the class (true or false). Typically, there is only one USER property in a class, by Qt convention.

- CONSTANT, another directive of type bool, indicates that the property value is constant.

- FINAL indicates that subclasses will not override this property. Note that this is really a comment to the developer; the meta-object compiler and run time do not currently enforce this.

In practice, when implementing your class, you generally specify the READ and WRITE values; occasionally you may come across a property that includes a RESET value.

> **CAUTION:** Don't forget that the Q_PROPERTY macro provides only the glue between your class and its properties! You must provide methods that implement the setter, getter, and reset operations if you specify them in a Q_PROPERTY macro.

Casting at Run Time

You are doubtless already aware of C++'s dynamic_cast, which lets you safely downcast or crosscast a pointer (returning 0 if the cast fails because of a type mismatch). Typically, you can't perform a dynamic cast across a plug-in boundary. Because Qt provides a cross-platform mechanism for managing plug-ins (in fact, Qt's support for different image types uses plug-ins to encapsulate the image format decoders), Qt needs a type-safe way to crosscast and downcast across dynamic library boundaries. To do this, Qt provides qobject_cast, a cast operation that's essentially the same in principle to dynamic_cast. In general when looking at Qt C++ code, you will likely see more use of qobject_cast than dynamic_cast, and it's generally a good idea to prefer it to dynamic_cast as well in your code. Another benefit to using qobject_cast is performance, as it uses the meta-object system rather than the C++ run time type inference.

> **NOTE:** We don't explicitly discuss creating plug-ins using Qt in this book. If you think you have a design that would benefit from using a plug-in architecture, take a peek at the Qt documentation on plug-ins (http://doc.qt.nokia.com/plugins-howto.html is a good place to start).

Managing Resources and Localization

Most applications—even many that have a minimal GUI—require resources as well as code. Images, sounds, and text—whether programmatic text, such as JavaScript to be used with the QtWebKit port or the text in the interface for windows, buttons, and so forth—must be packaged together with your application. Rather than taking the approach of providing a resource bundle with your executable, Qt takes the approach of statically compiling any resources into your executable. That way, you don't have multiple files to carry around with most applications, nor do you need to depend on a platform-specific mechanism, such as an application bundle.

You begin the process by specifying the resources your application requires in a resource collection file. The resource collection file is just a text file containing XML that describes the name and path to each required resource, like this:

```
<!DOCTYPE RCC>
    <RCC version="1.0">
    <qresource>
        <file>images/happy.png</file>
        <file>images/sad.png</file
    </qresource>
</RCC>
```

These files should already reside in your source tree (keeping them in your change control system isn't a bad idea, unless you're using one that doesn't handle binary files well), and the paths you provide to each <file> item are the paths relative to the resource collection definition file, as well as the paths to the resource when you load the resource in your application. You can name the resource file anything you like, as long as the filename ends with ".qrc."

To include the resource file in your application, just add a RESOURCES line to your project file indicating the resource file's location, like this:

```
RESOURCES += resources.qrc
```

To use a resource in your application, simply precede the location of the resource with a single colon and a solidus (":/"), like this:

```
QImage image(":/images/happy.png");
```

(We go into using Qt resources in more detail in the next chapter, in the section "Using Application Resources.")

> **NOTE:** Nearly any place you can specify a file path you can specify a resource path, too (just don't forget the leading :/ indicator in the path).

Small text resources, like those for labels, application error messages, and so forth, are best carried separately in a translation file created using Qt Linguist and the localization utilities `lupdate` and `lrelease` provided by Qt. You begin by ensuring that every string that needs a translation is marked using the function `tr`, provided by QObject. For example, when creating a button with the label "OK", we might write:

```
QPointer<QPushButton> button(tr("OK"), this);
```

The `tr` function is what will load the appropriate locale-specific string at run time; if a string is unavailable, it will default to the text you invoke it with.

Obviously, the thing you don't want to do is pick through thousands of lines of source code looking for `tr` invocations, so Qt provides `lupdate`, a utility to do just that. You must specify only the translation files to create in your project file and run Qt's `lupdate` command on your project file to create translation files (their names will end in .ts) containing every localizable string in your sources, headers, and Qt Designer files. Thus, the resource and localization parts of my project file might read:

```
RESOURCES = resources.qrc
TRANSLATIONS = myapp_dk.ts \
               myapp_en.ts \
               myapp_fi.ts
```

(The translation files include the source language name using the ISO-639-1 defined two-character code for the language.)

Once you create the initial translation files, your translator can use Qt Linguist to add the translated resources. Once that's done, you run `lrelease` over your project to compile the resulting release files. The resulting files are highly compressed and optimized for rapid access.

Occasionally, you might want to localize other resources, too—say, adding a localized version of a specific icon within your application. You do this using the XML in the resource collection file, by specifying the `lang` attribute of a specific qresource tag, like this:

```
<qresource lang="en">
    <file alias="images/flag.png">images/flag_en.png</file>
</qresource>
<qresource lang="fi">
    <file alias="images/flag.png">images/flag_fi.png</file>
</qresource>
```

Understanding Qt's Collection Classes

Like the C++ Standard Template Library (STL), Qt provides a number of type-safe collections through classes. These include sequenced collections through the use of the templates QList, QLinkedList, QVector, QStack, and QQueue, as well as associative containers through the use of QMap and QMultiMap, as well as QHash and QMultiHash. Finally, there is also QPair, which you can use to contain pairs of objects of arbitrary types.

For most applications needing to keep a list of items, QList is the logical choice. It's optimized for fast access, with only moderate penalties for insertion and deletion. If you find you need better performance for an updating list, try QLinkedList, which trades accessibility for performance when inserting or removing items. On the other hand, if QList doesn't meet your needs for access performance, there's also QVector, which stores its items in a contiguous region in memory, providing the fastest access but with considerable cost when inserting or removing items in the middle of the vector. QStack and QQueue provide convenience methods for implementing a stack using QVector and a first-in-first-out (FIFO) store using QList.

Associative maps let you store key-value pairs. Usually, you do this using a hash table; QHash and QMultiHash provide classic hash tables with arbitrary types for keys and values. You can also do the same thing with a binary search across a sorted set using QMap and QMultiMap. The "Multi" in QMultiHash and QMultiMap indicate that these templates can store multiple values for a single key, giving you additional flexibility.

These collections let you access items individually (using a method such as at or value) and iterate across the entire contents of the collection. These collections provide both STL-style iterators and a simpler Qt iterator to permit you to traverse the collection, visiting each item. The example at the end of the chapter shows you how to enumerate through the values in a QMap.

It's worth observing that the QString class, intended to represent strings of characters, isn't actually a collection class, but provides similar methods for inserting and removing characters from a string. The QString class also provides the usual methods you'd expect of a container of characters, including methods to format non-string values such as integers or floats, compare two strings, find and replace contents of a string, and so forth.

Using Signals and Slots

As we mentioned previously, signals and slots play a crucial role in Qt, enabling any two objects to communicate with each other without the need for clumsy interface definitions or callback functions. Declaring a signal requires only that the signal's object be a QObject and that the signal be declared with the signal's keyword in the class definition. In a similar vein, Qt's classic signal/slot example is that of a counter, wired to a button and slider. Our simple Qt counter class might look like what you see in Listing 4–1.

Listing 4–1. *An example declaring signals and slots*

```
#include <QObject>
class Counter : public QObject
{
    Q_OBJECT

public:
    Counter() { mValue = 0; }
    int value() const { return mValue; }

public slots:
    void setValue(int value);
    void increment();

signals:
    void valueChanged(int newValue)

private:
    int mValue;
}
```

This class derives from QObject, as you can tell from the class declaration and the inclusion of Qt's Q_OBJECT declaration at the top of the class declaration. This pulls in code generated by Qt's metaobject compiler. Any class that uses signals or slots must both be declared as a QObject *and* include the Q_OBJECT declaration.

> **WARNING:** Forgetting the Q_OBJECT declaration at the top of a class definition that inherits from QObject is one of the most common mistakes people make when they first start working with Qt. If you forget, you'll get an error such as Class declarations lacks Q_OBJECT macro (or something more confusing depending on what platform you're targeting) when you compile your class.

The class definition includes two slots and one signal. You can think of the signal declaration as an output of the class. When mValue changes, the class must emit that signal. As such, the signal itself does not have a method body; the prototype indicates the type signature and name of the signal.

Slots, on the other hand, do have method bodies; the slot's method body executes either when a signal connected to it fires, or if another piece of code invokes it. (After all, a slot really is just a method, albeit with special properties imbued by Qt.) For example, Listing 4–2 shows the definitions of setValue and increment.

Listing 4–2. *Implementing* Counter*'s slots*

```
void Counter::setValue(int _value)
{
    if (mValue != value) {
        mValue = value;
        emit valueChanged(mValue);
    }
}

void Counter::increment()
{
    emit valueChanged(++mValue);
}
```

As you can see, the slots perform the expected operation (copying the new value or incrementing the existing value) and then emit the signal using Qt's emit statement.

For a signal to notify a slot, you must first connect them. In keeping with the counter example, you might want to increment the counter every time the user presses a button and show the resulting count. Listing 4–3 has pseudo code that demonstrates this.

Listing 4–3. *Connecting signals to slots*

```
...
QPushButton *button = new QPushButton("Bump", this);
QLCDNumber *countLCD = new QLCDNumber(this);
Counter *counter = new Counter(this);
connect(button,    SIGNAL(clicked()),
        counter,   SLOT(increment()));
connect(counter,   SIGNAL(valueChanged(int)),
        countLCD,  SLOT(display(int)));
...
```

When the push button receives an appropriate event from the Qt main event loop, it emits the released signal. This in turn invokes the counter's increment slot, which emits a valueChanged signal accepted by the countLCD's display slot, which redraws itself to show the new value provided to the slot.

Performing Input and Output

Many newcomers and those unfamiliar with Qt often think that Qt is only a GUI abstraction layer, completely overlooking the support Qt provides for networking, file system access, and other key components in application development. As you see in Figure 4–1, Qt provides a clean abstraction for working with various kinds of I/O devices, including files and sockets, too.

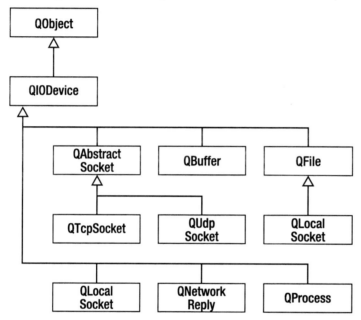

Figure 4–1. *Qt's hierarchy of I/O classes*

At the root of the I/O hierarchy is QIODevice. QIODevice defines familiar methods for managing a bidirectional stream of data, including:

- open, which prepares the device for reading and writing data.

- close, which terminates the device's interface for reading and writing and may release the system context (such as a file handle) associated with the instance.

- read, which reads up to the indicated number of bytes and returns them as an array of bytes.

- readAll, which reads the remainder of the available data and returns the data as an array of bytes.

- write, which lets you write an array of bytes to the device.

- peek, which lets you read ahead of the current file pointer.

- status methods, including isOpen, isReadable, and isWritable, indicating whether the stream is open, provides data, or accepts data, respectively.

- In many cases, you may not need to use the read and write methods at all. Many utility classes, such as the QXmlStreamReader class, accept QIODevice instances so you don't have to shuffle the data from one interface to another. We show you how to use the QXmlStreamReader in the section "Putting It All Together" at the end of this chapter.

Perhaps even more useful is the QDataStream class, which provides serialization of binary data to a QIODevice. For example, you might write:

```
QFile file("some.dat");
file.open(QIODevice::WriteOnly);
QDataStream out(&file);
out << QString("Hello World");
out.close();
```

The QDataStream class has bidirectional stream operators for types including: bool; eight-bit, sixteen-bit, thirty-two bit, and sixty-four bit int; float; double; and char – plus most Qt data types like QString, QColor, etc. You can configure the stream to indicate byte order and floating-point precision, as well as directly read or write the raw data for serializing your own data types.

Managing Multiple Threads

While Qt makes easy work of most I/O tasks, I/O brings its own issue: latency. While a QIODevice is working, your application waits; wait too long and your application performance will suffer as the UI thread stalls, blocking on pending I/O operations. In some cases, such as application launch, this isn't a problem. But in many cases (especially network I/O), it can be. Fortunately, to help with this and other tasks that can be run in parallel, Qt provides a platform-independent thread implementation, so you can move lengthy tasks to run in separate threads within your application.

The Qt class QThread is at the heart of Qt's thread support, and provides the usual semantics for creating, managing, and terminating a single thread. To create a thread, you simply subclass QThread and override its run method. At run time, you only need to create an instance of your thread class and invoke start. In turn, Qt spawns a platform thread and uses it to execute your run method. Once the run method exits, the QThread cleans up and releases the thread it used.

A thread may have (although it doesn't have to) an event loop that you can start by calling exec in your thread's run method. This makes it possible to connect signals and slots between your thread and other threads, such as the main thread on which the user interface of your application runs.

CAUTION: Although a thread can have an event loop, your graphical user interface code (widgets and painting) must all run on the main thread. Running user interface code—any code that triggers painting to the screen—on threads other than the main thread is not supported, and will yield unpredictable results.

The mechanics of managing the QThread are convenient, and made especially simple through the use of (you guessed it!) signals that the thread emits at various stages of its life. The methods QThread provides are:

- exit, which exits the run method and terminates the thread.

- isFinished returns true if the thread has run to completion, otherwise it returns false.

- isRunning returns true if the thread is still running in its run method.

- priority and setPriority let you obtain and modify the thread's priority.

- stackSize and setStackSize let you determine and set the thread's stack size. Be careful using this method, because many devices have a relatively small maximum stack size anyway.

- wait blocks the thread until either its run method exits, or the amount of time that you specify (the time value is in milliseconds).

QThread provides the following slots (also usable as methods, of course):

- quit, which terminates a thread's event loop.

- start, which starts a thread.

- terminate, which forcibly exits a thread. (In general, you should prefer using quit to terminate.)

NOTE: To terminate a thread, you can call exit from within the thread, or invoke the quit slot from outside the thread.

The signals that QThread provides are:

- finished, emitted when the thread's run method exits.

- started, emitted when the thread's run method commences.

- terminated, emitted if the thread is forcibly terminated.

Threads should be as independent as possible. Wherever you need inter-thread communication, you should use signals and slots in conjunction with a thread's event loop if you can. However, there's no getting around the fact that if your threads share resources such as mutable data structures, you simply have to synchronize access between threads. Qt provides the usual inter-thread synchronization primitives:

- QSemaphore provides synchronization for a specific number of identical resources.

- QMutex provides a mutually exclusive lock for a specific resource.

- QReadWriteLock is similar to QMutex, and is useful in that it distinguishes between read and write access to shared data, permitting multiple readers, while ensuring that only one thread is writing to your data.

- QWaitCondition permits one thread to wake other threads when some condition has been met.

Using Item Views with the Model-View-Controller Paradigm

As you would expect, Qt provides a host of user interface widgets to present things such as lists of items to the user. These widgets, such as QListWidget, provide an item-oriented interface to your application, where you provide items (perhaps from a collection your application maintains) that the user can manipulate (such as to make a selection). This sounds good in theory, but in practice it has limitations.

The key limitation is one of scalability—as the size of your collection increases, it's more work and more memory to keep essentially two copies (one for your application and one for the widget). Worse, if an item in your collection changes, you need to synchronize the widget's item list with your item list, which includes the need to repaint the widget.

Fortunately, there's a better way. Qt provides an implementation of the *model-view-controller* (MVC) pattern now commonplace in user interface development. The widgets QListWidget, QTableWidget, and QTreeWidget have corresponding classes, QListView, QTableView, and QTreeView, which each take a model of the data to present and monitor for changes, sharing data with the model to ensure both a small footprint and rapid updates.

THE MODEL VIEW CONTROLLER PARADIGM

The MVC pattern originated with the Smalltalk programming language and provides a concise way to structure an application's user interface around three related components:

- The *model* contains an independent representation of the data your application visualizes.

- The *view* is responsible for rendering the contents of the model in a specific (such as a list or table) way.

- The *controller* takes events from the user and performs the appropriate actions (for example, scrolling or collapsing part of the view), forwarding the application-specific behavior for handling the event to either the model or view.

MVC has been around long enough that there's a great deal written about it, and most GUI frameworks today support it. If you're unsure of how the pieces fit together after reading this section, take a look at Wikipedia or the Portland Pattern Repository at www.c2.com/cgi/wiki?WelcomeVisitors.

Understanding Qt's Model Classes

Qt provides a class hierarchy for models that are a little different than what you may have encountered on other platforms. While you can use a model with a single flat collection of objects such as a list, the Qt platform itself provides for a tree of two-dimensional tables such as the one you see in Figure 4–2. In the figure, we see a tree with a root that is a 4x4 table of items; the items at (0, 0) and (1, 3) each have child data, and so forth. While dizzying, this general representation provides the ability for a model to represent items in one dimension (lists), two dimensions (tables), and a hierarchy (such as a directory tree).

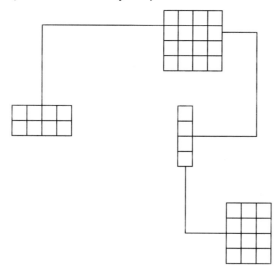

Figure 4–2. *An arbitrary model represented using Qt's abstract model structure*

Qt uses the QAbstractItemModel to encapsulate the full flexibility of a tree of tables; normally, a QAbstractListModel or QAbstractTableModel suffices, hiding the complexity of the tree unless you really need it.

In most cases, you don't even need to create your own model; instead you can use a QStringListModel for a one-dimensional list of QStrings, or a QStandardItemModel for one- or two-dimensional array, as well as data structured in a hierarchy.

The two-dimensional nature of the QTableModel is strongly reminiscent of a SQL database's tables, and it almost immediately comes to mind when you have data organized in rows with different facets of the data in each column. It shouldn't, however—in a Qt table model, *each cell in the table is independent of every other cell*. Think of a Qt table like a financial spreadsheet (not a well-formatted list!). Instead, if you have a list of items with different data per item—say, a list of location names with latitudes and longitudes—each location is a single item in a list.

To provide access to different facets of a single item, Qt provides *roles*. A role is a constant in an enumeration, and models return different data depending on the role you pass when you interrogate the model. Qt defines several roles by default defined by the Qt::ItemDataRole enumeration, including:

- Qt::DisplayRole, indicating the primary visible facet of a datum.
- Qt::DecorationRole, indicating a decoration (such as an icon) for a datum.
- Qt::EditRole, indicating the primary editable facet of a datum.
- Qt::SizeHintRole, indicating the desired size of the item for display layout purposes (this is the size the layout will try to accommodate, rather than the actual object's size).
- Qt::CheckStateRole, indicating whether the item is marked in some way (say, a list item bearing a check mark).

So, for example, the QListView uses the Qt::DisplayRole to indicate to the model what data is requested for display for each item. You can define your own roles, too, if you need to represent different kinds of data and find the Qt roles limiting in the kind of data being represented; just be sure that your first role has a value greater than Qt::UserRole.

When you set or get data from a model, you do so using a QModelIndex that indicates which datum you're interacting with as well as Qt's QVariant class. The QVariant class is a type-safe wrapper for most C++ and all Qt value types, including integers, floating-point numbers, and strings. You access the model's data through the data and setData methods; they use QVariant for encapsulating the actual values.

NOTE: There's even a way to add your own data types to those QVariant supports; see the documentation for QVariant at http://doc.qt.nokia.com/qvariant.html.

For example, here's how to access the first datum in a QStringListModel:

```
QStringListModel model;
…
QModelIndex index = model->createIndex(0);
QString datum = model->data(index, Qt::DisplayRole).toString();
```

Setting the data is similar:

```
QStringListModel model;
…
QModelIndex index = model->createIndex(0);
QString anEntry("hello world");
QString datum = model->setData(index,
    QVariant(anEntry),
    Qt::DisplayRole);
```

In addition to being able to set a datum within the model, you can manipulate the model in various ways. The most common things you're likely to want to use are:

- columnCount and rowCount indicate the number of rows and columns, respectively.

- insertColumn and insertColumns insert a column or columns after the indicated column.

- insertRow and insertRows insert a row or rows after the indicated row.

- removeColumn and removeColumns remove a specified column or columns.

- removeRow and removeRows remove a specified row or rows.

- data and setData let you manipulate a specific datum at a specific index in the model.

- index to create an index object that indicates a specific datum within the model.

As you manipulate a model with these methods, it emits signals so that the view or other code can be kept abreast of any changes within the model. Typically, when using a model, you don't need to worry about these signals, unless you're implementing your own model.

You needn't implement your own model most of the time. Qt also provides the QStandardItemModel, which provides a concrete implementation of a model you can use within your application for normal purposes. (We show you how to use the QStandardItemModel later in this chapter, in the section "Putting it All Together.")

SUBCLASSING A MODEL CLASS TO MAKE YOUR OWN MODEL

It's unusual, but you may find a case where you think you need to write your own model. Typically, you'd need to do this if you can't provide all the data at once—say, because of pending network or file system activity (however, Qt has support for SQL tables and file system directories through models it provides). Creating your own model isn't hard; you need only inherit from the appropriate base class (QAbstractItemModel, QAbstractListModel, or QAbstractTableModel for one- or two-dimensional or tree models, respectively) and override the methods that implement the structure appropriate for your data. You'll need to override two kinds of methods:

- Methods that describe the organization of your data, such as the rowCount and columnCount methods.

- Methods that permit access and mutation of your data, such as the data and setData methods.

In addition, when implementing the data-access methods, you'll want to be sure that you emit the appropriate signals when data changes in your model or the model's size itself changes. The Qt documentation provides good information about how to do this for pointers on creating both a simple list model and a tree model.

Using Qt's View Classes

Qt's view classes provide robust components that rely on a model for their data. QListView, QTableView, and QTreeView provide the fundamental UI classes many applications can use to provide a browsing metaphor for their data. These implement the abstract class QAbstractItemView, which defines the various methods, signals, and slots exposed by all view classes.

In general, you need to know very little about how a Qt view class works; it often suffices to drag one out in the GUI designer (or create one at run time, as you see later in this chapter in the section "Putting it All Together") and set its model, like this:

```
// In a class declaration inheriting from QMainWindow
QStandardItemModel *mModel;
QListView *mListView;
// Someplace in the GUI code
mListView = new QListView(this);
mStandardItemModel mModel = new QStandardItemModel(this);
mListView->setModel(mModel);
setCentralWidget(mListView);
```

Qt's design style calls for generally shallow class hierarchies, with a great deal of configurability being embedded in specific implementation classes, rather than dozens of classes providing slightly different behaviors. Thus, the QAbstractItemView has a number of properties affecting how an instance renders data, including:

- alternatingRowColors, indicating that the background of rows should alternate between two colors. rather than a single color.

- `autoScroll`, indicating that the control should automatically scroll when the touch drags over the view.

- `horizontalScrollMode` and `verticalScrollMode`, indicating whether the view should provide scrolling in the indicated direction.

- `selectionBehavior` indicating whether an item, row, or column can be selected.

- `selectionMode`, indicating whether one item or multiple items (perhaps contiguous) can be selected.

Unlike the classic implementation of model-view-controller, where the controller is a separate class with its own (usually application-specific) logic, Qt divides the responsibilities of the controller between the view and the application. The view handles the view-specific events, such as responding to events that would cause scrolling or item selection, and issues signals for user interaction that requires application logic, such as item activation and selection. These signals include:

- `activated`, indicating an item has received focus.

- `clicked`, indicating that an item has been selected with the primary selector such as a touch or mouse click.

- `doubleClicked`, indicating a double-click action.

- `pressed`, indicating the beginning of a click or double-click as the item receives the initial down component of a mouse or touch.

> **TIP:** On touch screen devices, you should always prefer `clicked` over the other signals. Users expect that an action should take a single touch.

In the next section, you see how wiring a signal from the `QListView` triggers an action when the user touches an item in the list.

Putting It All Together

Figure 4–3 shows our first prototype sample application "Shake", which connects to a Web service provided by the United States Geological Service (USGS) to show recent earthquakes around the world. (This application doesn't fully meet the design guidelines we set out in Chapter 2; in the next chapter we'll address that.)

Figure 4–3. *Our sample application*

Let's take a closer look at the source code, calling your attention to the construction of the user interface, and its use of model-view-controller, threads, and I/O.

Implementing the Application User Interface

The user interface for our application is admittedly simple, providing a single list of recent seismic events and a region showing the details of the event you select. The class MainForm, which extends QMainWindow supports the user interface. Listing 4–4 shows the MainForm class.

Listing 4–4. *The class declaration for* MainForm

```
class MainForm : public QMainWindow
{
    Q_OBJECT

public:
    MainForm(QWidget *parent = 0);
    ~MainForm();

public slots:
    void fetch();
```

```
private slots:
    void handleRequestFinished();
    void handleError(const QString& message);
    void handleItemClicked(const QModelIndex&);

private:
    WorkerThread* mBgThread;
    QuakeListModel* mEventModel;
    QSortFilterProxyModel* mSortedModel;
    QListView* mListView;
    QWebView* mItemView;
    QWidget* mMainView;
};
```

The UI itself uses a QListView to show the list of events, and a QWebView to show the results. (We talk more about the QWebView class in the next chapter.) The earthquake data is kept in the QuakeListModel, a simple subclass of QStandardItemModel that has a single helper method to permit easy storage of seismic data through a container class. In turn, the list view obtains the data through a QSortFilterProxyModel, which provides the data sorted so that the resulting list has the most recent item first. All of this is initialized in MainForm's constructor (shown in Listing 4–5).

Listing 4–5. *The MainForm constructor*

```
MainForm::MainForm(QWidget *parent)
    : QMainWindow(parent)
    , mBgThread(0)
    , mEventModel(new QuakeListModel())
    , mSortedModel(new QSortFilterProxyModel(this))
    , mListView(new QListView(this))
    , mItemView(new QWebView(this))
    , mMainView(new QWidget(this))
{
    mItemView->setHtml(tr("<body><p align=\"center\">"
        "Loading data... please wait</p></body>"));

    mSortedModel->setSourceModel(mEventModel);
    mSortedModel->setDynamicSortFilter(false);
    mSortedModel->setSortRole(QuakeListModel::When);
    mListView->setModel(mSortedModel);

    mListView->setSizePolicy(QSizePolicy::Expanding,
        QSizePolicy::Expanding);
    mItemView->setSizePolicy(QSizePolicy::Expanding,
        QSizePolicy::Expanding);

    mListView->setHorizontalScrollBarPolicy(Qt::ScrollBarAlwaysOff);

    QBoxLayout::Direction direction;
    if (height()>=width()) {
        direction = QBoxLayout::LeftToRight;
    } else {
        direction = QBoxLayout::TopToBottom;
    }
    QBoxLayout *layout = new QBoxLayout(direction, mMainView);

    layout->addWidget(mListView, 1);
```

```
    layout->addWidget(mItemView, 1);
    mMainView->setLayout(layout);

    setCentralWidget(mMainView);

    connect(mListView, SIGNAL(clicked(QModelIndex)),
            this, SLOT(handleItemClicked(QModelIndex)));

    fetch();
}
```

As you see immediately, we chose to manually create the UI, rather than use Qt Creator within the Nokia Qt SDK. The reason is only to show you that you can; you could easily use the user interface you created from Chapter 4 with Qt Creator. Regardless, the code creates the two visible elements and combines them in a single widget, set to be the main widget of the QMainWindow using QMainWindow's setCentralWidget method.

Perhaps the most interesting code in the constructor is the lines that link the QuakeModel instance with the QSortFilterProxyModel instance. As the name suggests, the QSortFilterProxyModel is a model in the object-oriented sense (it inherits from QAbstractItemModel), but doesn't contain any data. Instead, it provides a view with an ordered or filtered model (hence the "proxy" in its name) created using an indicated role. Here, the code:

  ▪ Tells the proxy model to use the data in the mEventModel model.

  ▪ Says the model should be sorted on demand, not automatically when items are added or removed.

  ▪ Tells the proxy model to present the data in the mEventModel sorted by a custom role, QuakeListModel::When.

In turn, the QListView accesses the data through the proxy model; behind the scenes the proxy model does some magic with its model indexes so that the model data appears to be sorted by time.

Once the user interface component and model is initialized, the constructor invokes fetch to obtain the latest seismic data.

It's worth mentioning that in the user interface, our error handling is admittedly primitive, but demonstrates that something needs to be done in the event of an error. In our case, we simply emit an error message, which the UI will present in a dialog indicating the nature of the error (Listing 4–6).

Listing 4–6. *Showing an error message*

```
void MainForm::handleError(const QString& message)
{
    QMessageBox box(QMessageBox::Critical,
                    tr("Error"),
                    message,
                    QMessageBox::Ok,
                    this);
    qDebug() << message;
}
```

Using the Network to Obtain Data

Listing 4–7 shows the fetch method, responsible for starting the thread to fetch the data.

Listing 4–7. *Starting the Qt thread for network access and data parsing*

```
void MainForm::fetch()
{
    if (!mBgThread)
        mBgThread = new WorkerThread(this, *mEventModel);
    connect(mBgThread, SIGNAL(finished()),
            this, SLOT(handleRequestFinished()));
    connect(mBgThread, SIGNAL(error(const QString&)),
            this, SLOT(handleError(const QString&)));
    mBgThread->fetch(
        "http://earthquake.usgs.gov/earthquakes/catalogs/1day-M2.5.xml"
    );
}
```

This code is quite simple. In addition to creating an instance of our worker thread, the code connects its signals to slots in the main view so that the main view can respond to success or failure in the attempt to obtain data from the network.

The thread itself is responsible for making the HTTP request and parsing the XML results. Construction of the thread (see Listing 4–8) initializes a hash with the XML tags we seek, and does the necessary connecting between signals and slots.

Listing 4–8. *Worker thread initialization*

```
WorkerThread::WorkerThread(QObject* owner,
                           QuakeListModel& eventModel)
    : QThread(owner)
    , mCancelled(false)
    , mNetManager(0)
    , mReply(0)
    , mEventModel(eventModel)
{
    // Initialize the hashtable of tags we seek
    mXmlTags.append("id");
    mXmlTags.append("title");
    mXmlTags.append("updated");
    mXmlTags.append("summary");
    mXmlTags.append("point");
    mXmlTags.append("elev");
    mXmlTags.append("link");

    mNetManager = new QNetworkAccessManager(this);
    connect(mNetManager, SIGNAL(finished(QNetworkReply*)),
            this, SLOT(handleNetFinished(QNetworkReply*)));
}
```

Performing the HTTP request, done in the fetch method with the URL you pass it, is very easy. Listing 4–9 shows how it's done.

Listing 4–9. *Making an HTTP request*

```
void WorkerThread::fetch(const QString& url)
{
    QNetworkReply *reply = mNetManager->get(QNetworkRequest(QUrl(url)));
    if (!reply) {
        emit error(tr("Could not contact the server"));
    }
}
```

It's worth noting that the QNetworkAccessManager's get method does not block; control returns to the main thread, and the manager performs the network request asynchronously. In fact, the real reason to encapsulate this part of the application in its own thread is the XML parsing, which can take a bit of time in a large document. When the network operation completes, the manager will emit the finished signal, which we handle in handleNetFinished (Listing 4–10).

Listing 4–10. *Handling the completion of the network transaction*

```
void WorkerThread::handleNetFinished(QNetworkReply* reply)
{
    // Start parser by starting.
    if (reply->error() == QNetworkReply::NoError) {
        if (!this->isRunning()) {
            mReply = reply;
            start();
        }
    } else {
        emit error(tr("A network error occurred"));
        qDebug() << QString("net error %1").arg(reply->error());
    }
}
```

Parsing the USGS Data Feed

The USGS data provides its data in well-formed XML. A specific seismic event might look like this:

```
<entry>
    <id>urn:earthquake-usgs-gov:ci:10756957</id>
    <title>M 3.8, Baja California, Mexico</title>
    <updated>2010-07-19T23:06:11Z</updated>
    <link rel="alternate" type="text/html" href="url"/>
    <link rel="related" type="application/cap+xml" href="url" />
    <summary type="html">
        <![CDATA
            html description of event
    ]]></summary>
    <georss:point>32.1465 -115.1627</georss:point>
    <georss:elev>-6300</georss:elev>
    <category label="Age" term="Past hour"/>
</entry>
```

This is contained within a root-level <feed> block. (For brevity, we've elided the actual URLs and HTML content describing the event.) The only catch in working with the data is that the <id> attribute uniquely identifies an event, but multiple <entry> items may have the same <id>. This can occur when the USGS provides updated information about a seismic event, such as after collecting more data and refining the estimate. Consequently, we must not only parse the XML <entry> items in the document, but also de-duplicate the data by ID, taking the most recent item when multiple items exist. Fortunately, there's an easy way to do this—accumulate the <entry> items in a hash indexed by the <id> field's value. Listing 4–11 shows the parsing and de-duplication that begins when the thread actually runs.

Listing 4–11. *Parsing and de-duplicating the XML results*

```
void WorkerThread::run()
{
    QuakeEvent anEvent;
    QXmlStreamReader xml;
    QXmlStreamReader::TokenType type;
    QString fieldName;
    QString value;
    QString tag;
    QMap<QString, QuakeEvent> events;
    bool successful = false;
    bool gotValue = false;
    bool gotEntry = false;

    xml.setDevice(mReply);
    while(!xml.atEnd())
    {
        // If we've been cancelled, stop processing.
        if (mCancelled) break;

        type = xml.readNext();
        QString tag = xml.name().toString().toLower();
        switch( type )
        {
            case QXmlStreamReader::StartElement:
                {
                    gotValue = false;
                    if (tag == "entry") {
                        gotEntry = true;
                    } else if (mXmlTags.contains(tag)) {
                        fieldName = tag;
                    } else {
                        fieldName = QString();
                    }
                }
                break;
            case QXmlStreamReader::Characters:
                // Save aside any text
                if ( gotEntry && !fieldName.isEmpty() && !gotValue)
                {
                    value = xml.text().toString();
                    gotValue = true;
                }
                break;
            case QXmlStreamReader::EndElement:
                // Save aside this value
                if (gotValue && tag != "entry") {
```

```
                    anEvent.set(fieldName, value);
                } else if (tag == "entry"){
                    events.insert(anEvent.id(), anEvent);
                    anEvent.clear();
                    gotEntry = false;
                    gotValue = false;
                }
                break;
            default:
                break;
        }
    }

    successful = xml.hasError() ? false : true;

    if (!mCancelled && successful) {
        mEventModel.removeRows(0, mEventModel.rowCount());
        mEventModel.insertRows(0, events.count(), QModelIndex());
        int row = 0;
        // Convert the hash into a list
        foreach(anEvent, events) {
            mEventModel.setData(row++, anEvent);
        }
        emit finished();
    } else if (!mCancelled) {
        emit error(tr("Could not interpret the server's response"));
    }
}
```

The QXMLStreamReader takes a QIODevice, so it's easily connected to either a file or a network result like this one. An event-generating stream-based parser, it's far more efficient to use than a DOM parser, although it requires a little more code. (This is a good trade-off, because neither the whole XML document nor the whole DOM must be stored in memory when using a streaming parser like this one.) In brief, we use the reader to walk through the stream a tag at a time, storing the characters bound by the tag. When the tag closes, the code looks to see if the closed tag was an entry tag. The parser accumulates data for the various sub-tags, creating a QuakeEvent in the hash for each <entry> tag indexed by its <id> tag. Once the parser completes scanning all tags, the code converts the hash to a list, enumerating the hash's entries and inserting them into the model. (Because our list view uses a proxy model that performs the sorting, it doesn't matter what order the hash's entries are inserted in the model.) After updating the model, the thread emits a finished signal so the UI knows that the download and parsing work is complete.

> **TIP:** A more robust sample application might store the previous results in a file so that data would be immediately visible when starting the application, and then replace the older data with that fetched from the network. See if you can make the modifications yourself. (Hint: Look at where the data is parsed.)

The QuakeEvent class is a data container and data helper class; it handles some of the messier bits of parsing the XML, such as converting the USGS time stamps into QDateTime instances that can be used elsewhere in the application. Listing 4–12 shows the class definition for QuakeEvent.

Listing 4–12. *The* QuakeEvent *class, representing a single seismic event*

```
class QuakeEvent {
public:
    QuakeEvent();

    QString id() const;
    QString summary() const;
    QDateTime when() const;
    QString where() const;
    qreal magnitude() const;
    QPair<qreal, qreal> position() const;
    qreal elevation() const;
    QString html() const;

    // Used by the XML parser
    void set(const QString& name, const QString& value);
    QString get(const QString& name) const;

    bool isEmpty() const;
    void clear();

    // For use when sorting by time
    bool operator<(const QuakeEvent& b) const;

private:
    QMap<QString, QString> mData;
    static bool mRegisterMetaType;
};
```

The class itself stores the various fields of data in a hash table, and the accessor methods do a bit of necessary screen scraping to obtain semantically valid values for each field. For example, Listing 4–13 shows the code necessary to extract a numerical magnitude and QString containing the human-readable location for a single event.

Listing 4–13. *Screen scraping the magnitude and location from the USGS data*

```
qreal QuakeEvent::magnitude() const
{
    QString title = mData.value("title");
    // Format of title is "M 2.6, Baja California, Mexico"
    QString mag = title.mid(2, 3);
    return mag.toFloat();
}

QString QuakeEvent::where() const
{
    QString title = mData.value("title");
    // Format of title is "M 2.6, Baja California, Mexico"
    QString where = title.mid(title.indexOf(", ")+2);
    return where;
}
```

Similar—albeit more complex—work is done to render the dates to a format usable by Qt for sorting quake events.

> **NOTE:** In a perfect world, there'd be no need for screen-scraping. Instead, the XML schema would provide specific tags for each bit of data your application requires. Hopefully, you get to define both sides of the transaction, or at least provide some input in the process of determining what data the client must parse. Screen-scraping is brittle and subject to potential failure; we use it here to show you how to obtain meaningful data from a Web service as a compromise between looking for a data service ideal to our task and free for everyone to use.

Displaying the Results

The great thing about working with the MVC paradigm is that nothing special is required to display updated content—stick some data in the model, and *poof!* The view updates itself. Consequently, there's little need for the handleRequestFinished slot, shown in Listing 4–14.

Listing 4–14. *Sorting the network results and helping the user*

```
void MainForm::handleRequestFinished() {
    mSortedModel->sort(0, Qt::DescendingOrder);
    mItemView->setHtml(tr("<body><p align=\"center\">"
        "Select an item for more details.</p></body>"));
}
```

This method simply performs the deferred sorting of the data by recency, and provides a bit of help text in the QWebView. A more complex application might need to do more here, such as manage a distraction graphic.

In the section "Implementing the Application User Interface," in the MainForm's constructor, we connected a slot to the mListView's clicked method. Listing 4–15 shows this slot.

Listing 4–15. *Displaying more data associated with an item*

```
void MainForm::handleItemClicked(const QModelIndex& which)
{
    QVariant html = mSortedModel->data(which,
                                  QuakeListModel::Description);
    qDebug() << html.value<QString>();
    mItemView->setHtml(html.value<QString>());
}
```

This method just sets the HTML for the QWebView to the verbose description of the seismic event, letting the user see a small map indicating the event's position and more information about the event.

Wrapping Up

In this chapter, we've touched on a number of aspects of Qt programming, including:

- Qt's introduction of signals and slots to facilitate decoupled communication between different objects.

- Qt's object model, including object properties that can be queried, hierarchical memory management, and resource management.

- Qt's collection classes, including lists and associative arrays (hashes).

- Using Qt's QIODevice with other classes for reading and writing data.

- Qt's facility for providing platform threads to multithreaded applications.

- Qt's support for MVC programming using a data model and view to ease the construction of data-centric applications.

With this information in hand and perhaps an occasional peek at the Qt documentation, you're on your way to building many kinds of applications that obtain or process data and present the results to users. In the next chapter, we'll build on this information to polish the application you've already seen by showing you how to include menu actions and multiple views within your application.

Chapter 5

Doing More with Qt

In the last chapter, we showed you the fundamentals of Qt as a porting layer and graphics environment. With what you learned, you can begin to design and build applications, but there's still quite a bit Qt offers that you haven't seen yet, some of it essential to most applications, we touch on that in the last chapter and expand upon it here.

This chapter shows you how to do more with Qt: including application resources, incorporating user actions in your application's user interface, implementing a custom widget, integrating Qt with web content, and accessing hardware features such as the positioning subsystem in the handset. We begin by discussing each of these facets of Qt individually with code snippets that demonstrate their use, and then we close the chapter with a revised version of Shake that shows how to integrate what you've learned in a running application.

Using Application Resources

For all but the simplest of applications, application resources—whether text, data such as XML-encoded default configurations, images, or sounds—play a key role. Over time, different operating systems and application frameworks have tackled the problem of carrying resources differently; some using parts of an application's binary, others using data files in specific locations or hidden from the user.

Qt provides a simple solution to the problem that works across all platforms, encoding resources as a part of the application binary's static read-only segment. Qt utility classes that deal with files can load any application resource as well. Qt accomplishes this by providing a resource compiler, rcc, as part of its tool chain; the resource compiler takes a collection of resources you specify and includes a copy of the binary data for each resource in the application binary. At runtime, you access the resources using QFile by providing a file path to the resource as defined in the collection of resources at compile time. You simply need only precede the path to the resource with a colon character to indicate that the path is to a resource instead of a file on the file system. Because most Qt classes that work with data can take data from files, in practice loading data from application resources is trivial for you to implement.

The Qt resource system stores your resources in a tree within your application, so you can create a logical hierarchy of resources, just as if they were on disk. The resource collection file lets you specify the relationship between the source resources in your project and the destination in the resource tree, although for simplicity it's usually best to have your source representation match the resource tree at runtime so you're less likely to be confused.

Including Resources in Your Applications

As you saw briefly in the previous chapter, including resources in your Qt application is especially easy if you use Qt Creator; to begin, you need to define a collection of resources to include. In Qt Creator, you do this by right-clicking the project in the Projects pane, and then choosing "Add New…" ➤ "Qt Resource File" from the dialog that appears. Qt Creator provides a resource editor to let you specify files for inclusion as your application's resources, or you can edit the resource collection manually.

When using the editor, you specify a resource's path in your source file hierarchy, the file name of the resource, and its path in the application resource tree. You can also provide a language, indicating that the resource should be loaded only when the specific language is active—handy if you're localizing your application with locale-specific icons, for example.

While the Qt Creator editor suffices for making small-scale changes to an application's resource collection, it's handy to understand the internal representation. Once you do, you can create tools to manage larger bodies of resources if your application requires it. A collection of resources is specified as a simple XML file with the suffix .qrc, like this:

```
<!DOCTYPE RCC><RCC version="1.0">
<RCC>
    <qresource prefix="/images">
        <file>images/map.png</file>
        <file>images/smallmap.png</file>
    </qresource>
    <qresource prefix="/js">
        <file>init.js</file>
    </qresource>
</RCC>
```

The root-level RCC node indicates that the file contains a collection of Qt resources. You indicate each path prefix in the resource tree using a qresource node; there can be any number of these nodes in your resource collection. In the qresource nodes are one or more file nodes, each providing a path (relative to the .qrc file) to the file that should be included as a resource. In this example, there are three files in two tree locations— two images in the images node, and a single (presumably JavaScript) file in the node named js. The images originate in the application sources' images directory, while the JavaScript file comes from the same directory as the resource collection file.

When working with multiple languages, the qresource node includes a lang attribute, set to the International Standards Organization (ISO) two-letter code for the language (such as "en" for English, "de" for German, and so on). If you specify a resource with a lang attribute and that language is not active at runtime, the resource loader will load the resource without any lang attribute, giving you a succinct way to specify both an international default and localized specific resources.

When you add a resource collection file to your project using Qt Creator, it will automatically update your project file by adding a RESOURCES declaration containing the path to your resource collection. In turn, Qt Creator uses qmake to create appropriate make file directives to compile the resource collection and include it in your application binary.

WHEN TO USE QT RESOURCES

The Qt resource system is so flexible that it's tempting to use it for all your resources. It comes with a cost, however: every resource you include in your application increases the data segment size of your application. If you're including a handful of bitmap images for buttons and a screen background, that's probably what you want. If there's a lot more, however, you should use the platform's native deployment format (see Chapter 8) and include larger resources as separate files bundled with your application. If you don't, your application will load more slowly and fail to load on devices with smaller amounts of RAM. This is especially true when your application runs from a USB-mountable medium such as a memory card, because operating systems disable demand paging to avoid losing parts of your application if the USB cable is removed.

Accessing Application Resources

In general, there is nothing specific that you need to do at runtime to access your application resources, other than provide a path to a resource file in the same way you'd provide a path to a file on the file system. The path to a resource always begins with a colon, like this: ":/images/map.jpg". You can provide a resource path to any API that takes a file path, including not just QFile, but other classes, such as QPixmap, which loads an image as a map of pixels (we'll have more to say about QPixmap in the next section, "Implementing a Custom Widget"). For example, here's a snippet from the implementation of a custom widget that loads an image from the application resource and draws it:

```
QPixmap map(":/images/map.jpg");
QPainter painter(this);
painter.setRenderHint(QPainter::Antialiasing);
QPoint pt(0,0);
painter.drawPixmap(pt, mMap);
```

Of course, in practice you'd want to load the pixmap once—say, at initialization time—rather than each time you paint the pixmap, but you get the idea.

Incorporating User Actions

It's one thing to use Qt's components to trigger actions—as you saw in the last chapter, both simple controls like buttons and complex ones like list views emit signals when the user interacts with them. However, there are times when you want to embed a call to an action within a screen, rather than attach the operation to a specific widget. For example, many applications have both list views and detail views, and you may want to have a means within the view to switch between views. (Shake does this, as you see later in the section "Putting It All Together".)

Rather than forcing you to handle this on a platform-by-platform basis, Qt provides an abstraction called an *action* that you can attach to a specific window. The Qt run-time library then performs device-specific gymnastics to present the actions you specify in device-specific ways, ensuring a common look and feel between Qt and other applications on the mobile device. To understand how this works, and to get a better feel for how your application fits with the rest of the device's user interface, it's worthwhile first to take a closer look at Qt's concept of a main window, and then delve into Qt actions in more detail.

Introducing the Qt Main Window

Figure 5–1 shows the layout of a typical Qt application's user interface on both Symbian (top) and MeeGo (bottom) devices. Both layouts reserve space for the following key components:

- The status bar, with annunciators for signal strength, GPS activity, new message alerts, and so forth. (These aren't shown in the diagram, which was taken from the Qt Simulator.)

- A trigger for the *options* menu of programmatic actions attached to the main window.

- The *central widget*, which occupies the bulk of the screen.

In addition, on Symbian devices there's room for two *soft keys* that lie below the screen's content region.

This layout is in turn a refinement of the Qt main window layout for desktop, which includes space for menu bars, toolbars, a dock widget, the central widget, and the status bar. On a mobile device, it's obvious that there's simply not enough room for all of these, so to simplify the user experience, Qt on mobile devices strips out all but the notion of a single menu and the central widget.

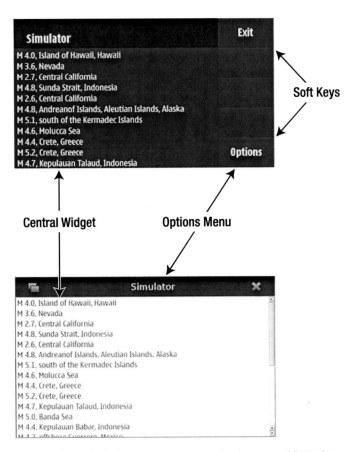

Figure 5–1. *The typical appearance of Qt applications on mobile devices*

When working with QMainWindow, Qt's class that represents your application's main window, you should be aware of three methods that help you manage this organization of your application's user interface.

The first two are the centralWidget and setCentralWidget methods. They let you get the currently established central widget and set it to a new widget. Your central widget can be—and often is—a single widget, such as a QListView or QWebView. If you need a more complicated layout, you can use a composite widget with layouts. Here's where Qt Creator really shines, because you can use it (simply right-click the project➤Add New...➤Qt➤Qt Designer Form) to create a new composite widget as your application's central widget. Once you do this, in your code you just create an instance of this widget, and then set it as the central widget for the main window.

The final method to be aware of is menuBar, which returns an instance of the Qt menu bar that hosts the options menu. Historically from the desktop, this menu bar would have multiple menus (e.g., "File," "Edit." and so forth), but on Nokia's mobile platforms, these menus are collapsed into the single options menu. You'll add actions to the menu bar that represent user actions, such as switching from one view to another.

Attaching Actions to the Main Window

Qt defines the QAction class as an abstraction of a user action. Actions act as containers for the notion of an action, which has user representations such as its menu text. On desktop platforms, actions bear a lot of additional optional information, including icons, status text, shortcut keys, and tool tip text. On mobile devices, all you'll care about mostly is its menu text, because most of the time you use an action, you are attaching it to a main window's menu bar to represent an options menu item.

> **NOTE:** Any widget can bear actions, however, but how widgets actually visualize and use those actions depends on the widget. For example, a toolbar collects actions and shows the actions as icons, while the options menu uses less space, but isn't immediately obvious or accessible to the user.

Using an action in the context of an options menu is easy: simply create it and add it to the main window's menu bar, like this:

```
QAction showListAction = new QAction(tr("Show List"), this);
mMainWindow->menuBar()->addAction(showListAction);
```

Actions emit the triggered signal when the user selects the action, so it's also necessary to connect the action's triggered signal to something that can handle the action, like so:

```
connect(showListAction, SIGNAL(triggered()),
        this,          SLOT(handleShowList()));
```

These four lines of code create an action that appears as the options menu item "Show List," add the action to the options menu, and then connect the item to the current class's handleShowList. So when the user selects the "Show List" item from the options menu, Qt invokes the method handleShowList. Note that by setting the showListAction's parent to this, there's no need to track it globally; when the creating object reaches its end of life, the Qt memory manager will destroy the action as well.

Implementing a Custom Widget

With Qt's rich collection of widgets, you might think there isn't much need or room for you to create your own widgets, but there are two reasons you might want to. First, there may simply not be a widget with the appearance and behavior your need; creating a new widget by composing simpler widgets or by performing the widget drawing and event handling yourself lets you create an entirely custom widget. Second, creating a custom widget is the trick to performing your own drawing in an application using other widgets. Qt provides the QWidget class, a base class to all widgets; when you create a widget, you subclass QWidget and override specific methods to indicate how your widget should set its size relative to its layout, handle incoming events, and paint its contents.

QWIDGET VS. QGRAPHICSITEM AND ITS KIN

A quick glance at Qt's class hierarchy will quickly point you to two competing widget hierarchies: QWidget and QGraphicsItem. What's the difference?

QWidget provides a traditional widget hierarchy with the notion of parent and children widgets in a container-based tree layout. It's been a part of Qt for a long time, and provides the basis for traditional component-oriented GUI applications for both desktop and mobile applications. It's best suited to those kinds of applications, where there's somewhere between a handful and a few dozen or so active widgets within a window at any time.

QGraphicsItem, on the other hand, is part of Qt's newer graphics view framework, a scene-based graphics rendering system that can handle large numbers of custom graphics items, including support for zooming and rotation. In the view framework, graphics items are lighter weight than widgets, and are managed by a graphics *scene* (consisting of a collection of objects) and visualized by a *view*. The framework provides simple primitives for shapes such as rectangles and ellipses, although of course you can provide your own custom items. These items can behave in ways very similar to widgets, including performing their own event handling and painting.

You might choose to use the Qt graphics view framework if you're implementing a very complex view system, such as a vector-based map renderer or complex game with its own canvas and many objects moving at once. While we focus on creating custom Qt widgets that interact with the QWidget hierarchy in this chapter, many of the concepts carry over to using the Qt view framework, and you can learn more about it at http://doc.qt.nokia.com/graphicsview.html.

Subclassing QWidget

To begin, your custom widget needs to implement QWidget and include the Q_OBJECT declaration. Listing 5–1 shows a trivial example:

Listing 5–1. *A trivial widget*

```
class MyWidget : public QWidget
{
    Q_OBJECT
public:
    explicit MyWidget (QWidget *parent = 0)
        : QWidget(parent) {}

protected:
    void paintEvent(QPaintEvent *) {
        QPainter painter(this);
        painter.setPen(Qt::blue);
        painter.setFont(QFont("Arial", 18));
        painter.drawText(rect(),
                         Qt::AlignCenter,
                         "Hello world");
    }

private:
    Q_DISABLE_COPY(MyWidget)
};
```

This widget simply paints the message "Hello World" at its origin. It does, however, demonstrate the basic requirements you must fulfill to provide your own widget:

- Your custom widget must inherit QWidget.

- Like any QObject-based class, your widget must include the Q_OBJECT declaration in its class definition.

- Your custom widget implements its functionality by overriding parent methods in QWidget. As you'll see in the section "Handling Incoming Events" later in the chapter, many of these methods are event handlers for specific Qt-based events passed to your widget.

- Instances of widgets are best thought of as unique objects, and thus can't be copied. To prevent the compiler from including default copy constructors for your widget, use the Q_DISABLE_COPY macro in private declarations in your class to ensure that the copy constructors for your widget remain private.

Specifying Your Widget's Size Hints and Policies

Previously you've learned about Qt's system of layouts, which let you specify how widgets arrange themselves in a container. A key part of the layout system is how widgets indicate their size preference and policies to the layout manager. They communicate this using two methods: sizeHint and sizePolicy.

The sizeHint method provides a hint to the layout manager how big the widget would like to be. It returns a QSize, which has width and height member functions to provide the dimensions, along with an isValid function that indicates whether the size is valid or not. (It also has convenience methods for performing arithmetic on sizes, including scaling a size to fit within a predetermined width and height.)

How the layout system interprets the sizeHint depends on the sizePolicy, which can have the following values for each of the horizontal and vertical axes:

- When the value is QSizePolicy::Fixed, the sizeHint-returned value is the only acceptable alternative, so the widget can never grow or shrink.

- When the value is QSizePolicy::Minimum, the sizeHint-returned value is minimal and sufficient. The widget can be expanded, but there is no advantage to it being larger.

- When the value is QSizePolicy::Maximum, the sizeHint-returned value is a maximum, and the widget can be shrunk if other widgets require the space.

- When the value is QSizePolicy::Preferred, the sizeHint-returned value is best, but the widget can be shrunk or expanded and still be useful.

- When the value is QSizePolicy::Expanding, the sizeHint-returned value is a sensible size, but the widget should get as much space as possible.

- When the value is QSizePolicy::MinimumExpanding, the sizeHint-returned value is minimal and sufficient. The widget can make use of extra space, so it should get as much space as possible.

- When the value is QSizePolicy::Ignored, the sizeHint-returned value is ignored and the widget be made as large as possible.

The widget returns these values when the layout invokes sizePolicy, which returns a QSizePolicy instance. Of course, you can override a specific widget's desired horizontal or vertical size policy by calling setSizePolicy. But in general when creating your own widget, it's easier to override sizePolicy altogether. Expanding our previous example, Listing 5–2 shows what we might write, with the methods you've already seen elided for brevity.

Listing 5–2. *Handling size preferences in a custom widget*

```
class MyWidget : public QWidget
{
    Q_OBJECT
public:
    explicit MyWidget (QWidget *parent = 0) …

    QSize sizeHint() {
        return QSize(80, 60);
    }
    QSizePolicy sizePolicy() {
        return QSizePolicy(QSizePolicy::MinimumExpanding,
                           QSizePolicy::MinimumExpanding);
    }
protected:
    void paintEvent(QPaintEvent *event) …

private:
    Q_DISABLE_COPY(MyWidget)
};
```

A widget with these methods would start small, filling a rectangle 80 pixels wide and 60 pixels tall, and grow to fit whatever space the layout could provide.

Handling Incoming Events

In addition to the signal-slot mechanism (which we discussed in the previous chapter in the section "Understanding Signals and Slots"), Qt provides for decoupled one-to-many application signals, Qt provides a rich event system based on its QEvent class and subclasses. All Qt applications have an event loop that accepts incoming events from the native system's event pump and converts those events to QEvent instances (or a QEvent subclass). It then forwards the events to appropriate receivers through QObject::event. The event receipt method in Qt. QObject::event (or its delegate) can choose to accept an event, handling it and marking it as accepted using

`QEvent::accept`. Or it can ignore the event, in which case the event may propagate elsewhere (such as to a containing parent widget).

> **TIP:** Don't confuse events and signals. They're complementary, but very different. A signal lets you set up a one-to-potentially-many notification by connecting a signal to one or more slots; events are directed to a specific receiver, usually via the parent-child layout of the widget hierarchy and the widget that has focus. While both use method dispatches in their implementation, signals go through Qt's metaobject system, while events passed through straight-up inheritance and method dispatches. In many cases, lower-level events sooner or later get transformed to higher-level signals. For example, a mouse-up event on a button will result in a clicked signal that you can easily process in your application.

The `QWidget` class provides its own event method, which internally checks the type of incoming events and calls one of a number of delegate methods, depending on the type of event. Table 5–1 shows a number of the events you likely want to intercept and handle in your widget.

Table 5–1. *Common QWidget Events and their Delegate Methods*

Event	Delegated to	Reason
QCloseEvent	closeEvent	Invoked when the widget is closed
QFocusInEvent	focusInEvent	Invoked when the widget is focused
QFocusOutEvent	focusOutEvent	Invoked when the widget loses focus
QHideEvent	hideEvent	Invoked when the view system hides the widget
QKeyEvent	keyPressEvent	Invoked when the user presses a key and a widget is focused
QKeyEvent	keyReleaseEvent	Invoked when the user releases a key and a widget is focused
QMouseEvent	mouseDoubleClickEvent	Invoked when the widget receives a double-click
QMouseEvent	mouseMoveEvent	Invoked when the user moves the mouse or drags on a touch screen
QMouseEvent	mousePressEvent	Invoked when the user presses a mouse button or presses the touch screen
QMouseEvent	mouseReleaseEvent	Invoked when the user releases a mouse button or releases the touch screen
QPaintEvent	paintEvent	Invoked when Qt needs the widget to draw itself
QResizeEvent	resizeEvent	Invoked when the widget's size changes
QShowEvent	showEvent	Invoked when the view system shows the widget

You've already seen one widget's `paintEvent`, which performs the simple task of drawing text. Many widgets also need to interact with the user, requiring them to process either mouse events or gestures (see the next section for more information about gestures).

Occasionally—especially when debugging someone else's code—you may want to intercept an event before it's delegated to the widget hierarchy or wherever it's headed. You can do this by installing an *event filter* on an object using `QObject::installEventFilter`. The event filter should be another `QObject` that implements `eventFilter`, a method that takes the object being monitored for events (the initial target of the event) and all events destined for the object. Use event filters sparingly, however, because intercepting the event mechanism is computationally expensive (your filter may receive a very large number of events) and may take a toll on run-time and battery performance.

Handling Incoming Gestures

While traditional mouse movement suffices for single-touch interaction on a touch screen, where mouse movement indicates dragging on the screen, Qt provides a gesture framework that handles user panning, pinching, and swiping. It lets you extend the gesture recognizer to interpret and handle application-specific gestures of your own. The framework uses the `QGesture` class to share information common to all gestures, gesture-specific subclasses such as `QPanGesture`, and the existing event system.

To indicate your widget can handle gestures, it must invoke `grabGesture`, passing the gesture ID (Table 5–2) of the gesture it can handle. (If you implement a custom gesture, the framework assigns it an ID when you register the gesture using `QGestureRecognizer::registerGesture`.)

As an example, here's how to recognize and act on swipe gestures, borrowed from Qt's Image Gesture example. The widget's constructor grabs the swipe (and other gestures), indicating to the gesture system that it wants to receive those gestures:

```
ImageWidget::ImageWidget(QWidget* parent)
    : QWidget(parent),
…
{
…
    grabGesture(Qt::PanGesture);
    grabGesture(Qt::PinchGesture);
    grabGesture(Qt::SwipeGesture);
…
}
```

QWidget doesn't define an explicit event handler for gestures, so we need to catch these gestures in QWidget's event method:

```
bool ImageWidget::event(QEvent* event)
{
    if (event->type() == QEvent::Gesture)
        return gestureEvent(static_cast<QGestureEvent*>(event));
    return QWidget::event(event);
```

```
}
```

The gestureEvent method referred to here isn't one in the QWidget class, but rather a
new method we implement that performs gesture-specific recognition and actions,
dispatching to specific handlers for each kind of gesture:

```
bool ImageWidget::gestureEvent(QGestureEvent *event)
{
    if (QGesture *swipe = event->gesture(Qt::SwipeGesture))
        swipeTriggered(static_cast<QSwipeGesture *>(swipe));
    else if (QGesture *pan = event->gesture(Qt::PanGesture))
        panTriggered(static_cast<QPanGesture *>(pan));
    if (QGesture *pinch = event->gesture(Qt::PinchGesture))
        pinchTriggered(static_cast<QPinchGesture *>(pinch));
    return true;
}
```

Table 5–2. *Default supported gestures in Qt and their IDs*

Gesture	ID
Tap	Qt::TapGesture
Tap and hold	Qt::TapAndHoldGesture
Pan (press-drag-release)	Qt::PanGesture
Pinch	Qt::PinchGesture
Swipe (press-drag-accelerate-release)	Qt::SwipeGesture

As the gesture recognizer interprets pointer movements and discerns gestures, it
generates QGestureEvent instances and passes them to any objects that have grabbed
the appropriate gestures via the object's event function, just as it passes any other
event.

Each of the individual gesture handlers called from within gestureEvent do the actual
gesture handling. This is where the rubber meets the road; you invoke gesture on the
incoming QGestureEvent to recover the gesture, determine its type and data, and then
perform the necessary widget-specific processing, such as panning, rotating, or
zooming. As you do this, you need to be cognizant of the gesture's state, because many
of them aren't instantaneous—think pinching, where the user may adjust the distance
between the two touched points repeatedly to see the same content at different zoom
levels. When using a gesture event, you often need to reflect this state in your own event
handling logic—say, by tracking the appropriate zoom level between events.

Creating your own gesture involves subclassing QGestureRecognizer and overriding its
recognize event, which takes the widget receiving input events, and performs the
filtering necessary to determine whether the incoming events in fact define a new
gesture, and parameters that can be discerned from the gesture. Writing a gesture
recognizer is beyond the scope of this book, but it's worth noting that gesture
recognition typically involves writing a small state machine, in which incoming events are

treated differently, depending on the previous events in the stream. When you create a gesture recognizer, you also can subclass QGesture to provide a custom gesture instance that has gesture-specific parameters, such as acceleration or a vector of gesture movement. For more information on writing a gesture recognizer, see Qt's documentation about the gesture framework at http://doc.qt.nokia.com/gestures-overview.html.

Painting Your Widget's Contents

Qt provides a trio of classes that permit you to perform painting—QPainter, QPaintDevice, and QPaintEngine. You use QPainter to paint on an output device, represented by QPaintDevice. QPainter delegates its work to a high-performance renderer via QPaintEngine, letting you render to raster images via the QImage class or using OpenGL or OpenVG on devices with hardware support for those standards. In practice, you use QPainter to perform painting and painting-related settings management, using a QPainter instance correctly configured to paint to the device's screen.

You can paint only when the view system is ready for you to paint; this occurs within your widget's paintEvent method on the main application thread. You already saw a small example in Listing 5–1, repeated again here:

```
void paintEvent(QPaintEvent *) {
    QPainter painter(this);
    painter.setPen(Qt::blue);
    painter.setFont(QFont("Arial", 18));
    painter.drawText(rect(),
                     Qt::AlignCenter,
                     "Hello world");
}
```

QPainter provides support for far more than just text drawing. Table 5–3 lists the primitive drawing functions QPainter provides.

Table 5–3. *QPainter drawing primitives*

Shape	Method
Arc (including a circle)	drawArc
Bezier curve	drawCubicBezier
Chord (circle segment)	drawChord
Convex polygon	drawConvexPolygon
Ellipse	drawEllipse
Erase a rectangle	eraseRect
Filled arc or circle	drawPie
Filled polygon	drawPolygon

Shape	Method
Filled rectangle	fillRect
Image	drawImage
Line	drawLine
Multiple lines	drawLines
Multiple points	drawPoints
Open polygon	drawPolyline
Picture	drawPicture
Pixmap	drawPixmap
Point	drawPoint
Rectangle	drawRect
Rectangles	drawRects
Rectangle with rounded corners	drawRoundedRect
Text	drawText

Drawing with QPainter uses its settings, including its font, brush, and pen. You describe each with a corresponding helper class (QFont, QBrush, and QPen) that encapsulates information such as the font metrics, color, and fill pattern. For example, you can get information and metrics information about a font with fontInfo and fontMetrics, or the color of a pen or brush using the color method. Colors have their own representation, too, using the QColor class, which includes support for interconversion between red-green-blue (RGB), hue-saturation-value (HSV), and the subtractive cyan, magenta, yellow, and key black (CMYK) color systems. The representation of colors includes an alpha channel, as QPainter rendering supports alpha blending during drawing.

When constructing complex shapes, especially repeatedly, you can use QPainterPath, a container class that lets you create a collection of graphical building blocks such as rectangles, ellipses, and so forth. QPainterPath objects can be used for filling, outlining, and clipping, and are more efficient than drawing the same shapes repeatedly because each shape in the composition need be drawn only once. It's especially handy when drawing complex widgets that have precomputed components, because you can compute and cache a QPainterPath as you construct your widget or when its data changes, and then paint it with a single call to QPainter::drawPath in your widget's paintEvent function.

By default, when you paint with QPainter, you're drawing on the device's coordinate system, usually screen pixels. Sometimes it's easier to think about rendering by adjusting the target coordinate system; QPainter lets you perform any affine transformation (linear transformation followed by a translation) of its coordinate system. You can use the following methods to adjust the coordinate system used by QPainter:

- scale to scale the coordinate system by an offset.

- rotate to rotate the coordinate system clockwise around its origin.

- translate to translate (shift by an offset) the coordinate system.

- shear to twist a coordinate system around the origin.

Another common operation you may want to perform is off-screen drawing. While Qt double-buffers drawing to prevent flickering, sometimes you need to perform off-screen drawing for other reasons, such as to composite multiple bitmaps to create a specific bitmap, or decorate a bitmap with text to be draw in multiple locations. Qt provides the QImage class and its subclasses as other concrete implementations of QPaintDevice. So you can create a QPainter using a QImage instance, and then drawing on the image using the QPainter. Qt provides four implementations of QImage:

- QImage class, optimized for fast input/output and direct pixel manipulation.

- QPixmap class, optimized for on-screen drawing.

- QBitmap class, an optimized QPixmap with a bitdepth of 1.

- QPicture class, a paint device that records and replays QPainter commands in a manner similar to QPainterPath.

Interestingly, QImage and its subclasses are Qt value classes like QString; because they use implicit data sharing, you can pass them around freely as you would other implicitly shared data classes like QString and QList. Under the hood, Qt's implicit data sharing handles one shared block for multiple instances, using copy-on-write to create multiple copies of the data only when necessary. To read about how Qt's implicit data sharing works under the hood, see Qt's documentation at http://doc.qt.nokia.com/implicit-sharing.html.

Integrating Qt Objects with Web Content

In the previous chapter we used Qt's WebKit integration to show HTML, but neither said much about its capabilities, nor took advantage of those capabilities. As it happens, Qt and WebKit are quite well-integrated through the QtWebKit implementation, which lets you not just render web content but enhance it by embedding QObject instances in the web content. QtWebKit is a full port of the open source WebKit engine, including rendering for HTML and XHTML, as well as Scalable Vector Graphics (SVG) documents, all styled using CSS and scripted using JavaScript. The most obvious use for QtWebKit is displaying web content or web-styled content in your application, but there are other things you can do, too, such as process web content into bitmaps for placement in your application (think of a wall in a platform game showing real-time data from a web-based news feed).

Linking Your Application with QtWebKit

Linking against QtWebKit in your application is easy—just be sure that WebKit is in your PRO file's QT variable, like this:

```
QT += webkit
```

Of course, C++ classes that access QtWebKit classes need to have access to QtWebkit's interfaces. The easiest way to do this is to include QtWebKit's headers any place you need them, like this:

```
#include <QtWebKit>
```

For faster compilation, you can always forward-declare the classes you're going to use in your header files, and include just the definitions you require, although there's no guarantee that under-the-hood QtWebKit headers are doing the same thing.

Displaying Web Content with QtWebKit

For most purposes, the first class in QtWebKit you use is QWebView. It's a descendant of QWidget that you first encountered in the last chapter when we used it to display the HTML content associated with an earthShake report in the USGS Really Simple Syndication (RSS) feed using the setHtml method. You could just as easily have it load web content from a remote server using its load method, like this:

```
QWebView* view = new QWebView(parent);
view->load(QUrl("http://www.apress.com/"));
view->show();
```

> **NOTE:** If you find yourself using Qt's graphics scene architecture and need to render Web content, use QGraphicsWebView instead. It inherits from QGraphicsItem and renders correctly in a QGraphicsScene.

The QWebView load method takes a QUrl, representing a URL; there are type coercion functions that let you supply a string and it'll be coerced to a URL at runtime, but it's better to be specific instead of relying on compiler magic to say what you mean.

QtWebKit's content loading is asynchronous, so it doesn't block the user thread. It signals its progress so that you can notify the user or take other action. It emits the loadStarted signal when the view begins loading, and periodically emits loadProgress whenever a web element of the page (such as an image or JavaScript segment) is fully loaded. When the entire page is loaded, the QWebView emits the loadFinished signal, passing true if the page is successfully loaded, or false if there is a failure.

You can control a QWebView's behavior using an instance of QWebSettings, available by calling QWebView::settings. You can change the font family and font size, but the most important things you can adjust are the web attributes that determine how QtWebKit behaves. The attributes include:

- Set by default, QWebSettings::AutoLoadImages specifies whether images in content should be automatically loaded.

- Set by default, QWebSettings::JavaScriptEnabled specifies whether JavaScript can be executed.

- QWebSettings::OfflineStorageDatabaseEnabled indicates whether HTML 5 offline data storage is permitted or not.

- QWebSettings::LocalStorageEnabled indicates whether HTML 5 local storage is enabled or not.

- QWebSettings::LocalContentCanAccessRemoteUrls indicates whether locally loaded documents are allowed to access remote URLs.

The last property is especially handy; using it and locally cached content, you can restrict browsing to local content.

QWebView relies heavily on its QWebPage object, which encapsulates the notion of a single web page. QWebPage, in turn, uses one or more QWebFrame objects to represent individual frames within the web page. You can obtain the QWebView's QWebPage instance by calling QWebView::page, and the main (parent) frame of a web page by calling QWebPage::mainFrame.

QWebPage's API is similar to QWebView, because QWebView is really a widget implementation that delegates its handling of web content to QWebPage. A common use for QWebPage (aside from obtaining the page's main frame, something you do to embed Qt objects into the JavaScript runtime, which we discuss more in the next section) is to use it to render web content to an image. You do this using the QWebPage's render function, by invoking it when the web page finishes loading (when its loadFinished signal fires). Listing 5–3 shows pseudocode from a class to do this drawn from the QWebPage documentation.

Listing 5–3. *Rendering a web page to an image*

```
class Thumbnailer : public QObject
{
    Q_OBJECT

public:
    Thumbnailer(const QUrl &url, QObject* parent = 0)
        : QObject(parent) {
        page.mainFrame()->load(url);
        connect(&page, SIGNAL(loadFinished(bool)),
                this,  SLOT(render()));
    };

    QImage thumbnail() {
        return thumb;
    };

signals:
    void finished();

private slots:
```

```
    void render() {
        page.setViewportSize(page.mainFrame()->contentsSize());

        QImage image = QImage(page.viewportSize(), QImage::Format_ARGB32);

        QPainter painter(&image);
        page.mainFrame()->render(&painter);
        painter.end();

        QImage thumb = image.scaled(400, 400, Qt::KeepAspectRatioByExpanding);

        emit finished();
    };

private:
    QWebPage page;
    QImage thumb;
};
```

The key work is in render, invoked when the web page finishes loading. It sets the page's view port—the virtual area where the page will render—to the QtWebKit-calculated size for the page, and then it creates a QImage in which the QWebPage will render the web page. Next, it creates a QPainter for the new QImage, and has the QWebPage render the web page into the image. Finally, it scales the image to a predetermined size, and indicates that thumbnailing is complete by emitting the finished signal.

Another common thing you may want is having fine-grained control over which URLs the web content can visit. This can happen if you're using QtWebKit to render content over which you don't have full control, and don't want to provide a full-on browser experience. Doing this is a bit trickier than thumbnailing, because you have to subclass QWebPage and override acceptNavigationRequest, which returns true if the QWebPage should handle the navigation request. To do this:

1. Subclass QWebPage.

2. Implement QWebPage::acceptNavigationRequest, performing your application-specific logic. You can look at the requested URL as well as the trigger for the navigation (form submission, clicked link, etc.) and determine whether to let the request pass or handle it yourself.

3. At runtime, create an instance of your QWebPage subclass and set it on your application's QWebView instance using setPage.

Embedding C++ Objects in QtWebKit's JavaScript Runtime

While it's quite handy to be able to embed a web view in your application, things get really interesting when you embed Qt objects into your web application. Using QWebFrame's addToJavaScriptWindowObject, you can add any QObject subclass to the JavaScript runtime associated with a web page. When you do this, Qt makes any properties the QObject provides available to JavaScript as slots, and signals as

JavaScript methods. For example, consider the class in Listing 5–4, which emits a signal when someone calls its `trigger` method.

Listing 5–4. The *WebActionProxy* class

```
class WebActionProxy : public QObject
{
    Q_OBJECT

public:
    explicit WebActionProxy(QObject *parent = 0)
    : QObject(parent) {
    };

public slots:
    void trigger() {
        emit triggered();
    };

signals:
    void triggered();
};
```

In itself, it doesn't seem that useful—until you embed it in a JavaScript context, like this:

```
mBackAction = new WebActionProxy(this);
mItemWidget->
    page()->currentFrame()->
        addToJavaScriptWindowObject("action",
                                    mBackAction,
                                    QScriptEngine::QtOwnership);
```

This adds a JavaScript object action that corresponds to an instance of `WebActionProxy`. On the C++ side in our Qt application, we can connect other QObjects to the `triggered` method, and then invoke them from JavaScript using something like the following HTML anywhere in the web content:

```
<p align="center">
  <button type="button"
          onclick="action.trigger()">Back</button>
</p>
```

This creates a button with the name "Back" that invokes the `WebActionProxy` method's `trigger` method, which in turn emits a `triggered` signal—behaving just like a `QAction` in a Qt view. We use this in Shake to permit the user to step back from an item view, which you see later in this chapter in "Putting it All Together."

> **NOTE:** While you could just embed any old object in your JavaScript this way, using a `WebActionProxy` object helps provide a clean abstraction between the JavaScript and C++ worlds, and makes for a more digestible example here.

The application of this should be obvious: not only can web content directly control the behavior of the C++ portions of your application, but with Qt you can weave JavaScript and C++ together, using each language's strengths. By presenting web-oriented user interface in HTML, you can rapidly prototype and control your presentation using CSS with simple scripts using JavaScript, while leveraging native performance and features using C++.

Embedding Qt Widgets into QtWebKit Pages

Not only can you embed Qt objects into a page's JavaScript runtime, but you can embed visible widgets in the page as well. This is handy if you want to use HTML and CSS to control the layout of Qt application components, although doing so is a little more finicky than simply embedding a QObject. QtWebKit supports QObject-based plug-ins, which are visible entities in the web content drawn by Qt widgets. For example, Figure 5–2 shows a QDateTime editor embedded in an HTML window.

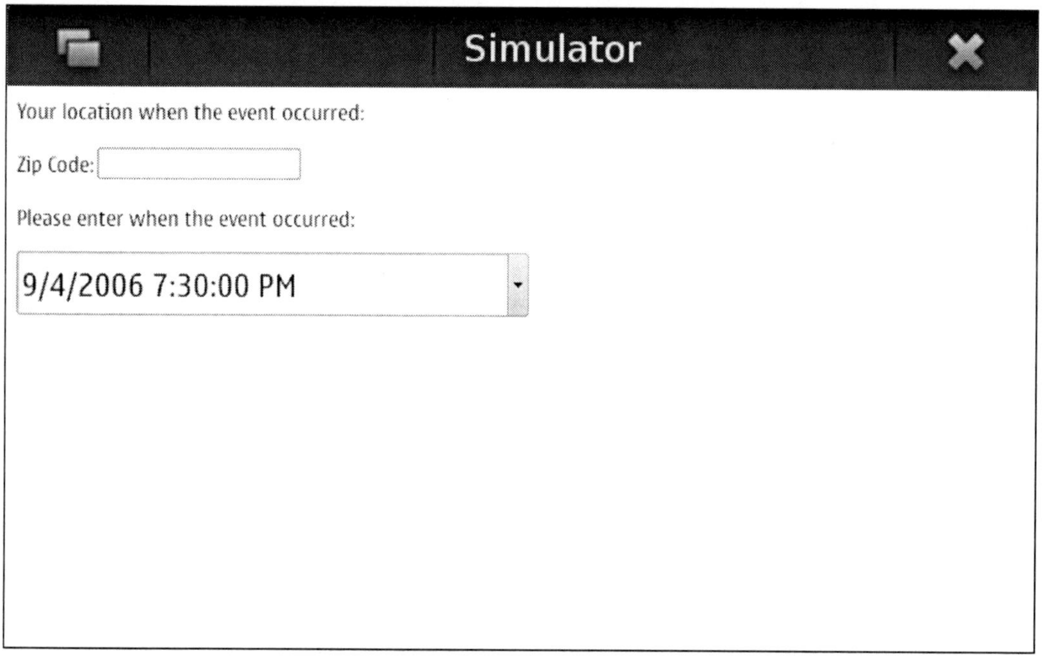

Figure 5–2. *Embedding a Qt widget into a QtWebKit page*

In the HTML, you might write:

```
<object type="application/x-qt-plugin"
    classid="MyDateTime"
    name="datetime"
    width="400" height="48">
</object>
```

This calls out to QWebPage's createPlugin method, which takes the name of a class to create along with the name-value parameters from the HTML origin of the object, and returns a QObject instance that is placed at the appropriate location in the HTML. This method might look something like this:

```
QObject *MyWebPage::createPlugin(
    const QString& classid,
    const QUrl& url,
    const QStringList& paramNames,
    const QStringList& paramValues)
{
    QDateTimeEdit *edit = new QDateTimeEdit(QDateTime()));
    return edit;
}
```

Of course, a real implementation might support several QObject plug-ins, and need to switch on the value of the classid variable.

Back in the QtWebKit environment, you can directly access the properties and slots (method invocations) of the resulting object named datetime from JavaScript, just as you could any other object proxied into the JavaScript runtime. The difference is that the object you created is *visible*, and draws when the web page is painted.

Extending Application Functionality with Qt Mobility

At first it's easy to be overwhelmed by the richness and depth of the porting layer that Qt provides. Experienced mobile developers may soon despair, however, asking where's the geolocation service APIs? How do I access the camera? Can I integrate with the native messaging stack? How do I access contacts?

Nokia provides the Qt Mobility application programming interfaces (APIs) to address these questions. Starting from the capabilities of mobile devices, these APIs may be equally relevant for desktop environments, especially as traditional desktop and mobile computing continue to converge through ultraportable laptops and other computing devices. Like the rest of Qt, Qt Mobility promises cross platform compatibility without sacrificing application performance by using C++, Qt's metaobject system, and signals and slots to provide a uniform programming environment throughout your Qt application's development. The APIs are provided as a collection of small libraries and headers you include within your application, using only the portions of the Qt Mobility API that your application requires.

As of this writing, Qt Mobility provides you with access to the following device features:

- Bearer management, permitting you to start and stop network interfaces, as well as use the system's support for selecting the best bearer interface for a particular application, given the networks available.

- The device camera, permitting you to capture still and video imagery.

- The contacts database, letting you create, edit, list, delete, and look up contact information.

- Device location, giving you an interface to both obtain device location and work with geographical information obtained from satellite or other sources.

- The document gallery, letting you use native applications to render data, such as captured photographs or multimedia.

- Control over feedback devices, such as on-board haptics.

- Messaging, letting you create, originate and receive Short Message Service (SMS), Multimedia Message Service (MMS), Multipurpose Internet Mail Extensions (MIME), and Transport Neutral Encapsulation Format (TNEF) e-mail messages.

- Multimedia, letting you play audio and video using the device's coders and decoders, as well as access the built-in FM radio if one exists.

- The organizer, where you can request calendar, scheduling, and other personal data from local or remote sources.

- Publish and subscribe, letting you share and access item values and obtain change notifications from a tree of values.

- Sensors, letting you access sensors for screen orientation, accelometry, and other applications.

- Service management for plug-in service discovery and use between applications for internal and external data sources.

- Basic system information to determine system-related information and capabilities, such as software versions, hardware features, available network types and status, and so forth.

- Versit document management to parse vCard (and eventually iCalendar) data.

The Qt Mobility interfaces have evolved considerably quicker than the existing Qt interfaces, a result primarily of mobile developer needs and the small, well-defined nature of each segment of the Qt Mobility API. Additionally, Nokia plans and frequently makes available *technology preview* releases of Qt Mobility, giving access to new APIs as soon as Nokia has finished coding and testing them. In the discussion that follows we give you a flavor for the capabilities and use of the first commercial release of Qt Mobility, so that as you design your application, you know what Qt Mobility features are available.

In the discussion that follows we touch on some of what we believe to be the most important and useful Qt Mobility APIs. For a thorough discussion of this fast-evolving part of Qt, see http://qt.nokia.com.

Using the Qt Mobility APIs

Before you use a Qt Mobility API in your application, you need to do several things:

1. Identify the Qt Mobility APIs you wish to use.

2. Update your application's PRO file to include the necessary configuration for that Qt Mobility API.

3. Re-run qmake by right-clicking on the project name and choosing "Run qmake."

4. Include the necessary Qt Mobility classes (from the Qt Mobility namespace) in your application.

5. On Symbian, update the platform capabilities to permit your application to use the desired API.

When you use Qt Creator to create a PRO file for your application, it includes two variables, CONFIG and MOBILITY. The CONFIG variable specifies particular build configuration options for your application (such as whether it's a Qt GUI or Qt console application), while the MOBILITY variable indicates which Qt Mobility APIs you wish to use. To use Qt Mobility APIs at all, you need to add mobility to the CONFIG variable, and then enumerate the desired Qt Mobility APIs, like this:

```
CONFIG += mobility
MOBILITY += location bearer
```

This example indicates that you want to use the location and network bearer APIs in your application. Under the hood, qmake uses the installed Qt Mobility configuration to determine the additional include paths and libraries for your application based on the value of the MOBILITY variable at build time. Table 5–4 lists each of the Qt Mobility API domains and the corresponding value to append to the MOBILITY variable.

> **CAUTION:** Don't forget to include the appropriate values for the MOBILITY variable! If you find you're getting build errors relating to missing include files or mismatches between the Qt Mobility namespace and your own namespace, or an inability to link, be sure and check your project's MOBILITY variable (and be sure you're appending values with +=, not assigning them with =).

Table 5–4. *Qt Mobility APIs and the values for the* `MOBILITY` *qmake variable*

Qt Mobility API	Value
Bearer Management	`bearer`
Contacts	`contacts`
Document Gallery	`gallery`
Feedback (haptics)	`feedback`
Location	`location`
Multimedia	`multimedia`
Messaging	`messaging`
Organizer	`organizer`
Publish and Subscribe	`publishsubscribe`
Service Framework	`serviceframework`
Sensors	`sensors`
System Information	`systeminfo`
Telephony Events	`telephony`
Versit (vCards)	`versit`

In the class declarations that use Qt Mobility classes, you need to do two things: include the Qt Mobility global declarations, and declare the Qt Mobility namespace so you don't have to declare the namespace containing Qt Mobility classes when you use a Qt Mobility class. You do this with the following two lines:

```
#include <qmobilityglobal.h>
QTM_USE_NAMESPACE
```

(If you include a specific Qt Mobility header, you can omit the inclusion of `qmobilityglobal.h` because it'll be included by the specific header.)

Of course, you also need to forward-declare Qt Mobility classes or include the relevant header files that declare those classes; as with Qt, there's usually an `include` file for each class. For example, to reference a position using the `QGeoPositionInfo` class, simply include the `QGeoPositionInfo` header, like this:

```
#include <QGeoPositionInfo>
```

As a general rule to help speed compilations, we like to forward-declare our classes in headers whenever possible, only including the actual class definition in source files when they're actually needed.

Finally, if you're writing an application targeted to Symbian, you need to be aware of Symbian *capabilities*. Symbian provides a robust security model, in which many APIs that may require user or operator trust are available only to applications that assert specific capabilities in their application binary. For example, before obtaining the device position, an application must be built including the Location capability; if the application doesn't bear this capability, the location request will fail with a platform security violation. You assert these capabilities in the application's PRO file, and the build system includes them in the binary package when building the application, like this:

```
symbian: TARGET.CAPABILITY += NetworkServices ReadUserData \
                              Location
```

Table 5–5 shows a list of the required capabilities for each of the Qt Mobility APIs. For more information about Symbian's capability model, see http://wiki.forum.nokia.com/index.php/Capabilities.

> **CAUTION:** Failing to provide a capability is a common source of grief when using Qt Mobility for Symbian. If your application simply fails to start, or exits immediately after starting or when you invoke an operation that's using a Qt Mobility API, be sure to check the capabilities in your application's PRO file. Mismatching capabilities frustratingly causes the system to terminate an application without warning, rather than giving you an error.

Table 5–5. *Qt Mobility APIs and the required Symbian capabilities*

Qt Mobility API	Value
Bearer Management	ReadUserData NetworkServices
Contacts	ReadUserData WriteUserData
Location	Location
Multimedia	UserEnvironment ReadUserData WriteUserData ReadDeviceData WriteDeviceData
Messaging	LocalServices ReadUserData WriteUserData NetworkServices UserEnvironment ReadDeviceData WriteDeviceData
Organizer	ReadUserData WriteUserData
Publish and Subscribe	Depends on the value being read or written.
Service Framework	None, although plug-ins may have specific requirements
Sensors	
System Information	LocalServices ReadUserData WriteUserData NetworkServices UserEnvironment ReadDeviceData WriteDeviceData
Versit (vCards)	None

1. NetworkControl is required for QNetworkSession::stop

2. Capability requirements are not yet published for the camera, document gallery, telephony events. or feedback APIs.

Note that if you add capabilities to your application, you may need to add a developer certificate, as well to assert those capabilities. You also may need to obtain additional signing from Nokia when publishing your application on the Ovi Store. For more information about certificates in the context of testing and publishing your application, see the section "Signing Your Qt Application for Symbian Devices" in Chapter 9.

Managing Bearer Networks

Today's devices typically have multiple means of accessing wireless networks, such as support for both WiFi and cellular wide-area networks. Most platforms allow the user to select the system's default configuration, which all applications should honor when accessing the network. This default may be a service network for wide-area network access, a particular Internet access point such as a WiFi network, or a default that prompts the user with available networks at each attempt to connect. The Bearer Management API lets you control when and how your application accesses the network by selecting a particular network interface or using the user-specified system default, without excessive prompting to the user.

The Bearer Management API consists of three classes: QNetworkConfigurationManager, QNetworkConfiguration, and QNetworkSession. The first class provides ways to determine whether the device is already online; detecting system network capabilities such as whether the application can start and stop interfaces; roaming across networks; obtaining a collection of all network configurations; or obtaining the default configuration. This last use, the most common one, occurs when your application needs to go online and should use the default connection, using code as you see in Listing 5–5. The second class, QNetworkConfiguration, represents a specific interface configuration, such as WiFi through a particular WiFi network with its associated security information. The QNetworkConfigurationManager provides these, and you use a QNetworkConfiguration with QNetworkSession, which opens a network session for your application.

Listing 5–5. *Opening the default network connection*

```
QNetworkConfigurationManager manager;
const bool canStartIAP = (manager.capabilities()
    & QNetworkConfigurationManager::CanStartAndStopInterfaces);
QNetworkConfiguration cfg = manager.defaultConfiguration();
if (!cfg.isValid()
 || (!canStartIAP
    && cfg.state() != QNetworkConfiguration::Active)) {
    QMessageBox::information(this,
                            tr("Network"),
                            tr("No Access Point found."));
    return;
}

session = new QNetworkSession(cfg, this);
session->open();
session->waitForOpened(-1);
```

Listing 5–5 does just this, beginning by determining if it is permitted to start and stop interfaces, and then determining the default configuration. If there's no default configuration and the network isn't already active, the code tests to see if it can start a new session; if it can't, it fails with an informative error. If, however, there's a default configuration, or the network is already running, the code opens the session, blocking the thread until the network completely opens(typically a few hundred milliseconds at most).

The QNetworkSession class offers a signal when a more suitable network session is available; by keeping a reference to the active QNetworkSession and listening for that signal, you can migrate a network connection to a more suitable access point. To do this:

1. Connect to the QNetworkSession's preferredConfigurationChanged signal.

2. In the slot that handles the signal, connect to the QNetworkSession's newConfigurationActivated signal.

3. In the connection that handles the preferredConfigurationChanged signal, invoke a migration to the new network by invoking QNetworkSession::migrate, or ignore the new network by invoking QNetworkSession::ignore.

4. If you invoke migrate, the connection will attempt to migrate, and when migration is complete, it willtrigger the newConfigurationActivated signal.

5. In the slot that handles the newConfigurationActivated signal, call accept to terminate the previous access point, or reject to reject the actual migration if the new network is unsuitable (for example, if the new network does not permit a connection to the remote host).

The Bearer Management Qt Mobility API was moved to Qt in Qt 4.7, so if you're developing with the Qt 4.7 release, you should use the classes provided in Qt 4.7 rather than the Qt Mobility API. To do this, simply remove the bearer value from the MOBILITY variable in your PRO file, and remove the declaration of the Qt Mobility headers and namespace from the relevant source files in your application.

Obtaining and Working with Device Location Information

The classes in the Qt Mobility Location API help you determine the device's location and manage the notion of precisely specified positions on the Earth's surface, abstracting the latitude and longitude, date and time, velocity, altitude, and bearing of the device when the data was captured. The Location API is explicitly source-agnostic, so under the hood it may be using the Global Positioning System (GPS), positioning through cellular or WiFi network data, or other methods.

To obtain the device's location, you must first obtain an instance of a position information source, which you can do by calling QGeoPositionInfoSource::createDefaultSource, which returns an instance of QGeoPositionInfoSource. This class emits the positionUpdated signal any time the system ascertains position information, so you connect your class to it and call startUpdates to request continuous updates, or requestUpdate to request a single update. We show how to do this in a full application later in the section "Putting It All Together," but Listing 5–6 shows the general idea.

Listing 5–6. Obtaining device position

```
class PositionInfo : public QObject
{
    Q_OBJECT
public:
    PositionInfo(QObject *parent = 0) : QObject(parent) {
        QGeoPositionInfoSource *source =
            QGeoPositionInfoSource::createDefaultSource(this);
        if (source) {
            connect(source, SIGNAL(positionUpdated(QGeoPositionInfo)),
                    this,   SLOT(positionUpdated(QGeoPositionInfo)));
            source->startUpdates();
        }
    }

private slots:
    void positionUpdated(const QGeoPositionInfo &info) {
        qDebug() << "Position updated: " << info;
    }
};
```

You can begin to receive continuous updates by invoking QGeoPositionInfoSource::startUpdates, and stop those updates by invoking QGeoPositionInfoSource::stopUpdates. You can control how often position reports are returned by invoking QGeoPositionInfoSource::setUpdateInterval, or what positioning methods you prefer using QGeoPositionInfoSource::setPreferredPositioningMethods. Note that different positioning methods have different power consumption characteristics, and the more often you obtain position data, the more you tax the device's battery. So it's best to be judicious about how often you poll.

The position data is returned as an instance of QGeoPositionInfo, a data container class that includes not just a QGeoCoordinate bearing the current device coordinates, but a time stamp indicating when the data was obtained. It also has zero or more attributes that indicate things such as the current direction, ground speed, vertical speed, magnetic variation from true north at that location, and the horizontal and vertical accuracy of the position data. The QGeoCoordinate includes information on the position latitude, longitude, and altitude, and provides helper methods for calculating the distance between two QGeoCoordinate instances as well as the bearing from one QGeoCoordinate to another.

New to Qt Mobility 1.1, the Location API includes an abstract interface to a device's store of landmarks, which may be managed by a native application such as a mapping or landmark application. This API provides QLandmarkManager, a utility class that lets you save, fetch, and remove both landmarks and categories of landmarks. Qt Mobility 1.1 also provides an interface based on server plug-ins that present map and navigation data through the notion of a geoservice provider that can provide mapping, routing, and location search results. Using the geoservice provider, you can request an instance of

QGeoMapWidget, a subclass of QGraphicsWidget that can present map data from the geoservice provider. As both the landmarks API and the geoservice API are evolving as we write this, consult http://doc.qt.nokia.com/qtmobility-1.1.0-beta/location-overview.html for more information on the new interfaces available in the Qt Mobility Location API.

Sending and Receiving Messages

Today's mobile devices include support for all kinds of messaging, and many applications benefit from integrating with those messaging solutions. Your application can receive low-cost push notifications via SMS or e-mail, and originating e-mail provides an asynchronous way for your application to interface with remote services. Then, too, there's the obvious: some applications need to permit the user to originate an e-mail with content: think of the "e-mail this story" link on web pages, placed in your application at strategic points in the content.

Qt Mobility's Messaging API provides a host of classes for interfacing with messaging; you can offer the device's native message composition interface, leverage existing installed message transports, including e-mail, SMS, and MMS, and access the native messaging store to pick out specific messages for your application. Two key classes provide the anchor for this functionality: QMessageService and QMessageManager. Together with a number of classes that abstract the notions of messages, recipients, message parts (attachments) message folders and message filters, it's a rich API that lets you use as little or as much of the platform's support for e-mail as you choose.

The QMessageService class gives you a simple interface for managing the messaging services themselves. Using QMessageService, you can:

■ Prompt the user to compose and send a message using the native messaging interface with the compose method.

■ Query for messages matching specific filter criteria using the queryMessages method.

■ Retrieve an undownloaded message's header or body (given only its unique ID) using the retrieve, retrieveBody, or retrieveHeader methods.

■ Send a message you've programmatically composed using the send method.

■ Show an existing message using the show method.

Sending a message is easy. Here's pseudocode to send an SMS message:

```
void MyClass::SendHello()
{
    QMessage message;
    message.setType(QMessage::Sms);
    message.setTo(QMessageAddress("+18885551212", QMessageAddress::Phone));
    message.setBody("Hello world!");

    if (mMessageService.send(message)) {
        sendId = message.id();
    } else {
        // Send failed
    }
}
```

mMessageService is an instance of the QMessageService class; its send message simply sends the message you pass. You can receive confirmation that the message has sent by attaching a slot to its stateChanged signal, like this:

```
MyClass::MyClass(QObject* parent)  : QObject(parent)
{
    connect(&mMessageService,
                SIGNAL(stateChanged(QMessageServiceAction::State)),
                this,
                SLOT(messageStateChanged(QMessageServiceAction::State)));
}

void MyClass::messageStateChanged(QMessageServiceAction::State s)
{
    if (s == QMessageServiceAction::Successful) {
        // message send successful
    } else {
        // message sending failed
    }
}
```

Received messages are automatically placed in the message store, which you can query for incoming messages. When querying for messages, you indicate the query criteria using the QMessageFilter class, which has methods that let you specify filter criteria, including:

- Message ID or a collection of message IDs using the byID method,

- Message priority by the byPriority method,

- Message time stamp using the byTimeStamp and byReceptionTimeStamp methods,

- Message recipients using the byRecipients method,

- Message sender using the bySender method,

- Message size using the bySize method,

- Message status using the byStatus method,

- Message subject using the bySubject method,

- Message type using the byType method.

You can combine independent filters using the & and | operations, just like boolean values. For example, you can search the messaging store for all high priority messages from someone@noplace.com using code like this:

```
QMessageFilter priorityFilter(
    QMessageFilter::byPriority(QMessage::HighPriority));
QMessageFilter senderFilter(
    QMessageFilter::bySender("someone@noplace.com"));
QMessageIdList results =
    QMessageManager().queryMessages(priorityFilter & senderFilter);
```

This code uses the QMessageManager, which provides an abstraction over the message store that lets you access individual messages. The QMessageManager class also provides signals indicating when a message was added to the store (such as by message composition or receipt), removed, or updated (such as when a message's body was fetched over IMAP).

You can obtain an individual message using its ID (obtained using one or more QMessageFilters and the QMessageManager's queryMessages method) and the constructor for the QMessage class, which can accept an ID and create an abstraction of the content of the message from its ID. The QMessage class is essentially a large data container, with a number of accessor and mutator methods to obtain message fields and message content, including:

- The to, cc, and bcc methods to obtain recipient information and the corresponding setTo, setCc, and setBcc methods to set recipient information.

- The attachmentIds, appendAttachments, and clearAttachments methods to obtain attachment information, append files to the message's attachment list, and clear the list of attached files.

- The date and receivedDate methods to obtain composition and receipt dates, and the setDate and setReceivedDate methods to set those values.

- The ID method to obtain a message's ID.

- The from method to obtain the message originator, and setFrom to set the message's originator.

- The subject and setSubject methods to obtain and manipulate the message's subject.

- The status and setStatus message to obtain or set the message's status (including the read status).

- The bodyId and setBody methods to obtain a reference to the ID for the body or set the body as a string or text stream using QString or QTextStream.

The class has several helper classes for data containment, such as QMessageAddress and QMessageAddressList to represent senders or recipients of a message.

Originating a message is easy. To let the messaging user interface do the hard work, you can invoke QMessageService::compose to have the messaging software provide its native composition interface to the user. If you need to originate a message programmatically, you create a QMessage object and use its setter methods to set the recipients, subject, body, and any attachments. Once you do this, invoke QMessageService::send method to send the message.

For examples showing how to use these methods in detail, consult the Keep In Touch example at http://doc.qt.nokia.com/qtmobility-1.0/keepintouch.html and the Message Services example at http://doc.qt.nokia.com/qtmobility-1.0/serviceactions.html on the Nokia web site.

Playing and Recording Multimedia

Qt Mobility's Multimedia APIs give you an easy way to harness the device's integrated coders and decoders (codecs) for audio capture, as well as audio and video playback. The Multimedia API is a good choice when rendering sounds or video for games and other entertainment, as well as streaming audio from remote sources like Internet radio stations. While Qt has Phonon, another multimedia framework that provides cross-platform compatibility, the Qt Mobility solution is the accepted path going forward. (There's also the Qt Multimedia framework, slated for addition into later versions of Qt 4.7 that has many of the same features.)

> **CAUTION:** Unlike all the other Mobility APIs we describe, the Multimedia API is *not* in the Qt Mobility namespace. When predeclaring or using the classes we discuss in this section, do *not* include the QTM_USE_NAMESPACE macro.

Audio playback couldn't be easier: create a player, create a URL to the (local or remote) source of the audio content, and invoke play:

```
QMediaPlayer *player = new QMediaPlayer;
player->setMedia(QUrl::fromLocalFile("beep.mp3"));
player->setVolume(50);
player->play();
```

The QMediaPlayer has slots that permit control of basic playback functions, making it easy to wire to existing UI controls, such as buttons and actions. These slots are as follows:

- The play slot starts media playback.
- The pause slot pauses media playback.
- The setMuted slot mutes or unmutes audio.

- Not supported by all codecs, the setPlaybackRate slot takes a qreal indicating a multiplier to the standard playback rate to speed up, slow down, or reverse playback (normal playback is indicated by a value of 1.0).

- The setPlaylist slot takes a QMediaPlaylist, a collection of media files, and instructs the player to play them in sequence. If the QMediaPlayer instance is playing a playlist, you can obtain that playlist by invoking playlist.

- The setPosition slot takes a number of milliseconds and sets the playback position to that number. You can obtain the current playback position by calling position.

- The setVolume slot takes a volume level as a percentage (from 0 to 100) and sets the playback volume. You can obtain the volume by invoking volume.

- The stop slot stops media playback.

The QMediaPlayer emits a number of signals you can use to monitor playback, including signals for buffering status (bufferStatusChanged), errors (error), media changes (mediaChanged), playback status (stateChanged), position (positionChanged), and volume (volumeChanged).

Playing video requires you to couple a QVideoWidget that renders the video stream to the player. This is a QWidget that integrates with the codec subsystem to render video data, so you can treat it as a standard widget in your application layouts. To wire a QVideoWidget to a QMediaPlayer, you need only pass the QMediaPlayer instance to the constructor of QVideoWidget, like so:

```
QMediaPlayer *player = new QMediaPlayer;
player->setMedia(QUrl::fromLocalFile("movie.mp4"));
widget = new QVideoWidget(player);
mainWindow->setCentralWidget(widget);
widget->show();
player->play();
```

Recording audio is a little trickier; not only do you need to set the output location (where the recorded audio will be stored), but you must select an audio device and a codec scheme. The Multimedia API encapsulates the notion of an audio source using the QAudioCaptureSource class, which offers the following methods:

- The isAvailable method, indicating if audio capturing is available.

- The audioInputs method returns a list of audio inputs (strings describing the kind of audio input).

- The setAudioInput method, which lets you set a particular audio input by its name, indicating that audio should come from that input device.

- The audioDescription method, which returns a string describing the named audio input source.

Once you select an audio input source (typically you would provide the list of sources in a configuration view using a QListView or QListWidget, and use the widget's signal to let you set the appropriate source), you create a QMediaRecorder to record the audio and configure it with a codec and destination for the data. Omitting the user interface for selecting an audio source, we might write:

```
source = new QAudioCaptureSource;
if (!source.isAvailable()) return;
// Select the first audio input device
source.setAudioInput(source.audioInputs()[0]);

QAudioEncoderSettings settings;
settings.setCodec("audio/mpeg");
settings.setChannelCount(2);

recorder = new QMediaRecorder(source);
recorder->setOutputLocation(QUrl::fromLocalFile ("audio.mpg"));
recorder->setEncodingSettings(settings);
recorder.record();
```

The QMediaRecorder interface shares some of its configuration responsibilities with the QAudioEncoderSettings (and QVideoEncoderSettings classes, on devices that support video capture), so you use it to determine the names and attributes of codecs. But then you actually delegate the configuration of a specific codec to the QAudioEncoderSettings (or QVideoEncoderSettings) classes. QMediaRecoder has other methods, including:

- audioSettings to determine the current audio encoder settings.

- videoSettings to determine the current video encoder settings.

- supportedAudioCodecs and supportedVideoCodecs to determine the supported audio and video codecs.

- metaData and setMetaData methods to obtain and set metadata in the encoded media stream.

- state and error to determine the recorder's current state and the last known error, if any.

As with the QMediaPlayer, the key actions a QAudioRecorder can take are actually slots, so it's easy to wire them to buttons or actions. These slots are:

- pause, to pause capture.

- record, to start recording.

- setMuted to mute the audio.

- stop to stop capture.

For an example demonstrating the Multimedia API, see the SlideShow example at http://doc.qt.nokia.com/qtmobility-1.0/slideshow.html.

Obtaining System Information

The System Information portion of the Qt Mobility API is perhaps the least exciting but the most important to many developers. It provides fundamental information about the system on which your application is running, and you can use that information to tune your application's presentation and performance. Using the API, you can obtain basic information about the host system, including:

- The power system status, including the battery level and presence of a battery or charger (using QSystemDeviceInfo).

- The input methods (keys, keyboard, single or multitouch, or mouse) the device supports (using QSystemDeviceInfo).

- The sound profile (silent, normal, loud, etc) selected by the user for ringtones and other alerts (using QSystemDeviceInfo).

- The International Mobile Equipment Identity (IMEI), a number that uniquely identifies the device (using QSystemDeviceInfo).

- The International Mobile Subscriber Identity (IMSI), a number that uniquely identifies the subscriber by the SIM in their device (using QSystemDeviceInfo).

- The device manufacturer and model number (using QSystemDeviceInfo).

- Whether or not the SIM is available (using QSystemDeviceInfo).

- The number of displays and display size (via the existing Qt class QDesktopWidget) and the color depth and brightness of each display (via QSystemDisplayInfo).

- The availability of specific features such as a camera or Bluetooth, the version number of the operating system or Qt installed, and the current country code and language (via QSystemInfo).

- Information about the supported networks, current and home mobile country, and network codes (via QSystemNetworkInfo).

- The ability to inhibit the screen saver when the handset is idle while your application is running, which may have deleterious battery effects (via QSystemScreenSaver).

- Available and total disk space on each storage media, such as the internal storage or a mounted card (via QSystemStorageInfo).

Getting information from QSystemInfo and its related classes is as easy as creating it and querying it, as the following pseudocode demonstrates:

```
QSystemDeviceInfo infoSource;
qDebug() << "imei: " << infoSource.imei();
qDebug() << "imsi: " << infoSource.imsi();
qDebug() << "manufacturer: " << infoSource.manufacturer();
qDebug() << "model: " << infoSource.model();
```

BEYOND QT MOBILITY: NATIVE INTERFACES

What if you look at the latest Qt Mobility APIs and don't find an interface you need? There's nothing that says that you can't access native device features from within your application; Qt and Qt Mobility are there to help you with a clean abstraction layer, not prevent your access to native APIs and services. You can always extend your application to include platform-specific libraries and headers and to write native code.

The best way to do this is to use the *pointer to implementation pattern*, a design pattern in which you provide a platform-independent class that exposes a public API and bears a private pointer to a private, platform specific implementation. You then use qmake and the build system to link the appropriate private implementation into your build, so that as you write your application, the platform-specific implementation is kept to a minimum of code. When you do this, you should:

- ▦ Use qmake and scopes to control which libraries, headers, and platform implementation files get included in different platform builds of your application.

- ▦ Use Qt signals and slots in your public API to give a consistent programming interface to the public consumers of your API.

- ▦ Insulate the public consumer from platform-specific exception handling (especially on Symbian, where the practice is to use a platform-specific exception handling mechanism instead of C++ exceptions) by translating platform-specific exceptions and error codes to signals or Qt error codes. (In general for portability, Qt prefers signals and error codes to using C++ exceptions.)

- ▦ Use Qt data types in the public interface, interconverting to platform data types where required when using native APIs.

An excellent discussion of these points with an example Symbian native implementation can be found on the Symbian Foundation's wiki at `http://developer.symbian.org/wiki/index.php/` `Using_Q5_and_Symbian_C%2B%2B`. Although focused on the Symbian platform, the guidelines presented there apply equally to writing platform-specific code for Qt applications on MeeGo as well.

Putting It All Together

In the last chapter, we showed you some basic Qt features using a prototype of Shake, our earthquake-reporting application that takes data from the U.S. Geological Survey and renders the result as a list of earthquake events, showing the data associated with a specific event. The application had several shortcomings, including a user interface that doesn't match the classic item list/item view paradigm of most mobile applications, an inability to determine how close you were to a particular event, and no good way to get a geographic overview of all of the events that have occurred.

For this chapter, we've extended Shake in several ways:

- ▦ The application now has separate list, item, and map views, as Figure 5–3 shows. As with other Qt mobile applications, the views are selected from the options menu, although selecting a list item also shows the item view.

- The map view demonstrates how to implement a custom widget that renders data from a Qt model.

- The application detail view includes more information about the event, including information from its summary and the title, and if information is available, your current distance from the reported event.

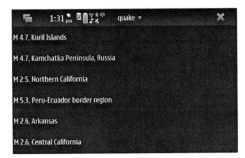

a. List view

b. Options menu

c. Item view

d. Map view

Figure 5–3. *The three screens of the final Shake application as written using Qt: in (a) the list view, (b) the options menu, (c) an item view obtained by touching a list item, and (d) the map view*

To do this, we:

- Refactored the application to use a separate application controller class to manage all of the various signals from the UI, network and Qt Mobility layer.

- Added actions to the main window options menu for view selection.

- Inserted a QObject that proxies QAction into the item view's QWebView, which now displays a "Back" button.

- Wrote a map widget that takes data from the application model and plots it over a Mercator projection map provided as a bitmap.

The following sections look at each of these changes in more detail.

Looking inside the Application Controller

When you launch Qt Creator to create a new Qt GUI application, by default it creates a subclass of QMainWindow, the object that will contain your application's user interface. As defaults go, it's not bad, but many applications don't really need to subclass QMainWindow. What they do need, however, is a *controller*—a QObject-derived class that has slots to accept the various signals from different components in the application. While you can certainly use a QMainWindow subclass to do this, as we did in the previous chapter, it seems in principle a poor idea, because there's an implied relationship with QMainWindow that simply doesn't exist. Because we were adding additional slots to our application to handle user actions and position information, this seems a good time to break the controller into its own subclass. First, we refactored *main.cpp* as you see in Listing 5–7.

Listing 5–7. *Shake's entry point.*

```
#include <QtGui/QApplication>
#include "maincontroller.h"

int main(int argc, char *argv[])
{
    QApplication app(argc, argv);
    MainController* controller = new MainController;
    int result = app.exec();
    delete controller;
    return result;
}
```

As you see, instead of creating an instance a QMainWindow subclass and showing it, we create our MainController instance, and it has a QMainWindow it shows as part of its initialization. Listing 5–8 shows the class definition for MainController in full, which we discuss over this and the next section.

Listing 5–8. *Shake's MainController class*

```
#ifndef MAINCONTROLLER_H
#define MAINCONTROLLER_H
#include <QObject>
#include <QPair>
#include <QMobilityGlobal.h>
#include <QGeoPositionInfoSource>
#include <QGeoPositionInfo>

class QSortFilterProxyModel;
class QProgressDialog;
class QModelIndex;
class QAction;
class QMainWindow;
class QStackedWidget;
class QListView;
class QWebView;
class WebActionProxy;
class WorkerThread;
class QuakeListModel;
class MapItemWidget;
```

```
QTM_USE_NAMESPACE

class MainController : public QObject
{
    Q_OBJECT

public:
    explicit MainController(QObject *parent = 0);
    ~MainController();

    void fetch(const QString& url);

public slots:
    void fetch();
    void handleRequestFinished();
    void handleError(const QString& message);
    void handleItemClicked(const QModelIndex&);
    void handleItemClosed();
    void handleShowMap();
    void handleShowList();
    void positionUpdated(const QGeoPositionInfo&);
    void addProxyObjects();

private:
    void createActions();

    QProgressDialog *mProgressDialog;

    WorkerThread* mBgThread;
    QuakeListModel* mEventModel;
    QSortFilterProxyModel* mSortedModel;

    QListView* mListWidget;
    QWebView* mItemWidget;
    MapItemWidget* mMapWidget;

    WebActionProxy* mBackAction;
    QAction* mShowListAction;
    QAction* mShowMapAction;

    QStackedWidget* mMainWidget;
    QMainWindow* mMainWindow;

    QGeoPositionInfoSource* mLocationSource;
    bool mLocationKnown;
    QPair<qreal,qreal> mLocation;
};

#endif // MAINCONTROLLER_H
```

At this point, there are three things to note about the main controller. First, it *has* a QMainWindow instance, rather than *being* one. In a moment, you'll see where we create and configure the main window. Second, it no longer uses a Qt Designer UI class; as you'll see more in a moment, we use a QStackedWidget to easily switch between different central widgets in the window. Finally, most of its methods are slots, because they're triggered by signals emitted from actions, the network thread, or other incoming events.

The constructor (Listing 5–8) is now responsible for setting up the entire user interface, which consists of creating the list view, web view, and map view, and a QStackedWidget to flip between each widget as the controller handles signals to change the user interface's main view.

Listing 5–8. *The controller constructor, where user interface setup takes place*

```cpp
MainController::MainController(QObject *parent)
    : QObject(parent)
    , mProgressDialog(0)
    , mBgThread(0)
    , mEventModel(new QuakeListModel())
    , mSortedModel(new QSortFilterProxyModel(this))
    , mListWidget(new QListView())
    , mItemWidget(new QWebView())
    , mMapWidget(new MapItemWidget())
    , mBackAction(0)
    , mShowListAction(0)
    , mShowMapAction(0)
    , mMainWidget(0)
    , mMainWindow(new QMainWindow)
    , mLocationSource(
        QGeoPositionInfoSource::createDefaultSource(this))
    , mLocationKnown(false)
    , mLocation(QPair<qreal,qreal>(0,0))
{
    createActions();

    mProgressDialog = new QProgressDialog(
                        tr("Fetching data..."),
                        tr("Cancel"),
                        0, 0);

    mSortedModel->setSourceModel(mEventModel);
    mSortedModel->setDynamicSortFilter(false);
    mSortedModel->setSortRole(QuakeListModel::When);

    mListWidget->setHorizontalScrollBarPolicy(Qt::ScrollBarAlwaysOff);
    mListWidget->setModel(mSortedModel);
    mListWidget->setContextMenuPolicy(Qt::NoContextMenu);

    mMapWidget->setModel(mSortedModel);

    connect(mListWidget, SIGNAL(clicked(QModelIndex)),
            this,        SLOT(handleItemClicked(QModelIndex)));

    addProxyObjects();
    mItemWidget->setContextMenuPolicy(Qt::NoContextMenu);
    connect(mItemWidget->page()->currentFrame(),
      SIGNAL(javaScriptWindowObjectCleared()),
      this,
      SLOT(addProxyObjects()));
```

```
    mMainWidget = new QStackedWidget(mMainWindow);
    mMainWidget->addWidget(mListWidget);
    mMainWidget->addWidget(mItemWidget);
    mMainWidget->addWidget(mMapWidget);
    mMainWidget->setCurrentIndex(kListWidget);
    mMainWidget->setContextMenuPolicy(Qt::NoContextMenu);
    mMainWindow->setCentralWidget(mMainWidget);

    if (mLocationSource) {
        connect(mLocationSource,
          SIGNAL(positionUpdated(const QGeoPositionInfo&)),
          this,
          SLOT(positionUpdated(const QGeoPositionInfo&)));
        mLocationSource->setUpdateInterval(kLocationUpdateIntervalMs);
        mLocationSource->lastKnownPosition();
        mLocationSource->startUpdates();
    }

    QTimer::singleShot(0, this, SLOT(fetch()));
#if defined(Q_WS_S60)
    mMainWindow->showMaximized();
#else
    mMainWindow->show();
#endif
}
```

After creating the actions for the options menu (more on that in a moment), the constructor creates a QProgressDialog, a stand-alone dialog class that provides a barber pole or progressive bar indicating progress. We'll show it when the network fetch begins, and hide it when the fetch completes. Next we set up the model, just as you saw in the previous chapter, and then set up the list's options to hide the horizontal scroll bar, use the sorted model, and not have a context menu for items. The code then creates and registers a QObject subclass with the QWebView, and connects to the QWebView's javaScriptWindowObjectCleared signal. That way, any time the JavaScript context changes, the same object is re-registered.

After that, the constructor creates the QStackedWidget mMainWidget and registers each of the view widgets with it. The QStackedWidget acts as a collection of widgets, and shows the widget indicated by its current index. We provide all three widgets to the stacked widget at once, and instruct it to show the list widget first by calling setCurrentIndex and passing the index of the 0th widget, the list widget.

Finally, the constructor configures the positioning interface (which we discuss in more detail in the next section) and sets a single-shot timer to commence the request before showing the main window.

Many of the slots in the controller are the same as the ones in the previous section, such as those that involve touching an item or when the network transaction completes. New are the action handlers for showing the list and the map, which involve triggered signals emitted by QActions. Those QAction instances are set up in createActions, which you see in Listing 5-9.

Listing 5–9. *Creating actions and adding them to the main window.*

```
void MainController::createActions()
{
    mBackAction = new WebActionProxy( this );
    connect(mBackAction, SIGNAL(triggered()),
            this,        SLOT(handleItemClosed()));

    mShowListAction = new QAction(tr("Show List"), this);
    connect(mShowListAction, SIGNAL(triggered()),
            this,            SLOT(handleShowList()));

    mShowMapAction = new QAction(tr("Show Map"), this);
    connect(mShowMapAction, SIGNAL(triggered()),
            this,           SLOT(handleShowMap()));

    // Add to the options menu
    mMainWindow->menuBar()->addAction(mShowListAction);
    mMainWindow->menuBar()->addAction(mShowMapAction);
}
```

The first action isn't a QAction, but a WebActionProxy, the class we showed you back in the section "Embedding C++ Objects in QtWebKit's JavaScript Runtime." Triggered when you press the back button, an HTML element, it simply brings you back to the list. The other actions are for showing the list and map, and are added to the main window's menu bar to be shown in the options menu.

Changes to the Network Request

We made two changes to how the network code works: we added a QProgressDialog to give some indication of progress, and added support for Qt Mobility's Bearer Management API to make sure that requests use the correct network in all places.

QProgressDialog provides a simple show/hide API that displays the dialog asynchronously when you need it. We create the dialog in the controller's constructor (Listing 5–8), and show it at the beginning of the fetch method using the following line of code:

```
if (mProgressDialog) mProgressDialog->show();
```

Later, in handleRequestFinished and handleError, we hide the dialog using

```
if (mProgressDialog) mProgressDialog->hide();
```

Incorporating the Bearer Management code isn't much more difficult; we changed WorkerThread::fetch to include the boilerplate default access point configuration, as you see in Listing 5–10.

Listing 5–10. *Requesting a URL after configuring the bearer network*

```
void WorkerThread::fetch(const QString& url)
{
    // Don't try to re-start if we're running
    if (isRunning()) {
        this->cancel();
```

```
        }

        // On Symbian, be sure we're using the desired access point.
        // MeeGo doesn't need this.
#ifdef Q_OS_SYMBIAN
        // Set Internet Access Point
        QNetworkConfigurationManager manager;

        const bool canStartIAP = (manager.capabilities()
           & QNetworkConfigurationManager::CanStartAndStopInterfaces);

        // Is there default access point, use it
        QNetworkConfiguration cfg = manager.defaultConfiguration();
        if (!cfg.isValid()
            || (!canStartIAP
            && cfg.state() != QNetworkConfiguration::Active)) {
            emit error(tr("No Access Point found."));
            return;
        }

        mSession = new QNetworkSession(cfg, this);
        mSession->open();
        mSession->waitForOpened(-1);
#endif

        QNetworkReply *reply = mNetManager->get(QNetworkRequest(QUrl(url)));
        if (!reply) {
            emit error(tr("Could not contact the server"));
        }
    }
}
```

This is exactly the code you saw in the section "Managing Bearer Networks," and it's enabled only for Symbian, the one platform right now that has full support for different bearer networks.

Determining the Device Position

In the constructor for the controller (Listing 5–8) you saw the following code:

```
if (mLocationSource) {
    connect(mLocationSource,
        SIGNAL(positionUpdated(const QGeoPositionInfo&)),
        this,
        SLOT(positionUpdated(const QGeoPositionInfo&)));
    mLocationSource->setUpdateInterval(kLocationUpdateIntervalMs);
    mLocationSource->startUpdates();
}
```

This code starts Qt Mobility's Position API to emit position information on a regular basis, invoking our positionUpdated slot when new position data becomes available. Listing 5–11 shows the method that handles that data, code that splits out the latitude and longitude and stores it in a QPair the way we stored position data in the previous chapter's example.

Listing 5–11. *Handling incoming position data*

```
void MainController::positionUpdated(const QGeoPositionInfo& update)
{
    if (update.isValid()) {
        QGeoCoordinate position = update.coordinate();
        mLocationKnown = true;
        mLocation = QPair<qreal, qreal>(position.latitude(),
                                        position.longitude());
    }
}
```

This position is global to the controller, and used only when we show a specific list item, when the user touches an item and the list view's clicked signal is emitted, invoking our handleItemClicked slot. Listing 5–12 shows the handleItemClicked method.

Listing 5–12. Formatting an earthquake report with position information and the back button

```
void MainController::handleItemClicked(const QModelIndex& which)
{
    QPair<qreal, qreal> where(mSortedModel->data(which,
        QuakeListModel::Latitude).value<qreal>(),
      mSortedModel->data(which,
        QuakeListModel::Longitude).value<qreal>());
    QString distance = QString(tr("unknown"));
    QVariant desc = mSortedModel->data(which,
      QuakeListModel::Description);
    QVariant title = mSortedModel->data(which,
      QuakeListModel::DisplayRole);
    if (mLocationKnown) {
        distance = QString("%1 km (%2 mi)")
                    .arg((qreal)gcdDistance(where, mLocation))
                    .arg((qreal)gcdDistance(where, mLocation)
                      / kKmPerMile);
    }

    QString html =
      QString(tr("%1<h1>%2</h1>\n%3\n<strong>Distance</strong>:%4\n%5"))
                .arg(kInitScript)
                .arg(title.value<QString>())
                .arg(desc.value<QString>())
                .arg(distance)
                .arg(kExitItem);

    mItemWidget->setHtml(html);
    mMainWidget->setCurrentIndex(kItemWidget);
}
```

This method has changed a lot, because we now no longer only show the bit of HTML provided by the USGS, but a title with the same information as in the list view, a distance (if we can compute one), and the back button.

This method starts by extracting the position of the earthquake event from the item in the model, as well as its description and title. If the location is known, a string containing the distance in kilometers and miles is computed using the Law of Haversines (http://en.wikipedia.org/wiki/Great-circle_distance), although we could have just as easily used Qt Mobility's own code to do the calculation. Then the entire item view's HTML is built up using a single template that has a (currently unused) JavaScript initialization, heading, USGS-provided description, our computed distance, and the HTML and JavaScript for the back button, which looks like this:

```
<br/><br/><br/>
<p align="center">
  <button type="button"
    onclick="action.trigger()">Back
  </button>
</p>
```

The `action` variable in JavaScript is just the `WebProxyAction` we created in `createActions`, back in Listing 5–9. It gets added to the JavaScript context each time the context gets cleared in our `addProxyObjects` slot, which you see in Listing 5–13.

Listing 5–13. *Adding a* `QObject` *to the web vie.*

```
void MainController::addProxyObjects()
{
    mItemWidget->
            page()->
            currentFrame()->
            addToJavaScriptWindowObject("action",
                                        mBackAction,
                                        QScriptEngine::QtOwnership);
}
```

Drawing the Map

The old saying "A picture is worth a thousand words" is definitely true when it comes to understanding the distribution of spatial data. We added the map to Shake to present earthquake data graphically, giving a quick glance as to where earthquakes had occurred and how big they were. Our goal when creating the map view to Shake was twofold: provide a map that displays something useful and show you the basic idea behind creating your own widget.

The result of this goal is the `MapItemWidget`, a simple class that draws markers of different sizes on a Mercator projection of Earth. The `MapItemWidget` gets its data from a model, so it additionally shows you how to watch a model's data for changes and re-renders when those changes occur. Listing 5–14 shows the class declaration for the `MapItemWidget`.

Listing 5–14. *The widget for rendering the map*

```
#include <QWidget>
#include <QPixmap>
#include <QModelIndex>
#include <QList>

class QAbstractItemModel;

class MapItemWidget : public QWidget
{
    Q_OBJECT
public:
    explicit MapItemWidget(QWidget *parent = 0);
    ~MapItemWidget();

    QSize sizeHint();
    QSizePolicy sizePolicy();

    void setModel(QAbstractItemModel* model);

public slots:
    void itemsChanged(const QModelIndex& topLeft,
                      const QModelIndex & bottomRight );
    void itemsReset();

protected:
    void paintEvent(QPaintEvent *event);
    void resizeEvent(QResizeEvent *event);

private:
    void initMap();
    void initMarkers();

    QPoint geoToWidgetCoords(qreal lat, qreal lon);

    QPixmap mMap;
    QSize mMapSize;

    QList< QPair<QPoint, int> > mMarkers;
    QAbstractItemModel* mModel;

    Q_DISABLE_COPY(MapItemWidget)
};
```

MOBILE DIGITAL CARTOGRAPHY

As we suggest, our goals here are to provide a glanceable view of where earthquakes occurred, and provide you with a digestable example that demonstrates how to create your own widget. The MapItemWidget is admittedly anemic if you're interested in presenting large-scale real cartographic data, or even in providing such basic operations as panning and zooming. If you need to show real data on real maps, what are your choices?

First, future versions of Qt Mobility will provide a maps and navigation API, letting device manufacturers provide plug-in map providers. Using the API, on devices with appropriate server applications, you can embed maps in your application, providing the full digital mapping experience found with the native hosting application. For many applications, this may be ideal, but does require that the application you're writing run on devices that have software serving maps to the Qt Mobility Layer.

Another option is to go with web-based maps like Open Street Maps or Google Maps. One solution would be to embed a QWebView within your application that displays a web-hosted map, using the Qt-JavaScript bindings to move information like the location of map markers from your application's data model to the JavaScript layer, thereby putting C++ objects directly on a map from the Web.

Either way you go, there's still substantial work, and most of that work is with the interfaces of a specific map provider, rather than what we want to show you here: how to create a custom widget. For more information about Qt Mobility's upcoming support for map rendering, see http://developer.qt.nokia.com/wiki/MapsNavigationAPI.

We can divide the widget's functionality into three broad areas: providing size hints to the containing widget, handling the drawing and placement of map markers, and map rendering. Listing 5–15 shows the code that provides the desired size hints for the widget.

Listing 5–15. Providing default size hints

```
const int kMinWidth = 320;
const int kMinHeight = 240;
QSize MapItemWidget::sizeHint() {
    return QSize(kMinWidth, kMinHeight);
}

QSizePolicy MapItemWidget::sizePolicy() {
    return QSizePolicy(QSizePolicy::MinimumExpanding,
                       QSizePolicy::MinimumExpanding);
}
```

Maps are useless when they're too small, so we provide a fairly large minimum size, indicate that our policy is to disallow anything smaller than that default, and grow to accept as much size as the layout will provide.

The map rendering and marker handling are closely related and also coupled with resizing the widget. This is because resizing the map involves redrawing the base map and relocating all of the map markers before redrawing them as well. For a given widget size, the map keeps two pieces of data to speed rendering: a pixmap containing the base map, an image of a map of the Earth in Mercator projection we found at WikiCommons (http://en.wikipedia.org/wiki/File:Mercator-projection.jpg), and the location and relative size of each map marker in widget coordinates. The location and size information is kept as a QPair, rather than a separate class; there's no reason not to use a separate class in this case, except that it makes the code longer, and QPair works just as well.

The base map and marker cache are all initialized whenever the widget resizes. This occurs when the widget is placed in a containing widget, as well as if the widget changes sizes (say, because the screen orientation changes). Listing 5–16 shows the initialization code, starting when the widget receives the resize event.

Listing 5–16. *Map widget initialization when the widget is resized*

```cpp
void MapItemWidget::resizeEvent(QResizeEvent *event)
{
    if (size() != mMapSize) {
        initMap();
        initMarkers();
    }
}

void MapItemWidget::initMap()
{
    // Load the map bitmap
    QPixmap map(":/images/map.jpg");

    QSize newSize(map.size());
    newSize.scale(size(), Qt::KeepAspectRatio);

    if (newSize!=map.size()) {
        mMap = map.scaled(newSize, Qt::KeepAspectRatio);
    }
    // Record the widget size so we only rescale when we need to
    mMapSize = size();
}

void MapItemWidget::initMarkers()
{
    // Always start from scratch
    mMarkers.clear();

    if (!mModel) {
        return;
    }

    for(int i = 0;  i < mModel->rowCount(); i++)
    {
        QModelIndex index = mModel->index(i, 0);
        qreal lat = mModel->data(index,
            QuakeListModel::Latitude).value<qreal>();
        qreal lon = mModel->data(index,
            QuakeListModel::Longitude).value<qreal>();
        qreal mag = mModel->data(index,
            QuakeListModel::Magnitude).value<qreal>();
        QPoint point = geoToWidgetCoords(lat, lon);
        mMarkers.append(QPair<QPoint, int>(point, mag));
    }
}
```

Handling the resizing event is easy—just reinitialize the map's base layer and cache of item positions if the new size isn't the same as the current size. Resizing the base map itself is also easy, thanks to Qt's handling of image formats; we simply reload the base map (which is an image larger than we expect any device screen to be, but not so unwieldy for today's devices) and scale it to fit within the new widget's bounds, preserving the map's aspect ratio. This isn't perfect—as you saw in Figure 5–2, the map ends up with black bands on the borders of the image—but it prevents additional stretching and tearing that would distort the map projection further.

Initializing the map marker position cache is a little trickier. Because there are a small number of items, we do this any time the map rescales or when the model changes (which you see later in Listing 5–18). In either case, we simply clear the cache of markers and then walk the model, projecting each point from its coordinates on Earth to its coordinate on the map using the private function geoToWidgetCoords (not shown here, but available in the sample code that accompanies this book). As you've seen elsewhere, we simply use the model itself to generate an index for each row in the model, and then extract the latitude, longitude, and quake magnitude from the model using its own data method.

With the cache always up-to-date, the map widget's paint function need only draw the base map and then loop over the cache of projected markers, plotting a rectangle for each marker, as you see in Listing 5–17.

Listing 5–17. *Drawing the map and its markers*

```
void MapItemWidget::paintEvent(QPaintEvent *event)
{
    QPainter painter(this);
    QPoint pt;

    pt.setX(size().width() /2 - mMap.size().width() /2);
    pt.setY(size().height()/2 - mMap.size().height()/2);
    painter.drawPixmap(pt, mMap);

    painter.setBrush(Qt::SolidPattern);
    for( int i = mMarkers.length(); i>0; i--)
    {
        QPair<QPoint, int> marker = mMarkers.at(i-1);
        pt = marker.first;
        int r = marker.second;
        painter.fillRect(pt.x()-r, pt.y()-r,
                         2*r, 2*r,
                         QColor(255, 0, 0));
    }
}
```

The code begins by calculating the upper-left-hand corner where to draw the map so it's centered horizontally and vertically. It then loops through the collection of map markers, painting a red-filled rectangle at each marker position. The rectangle's size is twice the magnitude of the earthquake on each axis, providing a slight idea as to the earthquake's relative magnitude without causing too much overlapping between adjacent earthquakes unless they're very close.

The remaining methods of the map widget are largely bookkeeping to manage the map model itself. as vou can see from Listina 5–18.

Listing 5–18. *Managing the view's model and its signals*

```
void MapItemWidget::setModel(QAbstractItemModel* model)
{
    if (mModel) {
        disconnect(mModel, 0, this, 0);
    }
    mModel = model;
    if (mModel) {
        connect(mModel, SIGNAL(dataChanged(QModelIndex,QModelIndex)),
                this,   SLOT(itemsChanged(QModelIndex,QModelIndex)));
        connect(mModel, SIGNAL(modelReset()),
                this,   SLOT(itemsReset()));
    }
    initMarkers();
    update();
}

void MapItemWidget::itemsChanged(const QModelIndex&, const QModelIndex &)
{
    initMarkers();
    update();
}

void MapItemWidget::itemsReset()
{
    initMarkers();
    update();
}
```

You first saw the map widget's setModel method invoked back in Listing 5–8; it needs to do four things:

1. Disconnect from all signals emitted by the old model, if there is one.

2. Cache a reference to the model so it can later get data from the model when it initializes or updates the list of map markers.

3. Connect slots to the model's dataChanged and modelReset methods, so that the widget can redraw any time the model data changes.

4. Re-initialize the cache of markers, so that the view updates with the new data.

The two slots that handle the model changes, itemsChanged and itemsReset, simply invalidate the entire cache and re-create the cache of markers. A more sophisticated view might keep a cache indexed by model index, so that the dataChanged signal's indices could be used to determine which items should be updated, and then update only the changed items. A good place to start in doing this would be to use a QHash keyed by QModelIndexes, with each entry in the cache being the projected point and its magnitude. However, given the number of items likely for the application (certainly less than one hundred), the infrequency of model updates (never, once the application has received its data), and the relatively low cost of handling a single item (a handful of floating-point operations) this complexity doesn't seem necessary.

Wrapping Up

In this chapter, we've covered a lot of ground. Armed with a basic knowledge of Qt, we've shown you how to create multiview applications that draw and present information from a variety of sources, including compile-time resources, device position, the Web, the device's messaging subsystem, local and remote multimedia, and system information.

In the next chapter, we largely set this knowledge aside, and turn to writing applications declaratively using Qt Meta-object Language (QML) and JavaScript, and how to bind applications written with these tools to parts of your application in C++.

Chapter 6

Introducing Qt Quick

Today, there are a lot of tools available for user interface development. In the past two chapters, you've seen a pretty typical approach taken by a platform vendor: provide robust APIs in a commonly known programming language (Qt with C++) to enable developers to create their products. This approach is not without its drawbacks. The cost of learning an entire new API set can be high for some, and even with an API as all-encompassing as Qt, there's still a lot of rote programming (think new and delete) you must do as you develop your application. Surely there's a better way.

To further streamline your development efforts—especially for new applications—Nokia provides Qt Quick, a *declarative* programming environment consisting of Qt Meta-object Language (QML), common components, and bindings to JavaScript and C++. In this chapter we show you what Qt Quick is, how to use QML, and how to connect QML applications to existing or new C++ and JavaScript. To give you hands-on examples along the way, we take the Shake applications in two directions: first an entirely QML-based implementation to show you how easy it is to write user interfaces using QML, and one that uses a QML interface with the C++ worker thread, XML parsing, and model to show you how to connect C++ code to QML. When you're through with this chapter, you'll be in position to create your own Qt Quick prototypes and full-fledged applications.

Declaring Your User Interface

Qt Quick takes a radically different approach to user interface development than you've seen previously in C++ with Qt. More like HTML than C++, Qt Quick uses QML, a JavaScript-like language to define your user interface. QML is a *declarative* language—instead of writing imperative statements that do things, you write declarations of your user interface objects. While at the top level both environments are inherently object-oriented, how you work at the level of individual statements is very different. In C++ with Qt, we might draw a new rectangle using pseudocode like this:

```
QRect rect(0, 0, 32, 32);
QPainter painter;
painter.setBrush(QBrush(Qt::red));
painter.drawRect(rect);
```

In QML, we'd simply write:

```
import QtQuick 1.0
Rectangle {
    height:200
    width: 200
    color: "red"
}
```

The QML example consists of a single object, of type Rectangle. This specific rectangle overrides three of Rectangle's default properties: height, width, and color. The height and width properties are each set to the integer value 32, and color is set to the string "red." Under the hood, the Qt Declarative module includes both a parser for QML and a renderer that renders QML to the screen.

QML can contain scripts, too—here's a button that changes its label to "Hello World" when it's clicked:

```
import QtQuick 1.0
Item {
    width: 200
    height: 100

    Text {
        id: label
        text: "Click Me"
        color: "black"
        anchors.horizontalCenter: parent.horizontalCenter
        anchors.verticalCenter: parent.verticalCenter
        font { family: "Helvetica"; pixelSize: 12; bold: true }
    }

    MouseArea {
        anchors.fill: parent
        onClicked: {
            label.text = "Hello World"
        }
    }
}
```

Here, we have a QML Item, the base element for all visible items in QML. It contains a Text object and a MouseArea that spans the entire size of the Item. We control the layout of the Text object and MouseArea using the anchors property, which indicates first that the text should be centered horizontally and vertically, and second that the MouseArea should fill its parent. The Text object is simply a label, with the initial text "Click Me" in black Helvetica bold font. The MouseArea contains a single bit of script that sets the object whose id is label—the Text item—to the string "Hello World"

You've already seen two examples of QML; now let's examine the nuts-and-bolts of the language.

Introducing QML

As you've seen, QML is declarative. Instead of saying how, you simply say what. With syntax based on JavaScript, QML gives you a concise syntax to specify a tree of objects with properties. Properties may be references to other objects, strings, or numbers, making it easy to edit QML using your favorite text editor—or by using Qt Creator's excellent support for the language. Let's look at the first `Rectangle` example again:

```
import QtQuick 1.0
Rectangle {
    height:200
    width: 200
    color: "red"
}
```

The first line simply instructs the QML interpreter to include the definitions provided by QtQuick 1.0; you can provide your own QML files to import as well, or import JavaScript to provide better separation between your user interface and business logic.

This QML defines a single object, a `Rectangle`. All QML objects are specified first by their type and then the properties of the object as name-value pairs separated by a single colon. Type names are capitalized, just like class names in C++. Here, we've written the properties one at a time, but we can put them on the same line and separate them with a semicolon, like this:

```
import QtQuick 1.0
Rectangle { height:200; width: 200; color: "red" }
```

Which you use is mostly a matter of personal preference for readability; we find that closely related properties requiring little explanation—say, the dimensions of an object— can be snuggled together on a single line. More important definitions, or those that require additional thought, should probably be placed on their own line and include a comment, like this:

```
import QtQuick 1.0
Rectangle {
    height:200; width: 200
    // Required by Sandy's UX documentation as of 5 November.
    color: "red"
}
```

Comments are written with standard C++ and JavaScript syntax, using either /* and */ for a block comment, or // to indicate that everything that follows until the beginning of the next line is a comment.

Values assigned to properties can be computed, too, using JavaScript syntax. For example, to create a rectangle whose width is twice its height, I might write:

```
import QtQuick 1.0
Rectangle {
    id: myRectangle
    height: 200
    width: myRectangle.height * 2
    color: "red"
}
```

Here, the expression includes a reference to the rectangle itself, now named using its id property. You can refer to other objects by their ID, too. The namespace is a tree identical to the objects you define, and a path to a specific object is simply the IDs of the objects along the path separated by periods. Of course, when referencing another property of the same object, you could just write `width: height * 2`.

A powerful feature of QML is that when you refer to another object in an expression like this, QML creates a *binding*: if the value of the referent changes, the QML runtime automatically recomputes the expression, updating the visual appearance if necessary. If later in our QML expression we change the value of `myRectangle.height` to 64, the `Rectangle` object will automatically change its width to 128 and re-draw, changing the appearance of the UI.

Properties are strongly typed; a property of one type may not be assigned a value of a different type. The QML type system includes the following basic types:

- The `action` type, which has the properties of a `QAction` (see Chapter 5) instance.

- The `bool` type, which may be `true` or `false`.

- The `color` type, which is a standard color name in quotes.

- A `date`, in the format `YYYY-MM-DD`.

- An `enumeration`, which can be any one of a set of named values.

- A `font`, which encapsulates the properties of a `QFont`.

- An `int`, representing an integer.

- A `list`, consisting of a list of objects.

- A `point`, with attributes for its x and y coordinates.

- A `real`, representing a real number.

- A `rect`, bearing attributes for its x, y, `width`, and `height` attributes.

- A `size`, with attributes for `width` and `height`.

- A `string`, which is a free-form collection of characters between quotes.

- A `time`, specified as `HH:MM:SS`.

- A `url`, which is a string that corresponds to the standard Uniform Resource Locator syntax.

- A `vector3d`, consisting of x, y, and z attributes.

You can introduce properties to your own object using the property declaration with a type, like this:

```
import QtQuick 1.0
Rectangle {
    id: window
    property bool loading: feedModel.status == XmlListModel.Loading
    ...
}
```

Here, we define the new property `loading`, whose value is dynamically computed based on the `status` property of another object.

Finally, it's worth noting that QML supports lists, collections of objects indicated between square brackets, like this:

```
Item {
    transitions: [
        Transition {…},
        Transition {…}
    ]
}
```

Here, the `transitions` property consists of two `Transition` objects, each with their own (here elided) properties.

Handling Signals in QML

Many Qt objects emit signals, and QML objects are no exception. You've already encountered one, MouseArea's `pressed` signal:

```
MouseArea {
    onPressed: {
        label.text = "Hello World"
    }
}
```

All signal handlers begin with on, and the remainder of a signal handler's name is the name of the signal; hence, `onPressed` is the signal handler for the MouseArea's `pressed` signal.

Some signals include an optional parameter, which is given a name and accessed as a variable in the script for the handler. For example, the `onPressed` signal handler has a mouse parameter, which you're free to use to determine characteristics of the mouse press, like this:

```
MouseArea {
    acceptedButtons: Qt.LeftButton | Qt.RightButton
    onPressed: if (mouse.button == Qt.RightButton)
            console.log("Right mouse button pressed")
        else if (mouse.button == Qt.LeftButton)
            console.log("Left mouse button pressed");
}
```

In this script you also see the `console` object used; like the JavaScript console object, you can use its log method to log strings to the console for print-style debugging.

> **TIP:** Nokia is working on a mixed-mode debugger for QML and C++ that will let you place breakpoints and inspect properties in both QML and C++. Until it's available, console logging is your best bet for debugging. Console log output appears on the application's standard output, so you can view it in the Application Output pane of Qt Creator or on the command line where you commenced execution of your application.

Speaking of JavaScript, you can import JavaScript into your QML, too. For example, in writing a game, we might want to encapsulate all of our game logic in a single file gamelogic.js. To include this file in our QML, we'd simply use an import directive at the top of the file:

```
import "gamelogic.js" as Gamelogic
```

This creates a top-level object named Gamelogic that has properties and methods for each of the fields and functions defined in the file. For example, if our gamelogic.js file defines a method startGame, we might create a start button in QML that begins the game with a declaration such as:

```
import QtQuick 1.0
import "gamelogic.js" as Gamelogic
Item {
    Id: start
    width: 60
    height: 32

    Text {
        id: startLabel
        text: "Start"
        color: "black"
        font { family: "Helvetica"; pixelSize: 12; bold: true }
    }

    MouseArea {
        onClicked: {
            Gamelogic.startGame()
        }
    }
}
```

You can also do the reverse. You can access properties of any QML object in JavaScript by referencing it as an object by its ID. For example, localization code written in JavaScript to set the text of the start button in gamelogic.js might read:

```
function localizeToEo() {
    ...
    startLabel.text = "Starti " // "Start" in Esperanto
    ...
}
```

Performing Animations in QML

With everything being declarations, you might wonder how dynamic behavior like animation gets represented in QML. While you can implement dynamic behavior in scripts, you can also provide *animations* across properties using the animation-on-property syntax, like this:

```
import QtQuick 1.0
Rectangle {
    width: 64; height: 64
    color: "blue"

    PropertyAnimation on x { from: 0; to: 64; duration: 1000;
        loops: Animation.Infinite }
    PropertyAnimation on y { from: 0; to: 64; duration: 1000;
        loops: Animation.Infinite }
}
```

This creates a blue rectangle that moves from the origin of the canvas to the position (64, 64), over a second.

There are other animation types that follow the same idea, transitioning from one value to another. For example, `ColorAnimation` animates changes in color values using QML's color type over Qt RGBA values, while `RotationAnimation` animates on the rotation of an object around its origin in degrees.

Sometimes you want to link a default animation to when a property changes; for example, you may want the rectangle to follow the mouse and animate to where the mouse is clicked. You can do this by adding `Behavior` elements and adding a `MouseArea`, like this:

```
import QtQuick 1.0
Item {
    width: 400; height: 400

    Rectangle {
        id: rect
        width: 64; height: 64
        color: "blue"

        Behavior on x { PropertyAnimation { duration: 500 } }
        Behavior on y { PropertyAnimation { duration: 500 } }
    }
    MouseArea {
        anchors.fill: parent
        onClicked: { rect.x = mouse.x; rect.y = mouse.y }
    }
}
```

Here, the `Behavior` declarations indicate that when x or y changes, the value should be animated over 500 milliseconds. We'll have more to say about anchors later, in the section "Creating the User Interface," later in this chapter.

Animations can be *eased*, that is, varied over time, according to one of various mathematical curves specified by the easing's type. For example, an animation may accelerate from its start, reach a maximum speed, then slow down to finally stop at its destination. The Easing property of animations has a number of attributes that control how the value should be varied. Its attributes include:

- type, indicating the mathematical function that the values follow as the animation is computed.

- amplitude, indicating a relative scale for the easing.

- overshoot, indicating how far past the final bound the animation should occur before returning to the final bound.

- period, indicating the degree of repetition between the overshoot value and the final value for some easing curves.

Qt defines a large number of easing curves, including linear, quadratic, cubic, and sinusoidal curves. We might want to add a bit of bounce to our rectangle animation by changing the PropertyAnimations like this:

```
Behavior on x {
    PropertyAnimation {
        duration: 500
        easing.type: Easing.InOutElastic
        easing.amplitude: 2.0
        easing.period: 1.5
    }
}
Behavior on y {
    PropertyAnimation {
        duration: 500
        easing.type: Easing.InOutElastic
        easing.amplitude: 2.0
        easing.period: 1.5
    }
}
```

Reviewing the Available Qt Quick Elements

Qt Quick elements can be broadly divided into two classes: things that are visible and things that aren't. Visible elements inherit from Item, and include the following:

- BorderImage, an image broken into nine tiles and can be used, for example, to create a resizable button that selectively scales only the middle area to retain an undistorted border.

- Image, an element that displays an image from a specific source.

- ListView, which provides a list of items provided by a model.

- Loader, a region that loads its QML from its source attribute (specified as a URL).

- Repeater, which lets you repeat an item-based component using content from a model.

- Text, a region that displays formatted text.

- TextEdit and TextInput, regions that permit the entry of multiple or single lines of text, respectively.

- WebView, which allows you to add web content to a Qt Quick view.

Each of these items can be created just as you saw us create Rectangle objects in the previous sections. Several items can coexist in a single layout; the QML for a user interface for a web browser in QML with a URL bar might look something like this:

```
import QtQuick 1.0

Rectangle {
    id: window
    width: 800
    height: 480
    TextInput {
        id: url
        anchors.left: window.left
        anchors.right: go.right
        anchors.top: window.top
        text: "http://qt.nokia.com/"
    }
    Rectangle {
        id: go
        anchors.left: url.right
        anchors.right: window.right
        anchors.top: window.top
        anchors.bottom: url.bottom
        Image {
            source: "go.svg"
        }
    }
    WebView {
        id: content
        anchors.left: window.left
        anchors.right: window.right
        anchors.top: url.bottom
        anchors.bottom: window.bottom
        source: "http://qt.nokia.com/"
    }
}
```

Here we've placed several items, using their anchor properties. Other visible items control the layout of their children and can be used to provide other means of item positioning, including:

- Column, a region that positions its child items so they are vertically aligned.

- Flow, a region that arranges its children side by side, wrapping as necessary,

- Grid, a region that positions its child objects in a grid.

- PathView is a cousin to Repeater, and lays out its model-provided items along a path.

- Row, a region that arranges its children horizontally,

We might modify the layout in the previous QML to better encapsulate the URL navigation line and "Go" button by placing them in a row, like this:

```
...
Row {
    id: navigation
    anchors.left: window.left
    anchors.right: window.right
    anchors.top: window.top
    TextInput {
        id: url
        text: "http://qt.nokia.com/"
    }
    Rectangle {
        id: go
        anchors.right: navigation.right
        width: 32
        Image {
            source: "go.svg"
        }
    }
}
```

Finally, some visible items don't actually draw anything, but instead accept user events for processing:

- Flickable, an item that appears to rotate around an axis as if it's being flipped over.

- GestureArea, used to enable simple gesture handling, such as panning, pinching, swiping, tapping, and so forth.

- MouseArea, a region that enables simple mouse event handling.

Each of these has signal handlers; for example, MouseArea has them for common mouse events including press, release, entry, and exit, while GestureArea has signal handlers for tap, tap-and-hold, pan, pinch, and swipe gestures.

Because changing the position, orientation, and scale of items is something you often want to do in user interfaces, Qt Quick defines the Translate, Rotation and Scale elements (subclasses of the Transform element), which you can assign to the transform property of a visible item. For example, the following specifies a rectangle rotated around its center by 45 degrees:

```
Rectangle {
    width: 100; height: 100
    color: "blue"
    transform: Rotation { origin.x: 50; origin.y: 50; angle: 45}
}
```

Note that when specifying a transform, the origin is relative to the object's position, not the center. In the previous example, the point (50, 50) is at the object's center, not offset to the lower–right-hand corner of the object.

Some visible elements, like the `ListView`, need a model of one or more items from which to draw their content. Models include the `ListModel`, a list of `ListItem` items, as well as the more flexible `XmlListModel` element, which draws its list items from an XML document using XPath expressions. (We use the `XmlListModel` element in the next section to represent the list of earthquakes from the USGS.)

A full list of the supported Qt Quick elements is available at `http://doc.qt.nokia.com/qdeclarativeelements.html`.

> **NOTE:** Qt Quick is undergoing heavy development and extension as we write this (Qt 4.7 has just been released), and this quick survey of the elements available to Qt Quick is probably already out of date. To keep with the latest information about Qt Quick, see
> `http://doc.qt.nokia.com/qtquick.html`.

Programming for the Web with QML

It's time to build a larger example: our Shake demonstration application, this time entirely in QML. In this section we'll build on the basics you've already learned, and introduce the powerful `XmlListModel` Qt Quick element that lets you fetch RSS feeds and parse out data from them using only XPath queries. Figure 6–1 shows our sample UI.

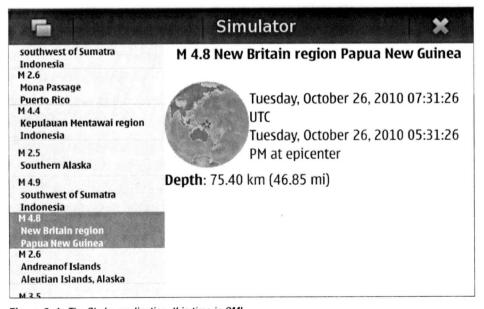

Figure 6–1. *The Shake application, this time in QML*

Before we begin, it's worth noting that the UI is completely different than that of a standard Qt application—here, pictured in the Qt Simulator with an N900 skin. If you're looking to create an application that closely resembles native applications with a look and feel identical to the native experience, QML may not be your first choice, because its presentation is a trifle more basic. As we write this, it doesn't have the necessary UI primitives or styles to match the native MeeGo or Symbian UI (this will soon be introduced by the Qt Quick Components). On the other hand, if you want to establish your own look and feel, or if you're writing a game or other application where it's okay to deviate from the native device UI, QML is an excellent choice.

Our application returns to the split-screen UI you first saw in the prototype in Chapter 4, with a few refinements. First, the event list on the left has a shaded background, and doesn't occupy precisely half the screen. Moreover, list items are formatted neatly, with an event's magnitude and region on separate lines. The basic functionality still remains, although for the brevity of this example, we don't include geolocation integration as we demonstrated in Chapter 6. It's easy to add through the Qt Mobility QML plug-ins (available since Qt Mobility 1.1), though, or you can do it through C++, which we will describe in the section "Mixing C++ with QML" later in the chapter.

Before we begin discussing the main user interface, you'll want to create a new QML project. To do this, launch Qt Creator and select "Create Project..." and then choose "Qt Quick UI" from the New Project dialog, as you see in Figure 6–2.

If all you want to do is run the application, you can do so using the `qmlviewer` command, which takes as its argument the name of a QML file to execute, like this:

```
qmlviewer main.qml
```

This works only on your development workstation; to display QML on the device, you'll use the wizard provided in Qt Creator (for versions after Qt Creator 2.1 beta), as we show you in the section "Displaying QML within a C++ Application" later in this chapter.

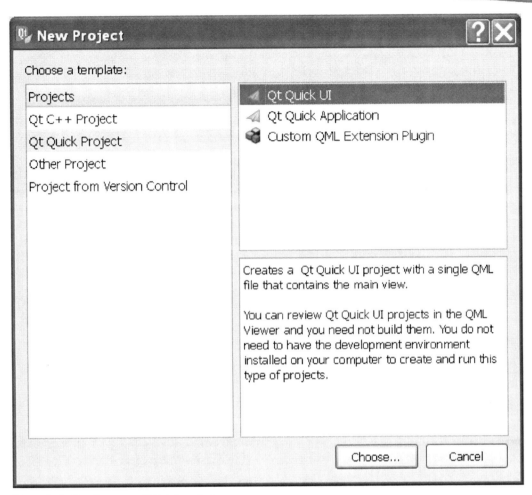

Figure 6–2. *Creating a new Qt Quick project*

Creating the User Interface

The user interface consists of two pieces: the list view, a ListView element, and the item view, a Text element. Listing 6–1 shows main.qml, the QML that defines the entire user interface (and the application's data model, as you'll see as we go along).

Listing 6–1. *The main UI for the QML version of Shake*

```
import QtQuick 1.0
Rectangle {
    property bool loading: feedModel.status == XmlListModel.Loading
    id: window
    width: 800
    height: 480

    Rectangle {
        id: listView
```

```
        anchors.left: window.left
        anchors.top: window.top;
        width: window.width/3
        height: window.height
        color: "#efefef"

        ListView {
            id: events
            property string text: window.loading ?
                "Loading data... please wait" :
                "<b><center>" +
                    feedModel.get(0).title.replace(",","\n").replace(",","\n") +
                    "</center></b><br/>" + feedModel.get(0).summary
            focus: true
            anchors.fill: parent
            model: feedModel
            delegate: QuakeListDelegate {}
            highlight: Rectangle { color: "steelblue" }
            highlightMoveSpeed: 9999999
        }
    }

    Text {
        id: itemView
        anchors.left: listView.right
        anchors.top: window.top;
        width: window.width - listView.width
        height: window.height
        wrapMode: Text.Wrap
        text: events.text
    }

    XmlListModel {
        id: feedModel
        source: "http://earthquake.usgs.gov/earthquakes/catalogs/1day-M2.5.xml"
        namespaceDeclarations:
            "declare default element namespace 'http://www.w3.org/2005/Atom';"
        query: "/feed/entry"
        XmlRole { name: "title"; query: "title/string()" }
        XmlRole { name: "summary"; query: "summary/string()" }
    }
}
```

The top level of the UI is a single rectangle, sized to fit the MeeGo device screen at 800×480 characters with the ID window. It has a single property, a Boolean value loading, which is true while the XmlListModel is loading the XML from the USGS.

Inside the main rectangle is a smaller rectangle containing a ListView, and the Text element that shows the details of a single earthquake event. We place the ListView in its own rectangle and position this and the Text element to be adjacent to each other, spanning the entire height of the containing rectangle using their anchor properties. They permit you to anchor item borders by referring to the borders of adjacent items.

The ListView itself has a property, the text to show for the current element. When the application starts, it simply shows a canned string indicating that the application is loading data; because QML maintains bindings between all the properties, as the list model's status changes, so does the window's loading property, and so does the text property of the ListView. The JavaScript expression for the text property creates a bit of HTML to present a rich-text version of the earthquake data that reiterates the quake's magnitude, location, and detail data the USGS provides.

A ListView doesn't draw its own items; instead, it relies on a *delegate*, a separate item that draws contents once for each item in the ListView's model. Listing 6–2 shows the QuakeListDelegate.qml (put it into the same directory as your main.qml file), our item for displaying a single item of the list.

Listing 6–2. *The delegate responsible for drawing a single list item*

```
import QtQuick 1.0

Item {
    id: delegate

    width: delegate.ListView.view.width; height: 60

    Text {
        text: title.replace(",","\n").replace(",","\n")
        color: delegate.ListView.isCurrentItem ? "white" : "black"
        font { family: "Helvetica"; pixelSize: 16; bold: true }
        anchors {
            left: parent.left; leftMargin: 15
            verticalCenter: parent.verticalCenter
        }
    }

    Rectangle {
        width: delegate.width; height: 1; color: "#cccccc"
        anchors.bottom: delegate.bottom
        visible: delegate.ListView.isCurrentItem ? false : true
    }

    Rectangle {
        width: delegate.width; height: 1; color: "white"
        visible: delegate.ListView.isCurrentItem ? false : true
    }

    MouseArea {
        anchors.fill: delegate
        onClicked: {
            delegate.ListView.view.currentIndex = index
            delegate.ListView.view.text = "<b><center>" +
                title.replace(",","\n").replace(",","\n") +
                "</center></b><br/>" + summary
        }
    }
}
```

The delegate has a single Text item that displays the title of an earthquake report as a series of three lines. It's in black for all items but the currently focused item, which is white and drawn over the highlight rectangle at the end of the listing. After the Text item is a dividing line one pixel tall. It provides separation between this and subsequent items. A MouseArea in the item filling the entire region handles clicks by setting the ListView's text property to the full text description of the event.

When the XmlListModel finishes loading or you click on an item, the QML runtime updates the ListView's text property. The itemView, a single Text element, displays this by setting its text property to shadow the text property of the event list itself.

Downloading the Data

The XmlListModel is a specific list model that handles both the fetching of an XML feed and parsing the feed into roles defined by XPath queries. The XmlListModel does the work of the WorkerThread in the previous chapters' examples, fetching the RSS feed and parsing it to provide title and summary attributes from the source XML available from the USGS. The fetch begins when the XmlListModel is created, and the status is updated after the load completes.

The ListView draws each item using the delegate you saw in Listing 6–2, obtaining the fields in each list item using the title and summary attributes extracted from a specific feed entry based on the entry's index. You can also fetch a specific XmlListModel's item using the get method and passing an index, as we do when we draw the 0th element after the loading completes.

The XmlListModel highlights a key feature of QML we've only hinted at: content can be fetched not just from the local device, but also over the Internet. Any element with a source property can present data from any URL, letting you freely mix local and remote resources in your Qt Quick applications. In fact, you can do this with whole Qt Quick items. The Loader element has a source property and at runtime replaces itself with the contents at the URL of its source element. That allows a Qt Quick application to load other QML from the Web.

Integrating C++ with QML

While QML is arguably a powerful environment, there are still uses for C++ in Qt development. For example, interfacing with platform enablers like QtDBus on MeeGo still requires some C++ work, even if your UI is entirely written in QML. Fortunately, it's easy to bind QML with QObject subclasses written in C++ using Qt's meta-object features, which we touched on in Chapter 4.

As you'll see in the section "Mingling QObjects with QML" later in this chapter, any QObject can be added to QML's object tree, exposing Qt properties as QML properties and slots as methods.

Other times you may just want to introduce a QML interface as a visible component of your application, either as all or part of your UI. The Qt Declarative library, on which Qt Quick is based, provides a collection of classes that let you do just this. The most obvious example is that when you want to ship a QML application on a mobile device, you'll need to create a QDeclarativeView in which to render your QML application.

Displaying QML within a C++ Application

Displaying QML in a Qt application is easy. Simply create an instance of QDeclarativeView and add it to your widget hierarchy. Then, set its source to the URL of the entry point to your QML application. For example, a player application for the previous section's QML is as simple as what you see in Listing 6–3.

Listing 6–3. *Rendering QML in an application's main window*

```
#include <QApplication>
#include <QMainWindow>
#include <QDeclarativeView>

int main(int argc, char *argv[])
{
    QApplication app(argc, argv);
    QMainWindow window();
    QDeclarativeView* view = new QDeclarativeView();

    window.setCentralWidget(view);

    view->setSource(QUrl::fromLocalFile ("main.qml"));
    window.showMaximized();

    return app.exec();
}
```

QDeclarativeView acts as a QWidget, so you can just set it as the central widget of the application's main window and give it some QML to render. In fact, if you choose a Qt Quick application from Qt Creator's "New Project," the resulting project includes an entry point (main function) whose body is very similar to what you see in Listing 6–3.

Mingling QObjects with QML

Through the rootContext method, the QDeclarativeView exposes a QDeclarativeContext, which provides an interface to QML's context within the QML engine that the QDeclarativeView uses to render its content. Using the QDeclarativeContent, you inject new QObject values to the context tree, providing the name that the QML content will use to access the QObject. When you do this, the QObject's properties become QML properties of the object in the QML context, and slots become methods that QML can invoke on the object.

As an example, let's imagine we wanted to reuse the model and network code from the previous chapter's example with the QML user interface we presented in Listing 6–1 and 6–2. In practice, this probably isn't a good idea, because the XmlListModel does what we need and requires less code, but this example will show you how you can introduce a model from C++ to QML and use it with QML's ListView.

The only change we need to make to Listing 6–1 is to remove the XmlListModel from the QML entirely; we'll replace it with our QuakeListModel using the code you see in Listing 6–4.

Listing 6–4. *Introducing a QObject into the QML context*

```
static const char* kUrl =
    "http://earthquake.usgs.gov/earthquakes/catalogs/1day-M2.5.xml";

int main(int argc, char *argv[])
{
    qRegisterMetaType<QModelIndex>("QModelIndex");

    QApplication app(argc, argv);

    QMainWindow window();
    QuakeListModel* model = new QuakeListModel(&window);
    WorkerThread* worker = new WorkerThread(&window, *model);
    worker->fetch(kUrl);

    QDeclarativeView* view = new QDeclarativeView();

    // The only thing we show is the declarative view.
    window.setCentralWidget(view);
    window.showMaximized();
    view->rootContext()->setContextProperty("feedModel", model);

    view->setSource(QUrl::fromLocalFile("main.qml"));

    return app.exec();
}
```

Listing 6–4 introduces a `QtDeclarativeView` to the main window, but only after it creates an instance of the `QuakeListModel` and `WorkerThread` to fetch the earthquake feed from the USGS server. While the thread is working, the code inserts the `QuakeListModel` instance into the declarative view's context using the line of code

```
view->rootContext()->setContextProperty("feedModel", model);
```

This assigns the model to the QML entity `feedModel`.

The `QuakeListModel` we presented previously doesn't provide status notifications as the worker thread does its work; we need to add a Qt property that indicates the feed status the worker thread will update as it fetches and parses the data. Listing 6–5 shows the modified interface to the `QuakeListModel`.

Listing 6–5. *Adding the status property to the* `QuakeListModel`.

```
class QuakeListModel : public QStandardItemModel
{
    Q_OBJECT

    Q_PROPERTY(int status READ status WRITE setStatus NOTIFY statusChanged)

public:
    QuakeListModel(QObject* parent = 0);

    enum {
        … // Role enum elided for brevity
    };

    bool setData(int row, const QuakeEvent& value);
```

```
    int status();
    void setStatus(int status);

signals:
    void statusChanged();

… // remainder of class follows
};
```

The status property uses the status and setStatus methods as its implementation, and setStatus must also emit statusChanged to provide QML's binding something to hook on to while watching for status changes. These methods (Listing 6–6) are trivial.

Listing 6–6. *Changes to the* QuakeListModel *implementation*

```
int QuakeListModel::status() {
    return mStatus;
}

void QuakeListModel::setStatus(int status) {
    if (status != mStatus) {
        mStatus = status;
        emit statusChanged();
    }
}

QuakeListModel::QuakeListModel(QObject* parent)
    : QStandardItemModel(parent) {
    QHash<int, QByteArray> roles;
    roles[Qt::DisplayRole] = "title";
    roles[QuakeListModel::Description] = "summary";
    setRoleNames(roles);
}
```

Listing 6–6 also shows a key change to the QuakeListModel's notion of its roles; for each named QML role, such as title, we need to provide the corresponding Qt::Role enumeration value. The QML context uses these when resolving the attributes referenced in specific list items while drawing the delegate for the list view. We do this when we construct the model by creating a QHash that links the QML attribute names to the Qt::Role enumeration values.

Next, the worker thread needs to update the model's status property throughout the HTTP transaction; for example, the beginning of the fetch method needs to look like this:

```
void WorkerThread::fetch(const QString& url)
{
    // Don't try to re-start if we're running
    if (isRunning()) {
        this->cancel();
    }
    mEventModel.setStatus(2); // XmlListModel.loading

    // Configure the access point, do the fetch, etc.
    // See Chapter 4 for details.
    …
}
```

The model's status also needs to be set at the end of run to signal the end of the transaction for success or error conditions, of course.

Wrapping Up

In this chapter, we've shown you how to use Qt Quick, Nokia's declarative environment for creating user interfaces using QML, JavaScript, and C++. By using QML entities like Rectangle, MouseArea, Item, Text, and ListView, you learned how to specify user interfaces by their contents, instead of C++'s imperative declarations in method definitions. You saw how QML uses properties and runtime binding to share data between user interface objects, automatically updating each object in its context tree as necessary. The process uses JavaScript to let you create programmatic linkages between one object's properties and another. We showed how that extended to both the JavaScript and C++ runtimes, letting you add JavaScript and C++ objects to your QML-based application. We also showed how to display QML content in a C++ application.

In the next chapter, we switch gears, and discuss Nokia's support for Web technologies, including HTML5, which lets you deploy existing or new web-based applications on Nokia's products. Take a walk to clear your head, and we'll be ready when you return!

Chapter 7

Developing with HTML5

One of the great things about Qt is its inclusion of QtWebKit and, with it, its excellent support for HTML5. Using HTML5, along with sister technologies CSS3 and JavaScript, you can build powerful standards-based applications that run simply in the web browser. Even better, you can easily build hybrid applications that combine the power of native Qt development, as we discussed in the past three chapters, with the ease and portability of web apps. Qt native development is the preferred method for developing Nokia apps, but HTML5, as supported in QtWebKit, is an acceptable secondary platform as well.

HTML5 is the fifth generation of HyperText Markup Language, the primary technology that has been used to author web pages and web applications since the beginning. HTML5 includes almost all the tags and features you have come to expect from web development (some tags that are rarely used or replaced with newer functionality have been deprecated) and adds many cool new features. We'll cover some of those features later in this chapter. CSS3 (usually when people talk about HTML5 they really mean HTML5 plus the related technologies CSS3 and JavaScript) stands for Cascading Style Sheets version 3. CSS was published as a W3C specification in 1996 as a means to clearly separate the content and styling in a web page. Now in its third generation, CSS3 adds powerful new features, such as animations, transitions, and transformations that allow web developers to add advanced graphic techniques with just a couple lines of code. Using CSS3 for these transforms also allows for hardware acceleration and, therefore, fast performance of these computationally complex graphics. (Note that CSS3 transformations provide the opportunity to use hardware acceleration, but do not guarantee that any given implementation does in fact implement this acceleration. The accelerated features will vary depending on the platform.) Last of the trio, JavaScript is a powerful scripting language that allows you to programmatically manipulate the Document Object Model (DOM) or perform other dynamic calculations.

These are the same industry standard technologies used to build the World Wide Web. Therefore, if you know how to build an application for the web, as do many developers today, it is just as easy to build an application for a mobile handset.

QtWebKit, the engine used to render HTML5, CSS3, and JavaScript, is a derivative of the WebKit open source project. (See `www.webkit.org`). This is the same browser core used by Google's Android, Apple's iOS, and most other mobile browser platforms. This means that web applications written using industry-standard HTML5 as supported by WebKit will run with little or no modification across most mobile platforms.

HTML5 Is an Industry Standard

The proposal for HTML5 came originally from the WHAT (Web Hypertext Application Technology) Working Group in June 2004 (www.whatwg.org/). At that time the W3C, keeper of most of the web standards we are discussing, was promoting XHTML as the next generation web markup language. The HTML5 team, including members from Apple, Opera, and Mozilla, argued for a more evolutionary approach to the next generation web, building on the existing HTML4 markup language. HTML5 became the starting point for a new W3C HTML workgroup in 2007. This workgroup operated with an openness policy that encouraged broad participation from the community, including non-W3C members. The first HTML5 public working draft was published on Jan 22, 2008.

Today, the group continues to operate with strong industry support from players such as Nokia, Google, Apple, Microsoft, IBM, and many others. The specification has not yet reached final status as a Recommendation and may not for several years. However, much of the work exists in a fairly stable state and is implemented in several browser engines, including WebKit and Gecko. The fact that most mobile players use these common engines ensures that support is mostly equivalent across different vendor platforms.

Let's get started by looking at some real HTML5 code.

Hello World in HTML5

A simple hello world application is a good place to start. A really simple hello world might look something like this:

```
<html>
<body>
<div>Hello World!</div>
</body>
</html>
```

The easiest way to get started is to save this code in a text file somewhere on your computer and call it hworld.html. Why not put it in your c:\temp directory? Now, fire up your browser and type file:///c:\temp\hworld.html in the navigation bar. You should see 'Hello World!' appear in your browser.

OK, that worked, but that code is about as exciting as pounding sand. Let's spice it up with some nifty HTML5 features. Let's add just a few lines so that our code now looks like this:

```
<html>
<body>

<style type="text/css">

  .box {
    float: left;
    margin: 4em 1em;
    width: 100px;
    height: 60px;
    border: 2px solid green;
    line-height: 60px;
    text-align: center;
    -webkit-transition: all 1s ease-in-out;
  }

  .rotate:active {
    -webkit-transform: rotate(180deg);
  }

</style>

<div class="box rotate">Hello World!</div>

</body>
</html>
```

Fire it up again in your browser and take a look. This time make sure that you have a browser that supports HTML5. We like to use either Chrome or Safari. Click and hold on the text in the middle of the box. Surprised? The box with the text in it should rotate 180 degrees, then rotate back when you release. A picture of ours is shown in Figure 7–1. Let's take a more detailed look at what just happened.

Figure 7–1. *Hello world rotated*

First, we added a style element that contains two CSS style rules for classes .box and .rotate. The .box class has some basic CSS that defines a box drawn around our text. It describes things like placement, size, text alignment, and so on. This is interesting stuff, but has long been a part of the web design toolbox. But wait, there is something new: a property -webkit-transition: all 1s ease-in-out. This tells the rendering engine that objects of class .box should be animated with a transition animation. The all parameter means that all the properties should be animated. 1s specifies a 1 second duration for the animation. And ease-in-out tells us to use this timing function (other options include linear or cubic Bezier functions).

Now look at the .rotate class. This tells us that when the class becomes active (meaning, for example, an object of this class is clicked by the user) it should be rotated 180 degrees. Finally, look at the div that contains our text. We have added class attributes telling the renderer that the div is part of the box and rotate classes. Notice that we're really playing here with CSS3, but as we said above, most people consider this generically part of HTML5 technology.

So, when we activate the Hello World text by clicking on it, it is rotated 180 degrees. And rather than seeing the text instantly flip upside down, the rotation happens in an animation over a 1 second duration. This is HTML5!

Hello World on a Handset

OK, we've seen our Hello World HTML5 app running on our desktop. Now let's try it out on our handset. First, we need to serve up the HTML from a server and not from a local file. (We'll look at using local files on a handset later in this chapter, but for now let's try it from a server like a traditional web page.) So throw hworld.html on a web server and let's try it from a handset.

There is one problem, though. Nokia's support of HTML5 is based on support of QtWebKit. Nokia is committed to making QtWebKit the default platform browser moving forward, but at the time this book is written the N900's browser is based on the Gecko rendering engine, and the Symbian platform browser is based on an older version of WebKit. This means that we need to build our own version of QtWebKit and install it on a handset. (Note that the Gecko rendering engine does in fact support most important HTML5 features. But for consistency we want to use QtWebKit for both platforms we are targeting.) Eventually this step won't be required and the platform browser that ships with the handset will run HTML5 apps without problem.

For now, the easiest way to build a QtWebKit browser is to build the fancybrowser example application that comes with the Nokia Qt SDK. To begin, browse to the directory C:\NokiaQtSDK\Examples\4.6\webkit (or similar). Here there are several interesting QtWebKit examples. Open the file fancybrowser.pro in the fancybrowser directory. Build the application just like any other Qt app as described earlier in this book.

For Symbian make sure your bearer management is properly established as described earlier in Chapter 5.

Now, fire up fancybrowser on either a Symbian or Maemo device and navigate to the site where you put the hello world content. Probably you need to type something like `http://mysite.com/hworld.html`. Try touching the Hello World text. Does it rotate like you expect? Yes, we're in business!

Using the HTML5 Application Cache

There is one concern, though, with running your web applications hosted on the network like this. You must be online to access your application. This is OK for a desktop computer that is plugged into a reliable network connection, but not so good for a mobile device. For a mobile device, network connections are frequently dropped, such as when driving through a tunnel, or potentially unavailable for long periods of time when out of a coverage zone. Luckily, HTML5 has some key features to enable web applications to work offline. We will discuss one such feature, local storage, later in this chapter. The other feature, the HTML5 application cache, is a nifty way to ensure your web pages are available even when the device is offline.

Caching is a technique normally implemented as an HTTP cache anyway, but HTML5 application cache is a new mechanism that allows you, the developer, to explicitly manage caching behavior for your application. The browser is told which files to place in the application cache by a manifest.

Imagine that our hworld application uses three files: `hworld.html`, `hworld.css`, and `hworld.js`. Having multiple files of these types is typical for most web apps. The head element for `hworld.html` might include these lines:

```
<head>
  <title>Hello World</title>
  <script src="hworld.js"></script>
  <link rel="stylesheet" href="hworld.css">
</head>
```

Normally if a user tried to open Hello World while there was no network connectivity, he would get an error because `hworld.js` and `hworld.css` are unavailable (unless they happened to already be in the local HTTP cache, but this is unreliable).

With HTML5's application cache, the developer can provide a manifest explicitly telling the browser to cache these three files. The manifest would look like this:

```
CACHE MANIFEST
hworld.html
hworld.css
hworld.js
```

This file should be saved as a text file called hworld.manifest and served up as type `text/cache-manifest`. You also need to add instructions to `hworld.html` telling the browser to use the manifest file. You do this by modifying the HTML element of `hworld.html` like this:

```
<html manifest="hworld.manifest">
```

Now, when the user goes to run the hworld web application, the browser will cache the files and make them available even when the user is offline. The offline cache mechanism also provides an API that allows the developer to have explicit control of the application cache.

The manifest file can contain three distinct sections indicating how different files should be handled:

- CACHE
- NETWORK
- FALLBACK

CACHE is the default section and says that the files in this section should be downloaded and stored in the application cache when they are accessed for the first time. Files under the NETWORK section are explicitly not cached and must be accessed over the network. This is useful when the application developer requires server side interaction, such as for tracking mechanisms. All requests to resources under NETWORK bypass the cache and are requested directly from their online location. Finally, FALLBACK allows the developer to specify resources that should be used if the primary resource is not available. The first URI is the resource, the second is the fallback. Both URIs must be relative and from the same origin as the manifest file. This is useful for the developer to put up an explicit warning or error message if some expected resource is not available.

A cache manifest with files in each section might look like this:

```
CACHE MANIFEST
CACHE
hworld.html
hworld.css
hworld.js

NETWORK
tracking.cgi

FALLBACK
offline.html
```

Once an application is cached, the browser will update the cached files only under three conditions:

1. The user has cleared her cache and the cached content is therefore no longer available.

2. The manifest file changed.

3. The cache is explicitly updated via JavaScript using the application APIs.

Full details can be found from the W3C specification for application cache at http://dev.w3.org/html5/spec/offline.html.

There is one last important point to keep in mind when using the HTML5 application cache. The application cache is by default disabled in QtWebKit, so you must explicitly enable it to use it. To do this, we need to set the appropriate property to true in the

QWebSettings class. To do this in our fancy browser example, you need to add these lines of code to the application:

```
QWebSettings *GlobalSettings = QWebSettings::globalSettings();
GlobalSettings->
setAttribute(QWebSettings::OfflineWebApplicationCacheEnabled, true);
```

So now we can create a web application, host it online, and flag it to be cached locally so that we can run it even when we don't have network access. But we are still missing a couple of things that we would get if we were running a full native application. First, the application must be run in the web browser and accessed by the user from a bookmark or explicitly entering a URL. The user does not click an icon on the home screen to launch the application. Second, the application is not downloaded and installed like a native application. On the one hand, this is a convenience to the user since it eliminates the overhead of application installation, but on the other hand it eliminates an opportunity for the developer to monetize his application by charging per download, such as when the application is sold from the Ovi Store. (We cover the Ovi Store in more detail in Chapter 9). To address these problems, let's learn about hybrid applications.

Hybrid Apps

Hybrid applications are a hybrid combination of native development, using Qt, and web development, using QtWebKit. In the last chapter we saw a sophisticated example of this where native Qt objects are embedded directly into a QWebView. In this section we focus on a simple hybrid application strategy where a very thin layer of native Qt code serves as a QtWebKit wrapper around generic HTML5 code.

In the example below, we use QWebView in a Qt C++ application, as we did previously to run our Hello World example. Another approach is to use QML to open a WebView. This would take only a few lines of code like this:

```
import QtQuick 1.0
import QtWebKit 1.0
WebView {
    url: http://nokia.com
}
```

Regardless of how we bring up the WebView, we can store our content locally on the handset then display it in a thin shell application.

Accessing Your HTML5 Content from the Local File System

The simplest way to create a hybrid application of this type is to write a thin Qt application using QWebView to render HTML5 content stored on the device in the local file system. Let's take a look at how to do this with our hworld example.

Our Qt application is called hybridshell and is available from www.apress.com for download. This app doesn't do much more than open a QWebView and display some content. The difference is that this time the URL points to content on the local file system rather than an http server on the network. To do this on Meego, for example, we use the command:

```
url=QUrl().fromLocalFile("/usr/local/share/web/hworld.html");
```

On Windows we probably want to put the content somewhere else that does not use an absolute file path. On Windows we would use this command:

```
dir.setPath("../hybridshell/hworld.html");
url=QUrl().fromLocalFile(dir.canonicalPath());
```

Just make sure that the file or files you are accessing are deployed to the device at the same time that you deploy your application binary. A convenient way to do this is to use the DEPLOYMENT variable in your .pro file. This is described in detail in Chapter 9.

> **NOTE:** At the time of this writing the deployment variable specified in the `.pro` file does not work correctly for Maemo when building with Qt Creator. To work around this, select the "build" project configurations for Maemo. Under "Build Steps," select the "Details" tab for the "Create Package" section. When the details pane is expanded, you will see a "Files to deploy" block. Here you can select files from your local file system and specify to where they should be copied on your remote device file system. This is a convenient place to specify your web content files.

There is one last thing we need to do. Many applications will need to access content on the network in addition to the content stored on the local file system. For example, in the Shake application that we present at the end of this chapter, we need to make an XmlHttpRequest call to download the earthquake feed data. By default, the QtWebKit security policy will block these requests. We need to explicitly enable this functionality by setting the LocalContentCanAccessRemoteUrls property to true like this:

```
QWebSettings *GlobalSettings = QWebSettings::globalSettings();
GlobalSettings->setAttribute(QWebSettings::LocalContentCanAccessRemoteUrls, true);
```

Run the application and there it is—our web content appears just like a web page, but now everything is local to the device. There is one last technique we should look at for building hybrid web applications: packaging the content as a resource in the application binary.

Storing the HTML5 Content as an Application Resource

Packaging files for the local storage system is nice, but it has the problem that you need to explicitly manage the placement of these files. Each platform needs the files placed in a slightly different location. An easier way to handle this problem is to include our content as an application resource. Qt allows us to access a .qrc file just as simply as accessing content from elsewhere. Just use qrc: rather than http: to indicate your HTML content is accessed from a resource. For our sample application we just make this substitution:

```
url=QUrl("qrc:/hworld.html");
```

Make sure to use Qt Creator to include your web content as application resources. Now, the content is bundled into your application binary. Management is much easier since we don't have to worry about moving around a bunch of external files. Be careful, though, too much web content stored as a resource will bloat the size of your application binary.

In this section we've shown how to use Qt to render HTML5 content using four different methods: a QtWebKit based browser that loads content off the net in the traditional manner, a QtWebKit browser that uses the HTML5 application cache to enable that same hosted application to be available without network connectivity, a hybrid app where the content is stored locally on the device file system, and a hybrid app where the content is bundled as a resource into the application binary.

In the next section we will take a more in-depth look at some of the new features in HTML5.

> **NOTE:** One last option for developing web applications is the Symbian Web Runtime. This is a Nokia proprietary technology where web files such as HTML, JavaScript, and CSS can be bundled into an archive package file and installed and run on the device like a native application. It is similar to the W3C widget standard defined here: `www.w3.org/TR/2009/CR-widgets-20090723/`. The Symbian Web Runtime will be supported on the Symbian platform for legacy applications, but is not the recommended development path moving forward.

More HTML5 Features

HTML5 has lots of new features. There are new elements such as the `<audio>` and `<video>` tags that give native support to multimedia formats that previously required additional third-party plug-ins. There are also a number of new semantic elements that allow authors to indicate the structural organization of the content. This is done with the introduction of tags such as `<header>`, `<article>`, `<figure>`, and others.

Three features: canvas, CSS transitions and transformations, and local storage are especially exciting. In the following sections we'll dive deeper into these new features.

Canvas

Canvas is a major new enhancement to HTML5. The `<canvas>` element is a resolution-dependent bitmap canvas which can be drawn on programmatically using JavaScript APIs. It is useful for rendering dynamic content, such as graphs or game graphics. Before we had `<canvas>`, web developers had to use plug-ins such as Flash.

To use `<canvas>`, you must first create the `<canvas>` element, just as you would with any HTML element. Then you draw on it using the supplied JavaScript API. Let's walk through some of the main ideas here with some examples.

When you create a canvas you specify the width and height of the canvas like this:

```
<canvas id="myCanvas" width="300" height="300">
```

Let's add some styling so that we can see the boundaries of our canvas:

```
<style type="text/css">
  #myCanvas {border: 1px solid black;}
</style>
```

Next, we need to add a spot where we can do some JavaScript to draw on the canvas. For this simple example, let's just execute a draw function every time the page is loaded like this:

```
<body onload="draw();">
```

Now, we can use draw to experiment with the drawing code for <canvas>. The simplest way to draw in canvas is by creating rectangles. Unlike SVG (SVG or Scalable Vector Graphics is another W3C standard based on XML used for drawing two-dimensional graphics) , no other primitive shapes such as circles or triangles are supported. You can also draw with lines and arcs, but let's talk about that later.

To draw, first you need to get the graphics context to draw in. Currently only two-dimensional graphics are supported, but in the future 3D may also be supported. We get the graphics context like this:

```
var canvas = document.getElementById('myCanvas');
var c = canvas.getContext('2d');
```

Once you have the graphics context, you use the fillRect function to draw a solid rectangle. You can also use the strokeRect function to draw the outline of the rectangle with no filling. The rectangle functions take four inputs: the x and y coordinates of the rectangle's starting position (usually the top left corner of the rectangle) and the width and height of the rectangle to be drawn. The coordinate system is arranged such that point (0,0) is the top left corner. Increasing x moves to the right, and increasing y moves down. This is shown in Figure 7–2 below.

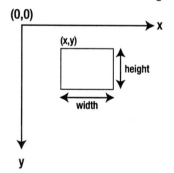

Figure 7–2. *The canvas coordinate system.*

You draw a rectangle like this:

```
c.fillRect (125, 10, 50, 50);
```

This gives us a nice black rectangle starting at the point (125, 10), and 50 pixels high and 50 pixels wide (notice we are actually drawing a square, since the height and width are the same—but still, the API refers to it as a rectangle so we will also). We can use the function fillStyle to spice it up a little. fillStyle let's you describe what kind of fill you would like. Let's add the line

```
c.fillStyle = 'red';
```

and you should see a red rectangle. Nice. OK, let's draw something more than just a rectangle. How about a stick figure? We already have the head. Let's add a body and arms. Just draw two more rectangles like this:

```
c.fillRect (142, 60, 16, 130); //body
c.fillRect (85, 100, 130, 16); //arm
```

Put it all together and you should see something like Figure 7–3 below.

Figure 7–3. *Head and body stick man*

Now, we have a problem, though. How do we draw the legs? We only know how to draw rectangles. In addition to rectangles, you can also draw lines starting and stopping from arbitrary points. To do this, you use the lineTo function to define a path. First you tell the canvas that you would like to start drawing a path with the beginPath function. Next, you specify the path by listing a series of points that are to be connected by lines. First you create the starting point with the first moveTo function call. When calling moveTo(x,y) and lineTo(x,y) you pass the x and y position of the point you are describing. You now call lineTo for as many points as you would like to specify. You can close the path with a closePath call, which takes you back to the first point you started with. Or you can just call stroke, which draws the subpath you described without closing it.

In our example we would like to draw some legs. Let's add these lines:

```
c.beginPath();
c.moveTo(150,180); //starting position
c.lineTo(200,270); //rightleg
c.stroke();
```

For the left leg we want to move to the starting point without actually drawing a line. This is kind of like picking the pen up from the piece of paper when drawing. Let's call a moveTo, then a lineTo to draw the left leg like this:

```
c.moveTo(150,180);
c.lineTo(100,270); //left leg
```

Finally, we want to make our lines look like the rectangles we drew earlier. To do that, let's add this styling call:

```
c.lineWidth=10;
c.strokeStyle='red';
```

Put it all together and our stick man should look like Figure 7–4 below.

Figure 7–4. *Stick man with legs.*

Our stick man is looking like a bit of a block head. But how do we give him a round head? We can use the arc call. It's like lineTo except that you specify an arc of a circle rather than a straight line. The parameters passed to arc are x, y, radius, startAngle, endAngle, and whether the direction is counterclockwise. The angles are expressed in radians and the value describing whether the direction is counterclockwise is boolean. (Remember from your high school math that 360 degrees equals 2π radians.) So, to draw our head, let's get rid of our block head and add a new arc path like this:

```
c.beginPath();
c.arc(150,35,25,Math.PI/2,3*Math.PI, false);
c.stroke();
```

Finally, our stick man has a real head as shown in Figure 7–5 below.

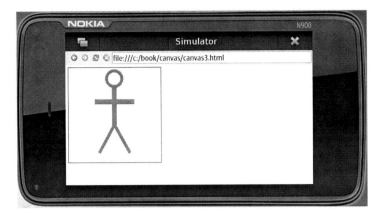

Figure 7–5. *Our stick man with a round head*

In addition to circular arcs, you can also use quadratic and Bezier curves to connect the points in your path. Let's talk about one last drawing feature in canvas before moving on.

You can apply transformations to the canvas. Let's consider this for drawing our legs. What if we wanted to continue to use rectangles to draw our legs rather than use paths as above. The problem before was that we can only draw rectangles aligned to the corner or the rectangular canvas. To get around this, now we can use a rotate function call to rotate the canvas much as we would a piece of paper before drawing on it. Before doing that, though, let's do a save function call. This saves the current state of the graphics context. By doing first a save before the rotate, we can then do a restore to restore the context to where it was before we did the rotation. This is like putting the paper back in the position it was in before we moved it.

One last thing we need to do is to translate the origin. By default the transformation will happen around point (0,0). We, however, want to rotate the rectangle with the origin of rotation near its top, so that it will be positioned properly as a leg. To add legs as rectangles rather than points, remove the code we had for creating a path and instead add these lines to draw the legs:

```
c.save();
c.translate(142,185);
c.rotate(Math.PI/6);
c.fillRect(0,0,10,100);
c.restore();

c.save();
c.translate(158,185);
c.rotate(-Math.PI/6);
c.fillRect(-10,0,10,100);
c.restore();
```

The stick man looks pretty much the same as he did in Figure 7–5 above, but this time we drew his legs using rectangles.

With that, we conclude our look at canvas. The examples we showed here, although controlled with JavaScript function calls, are in reality rather static. We draw a figure that could have just as easily been inserted as a static image. The real power of canvas comes when the API is used to create dynamic images. These could be used to power games or animations, or to generate dynamic graphs updated with the content.

Furthermore, there are several other aspects to canvas we did not talk about, such as using text and images on the canvas, compositing and clipping drawings, adding patterns and shadows, and animations. The canvas API is available for further study here: `http://dev.w3.org/html5/canvas-api/canvas-2d-api.html`. We leave these additional topics for investigation by the reader while we instead look at some new CSS3 effects.

Transitions and Transformations

Transitions and transformations are two cool new things in CSS. Transitions are implicit animations that occur when a CSS property is changed. Transformations allow elements to be translated, rotated, and scaled in 2D and 3D space. While technically not part of HTML5 (these are actually CSS features—not HTML), this new CSS functionality is one of the things people talk about when considering new features in HTML5.

Transitions

We already saw some of this in our `hworld.html` example earlier. Let's take a closer look now. Let's start with a typical CSS declaration. In the code below we describe properties for a class called box.

```
.box {
    margin: 20px 20px;
    width: 200px;
    height: 100px;
    border: 1px dashed green;
    text-align: center;
}
```

There are many available CSS properties. Here we specify that the box is placed 20 pixels from neighboring content. It has a width and height of 200 and 100 pixels. Any text placed in it is centered. And finally it is surrounded by a thin dashed green border.

Now, let's create some text and give it the class box like this:

```
<div class="box">
Transitions are cool!
</div>
```

Display this in an HTML5 compliant browser and it should like Figure 7–6. (Actually we haven't gotten to the new HTML5 stuff so it should like Figure 7–6 in pretty much any browser).

Figure 7–6. *Illustrating various CSS properties*

Now, we can do something clever. CSS allows us to define a selector for when the box is active. In this declaration we can change some of the CSS properties we defined above. Let's add this text:

```
.box:active {
  border: 8px solid red;
  font-size: xx-large;
  font-weight: bolder;
}
```

Now render this in your web browser. Click on it and you will see the border change to a thick solid red line. And the font gets bigger and bolder. Cool, right? Well, this is all just old school CSS. When you click on the box, the properties all change instantly. Now, let's add a CSS transition. Add these lines to the box declaration block:

```
-webkit-transition: all 1s ease-in-out;
```

Click on it and watch again. Now instead of a jump, you should see the properties smoothly animate from the start to the end property. This is a CSS3 transition!

In our transition line, we told the browser that all the properties that change should be animated. You can also explicitly set which properties are animated like this:

```
-webkit-transition-property: border;
```

Now when you click on the box, the border change is animated, but the text simply jumps from a small to large size. It is also possible to use different timing functions to describe the animation. We specified `ease-in-out`, but you can also use other functions. such as linear and cubic Bezier.

Now let's take a look at transformations.

Transformations

Transitions are nice, but you need transformations to start doing really cool things. Transformations are described with a new CSS property called –webkit-transform. This lets you move web elements by applying any of three types of transforms: translation, scaling, or rotation.

Translation means to move the element in the Cartesian plane. Scaling means to enlarge or shrink the element. And rotation means to rotate the element about an axis. When rotated about the z axis, the rotation happens on the view surface as you would expect in a 2D drawing. But you can also rotate about the X and Y axis. For example, a rotation about the X axis is like tipping the element away from you. You can also combine transformations.

Let's take the box we were using above and transform it in all three ways. We make it grow, move, and rotate at the same time. You do this by adding this line to the .box:active declaration block:

```
-webkit-transform: scale(2) translate(100px, 0) rotate(30deg);
```

Now when you click on the box it enlarges, spins, and moves to the right. The end result is a box that looks like Figure 7–7.

Figure 7–7. *Add some transformations*

Again, we have only scratched the surface on the topic of transitions and transformations. For further information, you can look at the W3C documentation here:

- www.w3.org/TR/css3-2d-transforms
- www.w3.org/TR/css3-3d-transforms
- www.w3.org/TR/css3-transitions

Local Storage

Earlier in this chapter we discussed using the application cache to enable offline HTML5 applications. There is one thing missing to make truly robust offline applications—local data storage. HTML5 gives you two methods to store data on your client: web storage and web database.

Web storage allows you to store values in key-value pairs. This is similar to the current cookie mechanism, but unlike cookies the key-value pair is not sent to the server with every request. Web database is a JavaScript front end to a local SQL database. This provides a robust method for your HTML5 application to access a local relational database even when offline.

Local storage is disabled by default in QtWebKit. To enable it, you must set the parameter QWebSettings::LocalStorageEnabled to true. You do this in the same way that we set QWebSettings::OfflineWebApplicationCacheEnabled to true for application cache above.

Web Storage

Let's talk first about web storage. There are two types of web storage supported: localStorage and sessionStorage. localStorage is meant to be more for storing long-term data. The data persists in local client storage even after the host browser window is closed. Also, the key-value pairs are accessible from any browser window.

sessionStorage is meant to be more of a temporary data store for a single browser window. The data can be accessed only from the window in which it was created and the data does not persist after the window is closed.

You store a key-value pair like this:

```
sessionStorage.setItem("item_price", theItemPrice);
```

and you retrieve the value based on querying the key like this:

```
var theItemPrice = sessionStorage.getItem("itemPrice");
// now do something with the value
document.getElementById('item_price').value = theItemPrice;
```

Note that these examples use sessionStorage, but the same functions can be used for localStorage. The syntax to use sessionStorage and localStorage is identical. The only difference are the rules for data persistence that we mentioned above.

Also, you can use sessionStorage.length to determine how many keys are stored in your local data store like this:

```
numKeys = session.storage.length;
```

Additionally, you can access a key based on a numeric index like this:

```
value = sessionStorage(index);
```

Finally, you can delete a single value like this:

```
sessionStorage.removeItem("item_price");
```

and delete all key-value pairs in your domain like this:

```
sessionStorage.clear();
```

Web Database

Web database provides a front end for a local SQL database. SQL, Structured Query Language, is an extremely popular standard to access relational databases. SQL itself is a large topic and is beyond the scope of this book. A good source of information for further investigation of SQL is the SQLite website at `www.sqlite.org`.

Let's explore some of the basics of using web database. First you need to create your web database. You do that with a call that looks something like this:

```
var db = openDatabase(shortName, version, displayName, maxSize);
```

Once your database is created, you do most of your work with the `executeSql` function. `executeSql` is part of a transaction object and is just a thin layer to pass SQL queries to your database. Using `executeSql` you do things like create tables, insert rows, and make queries. An example SQL query might look like this:

```
transaction.executeSql("SELECT * from items where color=?;",
    [myColor], dataHandler, errorHandler);
```

In this statement, the first argument is the SQL query passed to the local database to be executed. The second argument is an array of JavaScript values that can be used in the query. The third argument, `dataHandler`, is a callback function to handle the response. Finally, the last argument, `errorHandler`, is a callback for an error handling function.

In this chapter we presented only some of the more popular features of HTML5, which contains lots of cool features beyond the highlights we presented here. Furthermore, HTML5 is a dynamic standard. New features are constantly invented, with implementation following at an amazingly fast pace. For a current snapshot of the latest features supported in QtWebKit please look at the latest supported standards page at: `http://trac.webkit.org/wiki/QtWebKitSupportedStandards`.

Putting It All Together: Implementing Shake in HTML5

So far we've learned about various tools for building web applications based on HTML5 technologies. Let's put it all together with an example of building a more comprehensive web application. Let's take the Shake application we built in Chapters 4, 5 and 6 and, instead of using native Qt technologies, let's build it with web technologies.

The focus of this book is not to give an in-depth tutorial on web development. So instead, in this section we'll highlight some of the key points you'll want to understand to get Shake running as an HTML5 web app. For a more thorough understanding of what is going on, please download the complete source code from `www.apress.com` and explore on your own.

Web development is most easily done in an IDE designed for web applications. Any environment used for web applications will work fine, but some popular ones are Adobe DreamWeaver or Aptana Studio. Both of these environments have Nokia plug-ins to support the legacy Symbian Web Runtime platform. Even though we're not developing for the Web Runtime environment, some of the features and templates are still useful. For example, the Shake code we are building is based on the RSS reader example that comes with the Nokia Aptana plugin. You might want to take a look at those examples as well.

Now, let's consider how we are going to design Shake for HTML5. Just as in the native Qt application, there are three things we must do: download the XML feed, parse the feed data into usable pieces, and display the data to the user. Let's get started with the user interface.

Rather than build everything from the ground up, it is usually much easier to start with some kind of JavaScript library that provides a useful widget set. Since QtWebKit is a standards compliant HTML5 browser, any widget set that runs in HTML5 should work fine. jQuery or jQuery Mobile seem especially popular, but any library should work. For this example, let's use Guarana, a UI library built by Nokia based on jQuery. More information on Guarana is available from
http://wiki.forum.nokia.com/index.php/Guarana_UI:_a_jQuery-Based_UI_Library_for_Nokia_WRT

> **WARNING:** Guarana is no longer the target of active development and will likely be superseded by other widget sets in the future. However, at the time this book is written, Guarana is still the best available option from Nokia for mobile web widgets.

First, we need to include the reference to jQuery and Guarana in our code. For this, we need to add code that looks like this:

```
<link rel='stylesheet'
  href='lib/guarana/themes/themeroller/default-theme/Themeroller.css'
  type='text/css' media='screen'>
<script src="lib/guarana/lib/jquery/jquery.js"
  type="text/javascript" charset="utf-8"></script>
<script src="lib/guarana/lib/Guarana.js"
  type="text/javascript" charset="utf-8"></script>
```

Also, we need to set the appropriate path variables for Guarana. For this, we want this code:

```
<script type='text/JavaScript'>
NOKIA_PATH_JAVASCRIPT = 'lib/guarana/lib/';
NOKIA_PATH_STYLE_ROOT = 'lib/guarana/themes/nokia/base/';
</script>
```

We want to have two views for this application: our main view where we show the earthquake data and the about view where we give ourselves credit.

We use the templatedefault widget to get the basic view layout to look right. This gives us a title bar on the top with icons for home, menu, and back functionality, along with pull-down menus to let you navigate between views. After we add the templatedefault code the app should look like Figure 7–8.

Figure 7–8. *Shake gets started.*

Next, we want to create our two views. Let's take a moment to understand how views work. The best way to think about the Nokia.view class is as an abstract class that must be extended to form more specific types of classes, which you then use to create object instances for your application. You do this by creating callback functions that are called as certain view events are handled. These callback functions are passed as function arguments when the view is defined with the Nokia.view.extend function. Some significant events for which you can define callback functions are:

- init
- renderUI
- bindUI
- syncUI
- show
- hide

As expected, init is called to initialize the view. The next three callbacks — renderUI , bindUI, and syncUI — are part of the view lifecycle. These are abstract (empty) methods and need to be overridden for each view. renderUI is the method responsible for creating and adding the HTML nodes the view needs. It is usually the point where the DOM is first modified by the view. bindUI is the method responsible for attaching event listeners that bind the UI to the view. And syncUI is the method responsibly for synchronizing the state of the UI based on the current state of the view. show is called when the widget is shown, and hide is called when the view is hidden.

Let's take a look at the first view from our application. First, the view is defined using the Nokia.view.extend function and the init function is overridden. In this example init does nothing.

```
var FirstView = Nokia.View.extend({
  /*
   * Lifecycle
   */
init: function() {
  //console.log("initialize FirstView view");
},
```

Now, let's look at renderUI. This is where the HTML for the node is created. In this case, it is just some simple text. Later, we will add the HTML for our earthquake data in this section.

```
renderUI: function() {
  this._viewHeader = Nokia.dom.parseHTML('<p class="nokia-view-header">First View Header
First View Header' +
  'First View Header First View Header First View Header First View Header First View
Header First View Header' + '</p>');

  Nokia.dom.append(this.getContainer(), this._viewHeader);
},
```

The HTML markup is attached to the DOM using the Nokia.dom.append function. This is typical jQuery syntax. Next, look at bindUI and syncUI.

```
bindUI: function() {
  this._viewHeader.click(function() {
  //console.log('Clicked on Header');
  });
},

syncUI: function() {
  this._viewHeader.CSS('color', 'red');
},
```

bindUI is where listeners would be bound. In this case, bindUI does nothing but log that the view was clicked. syncUI causes the text in this view to be colored red.

show does a lot of activity when the view is actually shown. The items in the menu (selected by the menu icon in the title bar) are set to the appropriate values. The title bar is updated with the appropriate view name and other elements in the title bar are also updated. And finally, this.getContainer.show is called to show the entire view.

```
show: function() {
    if (feedName==null){
        viewManager.show(1);
                    }
    var template = this.getTemplate();
    var topBar = template.getHeaderTopBar();

    floatingMenu.destroy();

    floatingMenu = new Nokia.FloatingMenu({
                autoRender: false,
                element: '.nokia-template-header-icon-menu',
                elementHoverClass: 'nokia-template-header-icon-menu-hover',
                offsetTop: 60,
```

```
            items: [
                                {label: 'About', callback: function() {
    viewManager.show(1) }},
                                {label: 'Refresh', callback: function() {
    window.location.reload(); }}
                            ]
        });

        defaultTopItems[2] = {
            classname: 'nokia-template-header-icon-menu',
            callback: function() {
                    floatingMenu.render().toggle();
                }
        };

        defaultTopItems[4] = {
            classname: 'nokia-template-header-title',
            label: feedName
        };

        defaultTopItems[6] = {
            classname: 'nokia-template-header-icon-close',
            pressedStateClass: 'nokia-template-header-icon-hover',
            callback: function() {
                window.close();
            }
        }
        topBar.setItems(defaultTopItems);
        this.getContainer().show();
        }
}
```

The views are now defined. Now we instantiate the two views and add these views to the viewManager using the viewManager.Add function.

```
viewManager.add(new FeedsView());
viewManager.add(new AboutView());
```

The last significant piece of code is here:

```
Nokia.use('template-default', init);
```

This tells the Nokia Loader to dynamically load the library code for template-default, and then execute the init function.

Adding UI Components to the Views

Our views are set up. Now let's think about making the views look like something we want. For the Shake view we want to show a list of seismic events as grabbed from the USGS. We want to add the ability to click on each event to get more details and an image showing where the quake hit. One way to do this is to make each event take you to a new full screen view with the additional information. Another, nicer way, though, is to use the accordion widget. Let's add it to our application.

First, we need to add a <div> for the accordion to the FeedView HTML with a recognizable div id. This div id is then referenced when the accordion is instantiated. To do this, let's add this code to the RenderUI callback in the FeedView we created above.

```
renderUI: function() {
  this._viewHeader = Nokia.dom.parseHTML('<div class="widget-view">'+
    '<div id="accordion"></div>'+
    '</div>');
  Nokia.dom.append(this.getContainer(), this._viewHeader);
}
```

Now we've added the appropriate <div> to the view HTML. Next, we need to populate the <div> with the appropriately structured content, and then instantiate the accordion. Eventually we will populate this with the data we pull from the USGS, but for now let's get the structure right with some dummy data. Let's populate the data in a function called setFeedItems. This nicely contains this functionality so we can use this same function later for the real feed data. So now, create this function:

```
function setFeedItems(items)
{
  // start by removing all current feed items
  $('#accordion').children().remove();

  // create new feed items and add them to the main view
  for (var i = 0; i < items.length; i++)
  {
    var item = items[i];
    $('#accordion').append('<a ref="JavaScript:void(0);"> quake ' + i + ' title </a>');
    $('#accordion').append('<div> <p>item 1 </p><p>item 2</p></div>');
  }
}
```

Note that this again makes significant use of jQuery syntax. For now, let's call this function from the show callback of the FeedView using some dummy data. Just add this line to the FeedView callback:

```
setFeedItems([1,2,3]);
```

Last, we need to add the code to instantiate the accordion to our setFeedItems function. SetFeedItems() should look something like this:.

```
window.accordion1 = new Nokia.Accordion({
    element: '#accordion',
    collapsible: true,
    multiple: false,
    closed: true,
    toggle: function(event, header, content) {
    },
    create: function() {
    },
    open: function(event, header, content) {
    },
    close: function(event, header, content) {
    }
  });
```

This code instantiates a new Nokia.Accordion object. The first element says that `<div>` with div id = 'accordion' that we set earlier will become the container for the accordion. The other options specify various configurable options for the widget. The accordion widget, for example, has a configuration option to set whether or not it is collapsible. Each widget has its own set of options that you can find from the documentation provided earlier.

One last thing we need to do is to add 'Accordion' to the Nokia.use function call that specifies which libraries are to be loaded. To do this, update the function call to look like this:

```
Nokia.use('template-default', 'accordion', init);
```

If all goes well, your app should work as before, but now you should see an accordion view filled with dummy earthquake data. Take a look at Figure 7–9 to see what it should look like. Now let's get some really USGS data and plug it in.

Figure 7–9. *Shake with the accordion UI widget*

Fetching and Parsing the Data

Next, we need to download and parse the XML data from the USGS. Let's use XmlHttpRequest to request the XML data. After that, we can put together some simple JavaScript to parse the result and put in HTML formatting. Finally, we plug it into the accordion widget and we are done.

There are many examples for how to request and parse XML feeds available elsewhere, so we won't go into detail here. The example code here was based on an RSS reader example that came with the Nokia Aptana plug-in.

One really cool thing about this code is that the markup in the summary received from the USGS XML feed includes an `<img>` tag. Without doing any fancy coding or image handling, the summary information for each quake shows a thumbnail for each quake's location in addition to the text giving details. We didn't need to do anything special to render the image. We just pasted the `<img>` tag as we got it from the USGS and it works!

Let's do one bit of HTML5 magic to liven things up a bit. Inside the `image` element, let's add this class declaration:

```
class='quakeImage'
```

And later in the CSS file, let's add this declaration block:

```
.quakeImage:active {
    -webkit-transition: all 1s ease-in-out;
    -webkit-transform: scale(5) translateX(50px);
}
```

Now, when we click on the image, we use the `-webkit-transform` property to make the image grow and move to the right. With just a couple of lines of code we were able to add a nice zooming effect.

Packaging the App

Finally let's package our app into a hybrid app. In this case let's package the content as resources just so we don't have to worry about installing files. Let's package and install as we did earlier in this chapter and we're done!

Figure 7–10 below shows our completed Shake application built using HTML5 and associated technologies and running in a QtWebKit container.

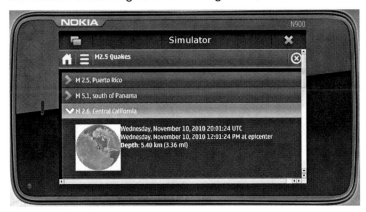

Figure 7–10. *Shake is complete*

Links for further information

Because of space considerations, we could not give the depth many topics deserve. We encourage you to continue exploring these technologies on your own. Here are some sources of additional information:

- Tutorials on web technologies: www.w3schools.com
- The full HTML5 specification: dev.w3.org/html5/spec/

- An excellent example of a Cartoon Reader written using hybrid Qt and HTML5 technologies, including local storage:
  www.forum.nokia.com/info/sw.nokia.com/id/269f8716-ca61-4036-9b6a-f567f0184f0b/QtWebKit_Cartoon_Reader_Example.html

- Tips on power management:
  www.forum.nokia.com/main/resources/development_process/power_management/.

- JavaScript performance best practices:
  wiki.forum.nokia.com/index.php/JavaScript_Performance_Best_Practices#JavaScript_Performance_Best_Practices.

Wrapping Up

In this chapter we presented the basics you will need to know to write HTML5 applications for Nokia. We showed you how to build a QtWebKit-based browser and we showed several techniques for running your HTML5 application offline. We highlighted some of the more nifty HTML5 features, such as canvas, CSS transitions and transformations, and local storage. Finally, we re-implemented Shake, the application we built in the past three chapters with native Qt technologies, this time using HTML5.

Next up, we'll show you how to test and distribute your application.

Distribute

Chapter 8

Testing Your Application

As you near the completion of your first application, it's time to turn your attention to what's often called "the other 80 percent"—that is, the work that remains after you've done the first 80 percent. It doesn't need to be overwhelming, but the truth is that there's more to delivering a quality application than just the design and the code. As you wrap up application development, you should be thinking about testing and integration with other systems and even simple things like establishing your application's brand message through the artwork and copy you'll submit to the Ovi Store (which we discuss in the next chapter).

In this chapter, we examine application testing, giving you some tips and tricks as to ways you can best use Nokia tools to support your testing. These include QTest, Qt's test framework, which as you'll see, you can use throughout your development cycle to help you reach your quality goals. We close the chapter with an example using QTest to show you how easy it is to verify application quality as you go through the use of unit tests.

Preparing to Test

Although there has been a lot of discussion in recent years about the nature of testing that's appropriate in software development, there's no question some of it is absolutely necessary. When you plan your testing, you should be sure to think about the kinds your application will require and how much time and effort they will take.

You should begin with a *test plan*, a concise list of *test cases* that you automatically or manually execute at regular intervals (say, daily or weekly). Each test case should describe a single test, including the initial configuration, the steps to perform the test, and the expected results. A good test plan, coupled with investigative work, can give you an idea of the *test coverage*—that is, the percentage of the application's functionality that is testable and how much of that testing you can automate.

Your testing may be *functional*, as well as *non-functional*. Functional testing includes everything to do with the actual operation of your application—things like its business logic to ensure that it operates correctly. Non-functional testing includes all areas of your application that have to do with its performance outside of correct operation. That's a lot: out-of-memory conditions, signal loss, position/GPS loss, servers not being available due to downtime or unplanned load, and so on. Non functional testing is also often thought of as *adversarial* testing. It explores how your application performs in adverse situations. When planning your tests, be sure to include at least as much adversarial testing as functional testing, because it's impossible to really know just what situations your application will encounter. The execution environment, after all, is mobile, will both move in and out of signal coverage, and experience periods of heavy and light use, leading to periods of heavy heap and persistent storage use.

What most people think of testing is *dynamic*—that is, testing that occurs while the application is running. Dynamic tests include:

- *Manual* testing, in which you or a tester puts your application through its paces with the guidance of a test plan.

- *Unit tests, which* exercise a single class programmatically (more on doing this with Qt later in this chapter in the section "Using Unit Tests to Verify Functionality").

- *Integration* tests, which examine your application as it works with other portions of your application's system, such as back-end servers.

- *Analysis* tools like valgrind (http://valgrind.org) that explore run-time performance with regard to memory and other resource usage (not available for Symbian, however).

Equally—and perhaps more—important is *static* testing, which includes any nonexecution examination of your source code. Buddy checks or code reviews are a great way to catch common programming errors and cross-train participants on your developer team, as well as think through tricky problems together. Tools abound for verifying your application as part of the compile cycle; an easy one is the compiler's own warnings.

TESTING AS YOU GO ALONG

There's a lot you can do today to ensure that your application works correctly tomorrow. Much of this falls under the category "test-driven development." The Internet has a lot of information that can guide you toward a test-driven development cycle. Some places to start include:

- Daily builds. You should build your application daily, if not more often, from your change control system. The resulting build should be at least smoke-tested to make sure that no major problems have crept in—and, if they have, development should stop while you determine the root cause and fix it.

- Buddy reviews. Even if you don't go as far as a formal code review for all the code in your application, working with a buddy to review the code you commit to your change repository can help you spot both obvious and tricky coding errors.

- Compiler warnings. Compiler warnings are there for a reason: they tell you that you're doing something that isn't safe to do. After years of experience, we liken a compiler's warnings to guards on power tools in the garage. Sure, you can flip up the guard and continue working, but is it worth it? Probably not. Adopt a zero warnings, no-exceptions policy for your code; you won't regret it.

■ Use multiple compilers. Although C++ language compatibility has improved dramatically in the past decade, not all compilers are created equal. Some, including GCC, provide very good warnings that can help you prevent esoteric bugs. Consider using multiple compilers from different vendors if you can when you're doing cross-platform development. You can do this by using Microsoft Visual Studio for your simulator testing, and then compiling for device (which uses a different compiler), for example.

■ Run early and run often on device. You're developing an application for mobile, and with today's tools, there's little excuse to spend all of your time in a simulator. Worse, all a simulator does is simulate; you should run your application often on hardware to explore its actual performance. The simulator is an excellent tool for rapid iteration on your user interface, but there's no replacement for actually seeing your application on a device.

NOTE: Unfortunately, as we write this, the Symbian build environment is apt to emit warnings of its own when you compile, making a zero-warnings policy difficult. One strategy is to use compiler pragmas to turn off certain warnings, but we find it easier to periodically (say, daily) skim the warnings from an otherwise working build and make sure nothing has crept in. If you've got a lot of files in your project, once the number of files is stable, you can capture the output and use a tool like diff to verify that the warnings remain the same. With luck and effort on the part of Nokia, this problem will improve soon.

Using Qt's Test Framework

Inspired by the various unit testing frameworks evangelized by the extreme programming community, Qt provides a framework for implementing unit tests for classes using Qt. This framework, called QTest, is a small, self-contained library that invokes tests provided by a class that you write and lets you test components in your application. With a bit of creativity, you can extend your tests within QTest to test not just single classes as recommended by the unit test paradigm, but also test classes in combination or perform simple integration tests. Implementing both the test runner and the basic primitives for result verification and benchmarking, QTest is a lightweight, self-contained thread- and type-safe library you can use to quickly create tests for your application.

Introducing the QTest Test Framework

QTest's test runner uses Qt's meta-object protocol to introspect the methods in a class you provide to determine what must happen at run time. This makes test definition very easy for you. You only need to provide a class derived from QObject that defines slots implementing the tests that you want to run. QTest treats several slots in your test class in special ways to determine what slots correspond to tests and give you a way to control the test environment setup and teardown:

- The test harness invokes the slot initTestCase before any tests are run.

- The test harness invokes the slot cleanupTestCase after all tests are run.

- The test harness invokes the slot init before each test is run.

- The test harness invokes the slot cleanup after each test is run.

- The test harness invokes each slot in turn, invoking first the slot init, and then the first slot it encounters, and then the slot cleanup, and then init, the next slot, and then cleanup, and so on, until all slots are run.

By design, your individual test cases should be independent; a test case should not rely upon the performance of a previous or subsequent test case. This is a key reason for providing the initTestCase and init methods, where you can separate key initialization for all test cases, and clean up after a single or all test cases using cleanup and cleanupTestCase.

> **CAUTION:** Don't confuse init with initTestCase (or cleanup with cleanupTestCase). It's easy to get confused, because you tend to think of each test in your class as an individual test case—so there's the temptation to write initTestCase for per-test initialization. It's exactly the reverse, however.

Listing 8–1 shows perhaps the most trivial of tests.

Listing 8–1. *A trivial test class*

```
#include <QtTest/QtTest>
class TrivialTest: public QObject
{
    Q_OBJECT
private slots:
    void () trivialTest
    { QVERIFY(1 == 1); }
    void anotherTrivialTest()
    { QVERIFY(0 != 1); }
};
QTEST_MAIN(TrivialTest)
#include "trivialtest.moc"
```

Before we look at the test slots, let's pause briefly and look at the additional stuff after the test. The compiler will expand the QTEST_MAIN macro to provide an entry point function and invoke your test methods. The second line with the #include includes the output from the meta-object compiler, required anytime you define a QObject derivative in a C++ class instead of a header. Not shown in Listing 8–1 is the .pro file; in addition to including the source file for *TrivialTest.cpp*, it needs to include the QTest configuration. If you've got the qmake executable in your path, an easy way to make a .pro file for a QTest test class is to use qmake on the command line, like this:

```
C:\Book\Tests>qmake -project "CONFIG += QTest"
C:\Book\Tests>qmake
C:\Book\Tests>make
```

In project mode, qmake will make a *.pro* file for you that includes the source files in the current directory, as well as the CONFIG variable, including the QTest libraries and headers.

If you don't, you can create one using Qt creator by performing the following in the Nokia Qt SDK:

1. Choose "File>New File or Project"…

2. Choose "Other Project" from the upper left-hand pane of the window that appears.

3. Choose "Qt Unit Test" from the list in the upper right-hand pane.

4. Click "Choose…"

5. Enter a name and path for the unit test and click "Next."

6. Choose at least the Simulator Qt options for your build system, and optionally choose device targets as well and click "Next."

7. Choose any modules upon which your unit tests will depend, such as QtNetwork for networking and click "Next."

8. Fill out the form describing the first unit test in your test cases and click "Next."

9. Click "Finish."

Returning to the body of the test functions, the QVERIFY macro is one of several provided by QTest to facilitate instrumentation for test passes and failures. These are:

- QVERIFY verifies that a condition is true and causes the test to fail if it's not.

- QVERIFY2 operates the same as QVERIFY, but includes a verbose message to be output if the condition fails.

- QCOMPARE performs a type-safe comparison of an actual value to an expected value. When comparing floating-point (single or double precision), it uses the Qt function qFuzzyCompare to better support approximate comparisons using floating-point representations.

- QSKIP stops execution of the current test without adding a failure to the test log. It does, however, indicate that the test was skipped for the reason you provide when invoking the macro.

- QBENCHMARK benchmarks the code block that immediately follows the macro, running it multiple times if necessary to obtain benchmark data. You can require the benchmarked code only be run once by using QBENCHMARK_ONCE, although the elapsed time may be reported as zero, if the execution time is too short to be measured by the benchmark system.

Unit Testing the QuakeEvent Class

Let's take a look at an actual unit test, one we wrote for the QuakeEvent class. Listing 8–2 shows the unit test itself.

Listing 8–2. *The unit test for the QuakeEvent class*

```
#include <QtCore/QString>
#include <QtTest/QtTest>
#include <QDebug>
#include "quakeevent.h"

class TestQuakeEvent : public QObject
{
    Q_OBJECT

public:
    TestQuakeEvent();

private:
    QuakeEvent *mEvent;

private Q_SLOTS:
    void initTestCase();
    void cleanupTestCase();

    void init();
    void cleanup();

    void testConstructor();
    void testSetGet();
    void testIsEmpty();
    void testClear();
    void testComparator();

    void testId();
    void testSummary();
    void testWhen();
    void testWhere();
    void testMagnitude();
    void testPosition();
    void testElevation();
    void testHtml();
    void testDistanceTo();
```

```cpp
};

TestQuakeEvent::TestQuakeEvent()
{
}

void TestQuakeEvent::initTestCase() {
    mEvent = new QuakeEvent();
}

void TestQuakeEvent::cleanupTestCase() {
    delete mEvent;
}

void TestQuakeEvent::init() {
    mEvent->clear();
    mEvent->set("title",   "M 2.6, Hawaii region, Hawaii");
    mEvent->set("point",   "19.9770 -156.8687");
    mEvent->set("elev",    "-7900");
    mEvent->set("summary", "<img src=\"http://earthquake.usgs.gov¬
/images/globes/20_-155.jpg\" alt=\"19.977&#176;N 156.869&#176;W\"¬
 align=\"left\" hspace=\"20\" /><p>Monday, September  6, 2010 15:¬
19:09 UTC<br>Monday, September  6, 2010 05:19:09 AM at epicenter<¬
/p><p><strong>Depth</strong>: 7.90 km (4.91 mi)</p>");
}

void TestQuakeEvent::cleanup() {
    mEvent->clear();
}

void TestQuakeEvent::testConstructor() {
    QuakeEvent *e = new QuakeEvent();
    QVERIFY(e->isEmpty());
    delete e;
}

void TestQuakeEvent::testSetGet() {
    mEvent->set("arbitrary", "value");
    QVERIFY(mEvent->get("arbitrary")=="value");
}

// Failures may indicate a problem with either
// isEmpty or clear
void TestQuakeEvent::testIsEmpty() {
    QVERIFY(!mEvent->isEmpty());
    mEvent->clear();
    QVERIFY(mEvent->isEmpty());
}

// Failures may indicate a problem with either
// isEmpty or clear
void TestQuakeEvent::testClear() {
    QVERIFY(!mEvent->isEmpty());
    mEvent->clear();
    QVERIFY(mEvent->isEmpty());
}
```

```cpp
void TestQuakeEvent::testComparator() {
    QuakeEvent *e = new QuakeEvent();
    e->set("summary",      "<img src=\"http://earthquake.usgs.gov¬
/images/globes/20_-155.jpg\" alt=\"19.977&#176;N 156.869&#176;W\"¬
 align=\"left\" hspace=\"20\" /><p>Monday, September  6, 2010 15:¬
19:09 UTC<br>Monday, September  6, 2010 05:19:09 AM at epicenter<¬
/p><p><strong>Depth</strong>: 7.90 km (4.91 mi)</p>");
    QVERIFY(*mEvent < *e);
    delete e;
}

void TestQuakeEvent::testId() {
    mEvent->set("arbitrary", "123456789");
    QVERIFY(mEvent->get("arbitrary")=="123456789");
}

void TestQuakeEvent::testSummary() {
    QVERIFY(mEvent->summary() == "M 2.6, Hawaii region, Hawaii");
}

void TestQuakeEvent::testWhen() {
    // Ideally this would test a number of dates and times
    QDateTime when(QDate(2010, 9, 6),
                   QTime( 15, 19, 9), Qt::UTC);

    QVERIFY(mEvent->when() == when);
}

void TestQuakeEvent::testWhere() {
    QVERIFY(mEvent->where() == "Hawaii region, Hawaii");
}

void TestQuakeEvent::testMagnitude() {
    float mag = (float)mEvent->magnitude();

    QCOMPARE(mag, (float)2.60);
}

void TestQuakeEvent::testPosition() {
    qDebug() << mEvent->position();
    QCOMPARE((float)mEvent->position().first,  (float)19.977);
    QCOMPARE((float)mEvent->position().second, (float)-156.869);
}

void TestQuakeEvent::testElevation() {
    QVERIFY(qFuzzyCompare(mEvent->elevation(), -7900.0));
}

void TestQuakeEvent::testHtml() {
    QVERIFY(mEvent->html() ==
                      "<img src=\"http://earthquake.usgs.gov¬
/images/globes/20_-155.jpg\" alt=\"19.977&#176;N 156.869&#176;W\"¬
 align=\"left\" hspace=\"20\" /><p>Monday, September  6, 2010 15:¬
19:09 UTC<br>Monday, September  6, 2010 05:19:09 AM at epicenter<¬
/p><p><strong>Depth</strong>: 7.90 km (4.91 mi)</p>");
}
```

```
void TestQuakeEvent::testDistanceTo() {
    qreal distance = mEvent->distanceTo(
        QPair<qreal, qreal>(37.0, -122.0));
    QCOMPARE((float)distance, (float)3870.68);
}

QTEST_APPLESS_MAIN(TestQuakeEvent);
#include "tst_quakeevent.moc"
```

These tests show a common pattern in unit tests, in which there's at least one test per method of the object under test. Our tests are self-explanatory, so rather than walking line-by-line, we'll just call out a few of the high points.

First, with a few exceptions, the test reuses a single QuakeEvent object, rather than creating one for each case. This increases performance (fewer memory allocations), but requires that the basic object recycling interface that the QuakeEvent::clear method promises be working correctly. As each test case starts, the init method initializes the unit test's mEvent field with known content hand-scraped from the USGS web site's feed. When the test is completed, the cleanup method clears the mEvent field, ensuring that each test enters and concludes with the recycled object in a known state.

Second, tests that require their own object—either one that hasn't been initialized, like the testConstructor test, or one that requires more than one QuakeEvent object, such as testComparator—simply create a second object and initialize them as the logic behind the test case requires.

Third, the test for QuakeEvent::when is probably a little underpowered; you remember from Chapter 5 that it scrapes the date from a text string and requires exact matching of month names; a good test case would probably set several different date strings on the QuakeEvent and check that each date gets parsed correctly. (Even better would be one that includes invalid dates and protects against crashes or bizarre failures.) However, the code we wrote was reviewed, which provides some confidence, and such an example could become tedious for you to read very quickly.

Finally, unit tests that compare floating-point numbers are notoriously finicky to get exactly right. Thanks to the vagaries of floating-point arithmetic, you should always declare the precision you desire and use either qFuzzyCompare or QCOMPARE (which uses qFuzzyCompare under the hood). If you don't, you can get all kinds of odd results, especially when computing with double-precision floating-point numbers or when matching single-precision and double-precision arithmetic. Here, given the nature of the input and results, single-precision arithmetic is ample, so it's all we do.

Testing Signals and Slots Using QTest

Many times when you're writing a test for a class, you realize that what you want to test is a signal's emission, not just the results of a function. For example, if you write a new model, you want to ensure that your model correctly emits the QAbstractItemModel's signals like dataChanged as the contents of the model changes.

Fortunately, Qt has a class that enables you to examine the results of any signal emission, QSignalSpy. Implemented as a list of QVariant lists, each signal it catches appends a list of signal arguments to its main list, letting you eavesdrop on the signal process itself. Listing 8–3 shows a typical use.

Listing 8–3. *Using QSignalSpy to test signal emission*

```
QSignalSpy spy(myObject, SIGNAL(something(QString, int)));
// trigger signal emission
myObject ->emitsSomething();
// Check the resulting types
QList<QVariant> arguments = spy.takeFirst();
QVERIFY(arguments.at(0).type() == QVariant::QString);
QVERIFY(arguments.at(1).type() == QVariant::Int);
// Check the resulting values
QVERIFY(arguments.at(0).value<int>() == 1);
QVERIFY(arguments.at(1).value<QString>() == "hello");
```

The code begins by connecting a stack-stored QSignalSpy instance to a custom QObject that emits the something signal, passing a QString and an int. It next calls the hypothetical method emitsSomething, which presumably emits the something signal. The arguments to this signal are stored in the QSignalSpy as its first element; each of the signal's arguments is stored as a separate QVariant instance (which we first mentioned in Chapter 5) in a QList of arguments.

The code performs the tests themselves on the arguments to the signal, first verifying the type of each signal argument, and then verifying the value. The QVariant's type method returns the C++ type of a QVariant as a Qt-enumerated value, while its templated value function returns the value, optionally coerced to the specific type you pass as a template argument.

Testing User Interface Code Using QTestEventList

If you're interested in performing automated testing on user-interface classes, little we've shown you so far provides much help. As your user interface should primarily connect to your business logic through signals and slots, writing unit tests that use QSignalSpy lets you create an instance of pieces of your user interface (say, a custom widget or a panel of related widgets) and test that they emit appropriate signals.

However, to do this, when you test a user interface class, you want to simulate user events, such as key or mouse events. This is especially true if you're creating your own widget or if you want to script an interaction with a component such as a view in your application. QTest also includes the QTestEventList class, a class that lets you create a list of events and then pass them one at a time to a child object of QWidget. At its heart, it's simply a QList of test event objects, which get invoked on the widget one at a time when you invoke its simulate method. QTestEventList provides methods so that you can add following events to the list:

- A key click or clicks (by Qt::Key code, ASCII character, or QString) by calling addKeyClick or addKeyClicks (for multiple key clicks).

- A key press by calling addKeyPress (passing either the Qt::Key code or an ASCII character).

- A key release by calling addKeyRelease (passing either the Qt::Key code or an ASCII character)

- A mouse click by calling addMouseClick and passing which mouse button (Qt::MouseButton), any keyboard modifiers (Qt::KeyboardModifiers), and the point where the click should be simulated (QPoint).

- A mouse double-click by calling addMouseDClick and passing which mouse button (Qt::MouseButton), any keyboard modifiers (Qt::KeyboardModifiers), and the point where the click should be simulated (QPoint).

- A mouse button press or release event by calling addMousePress or addMouseRelease and passing which mouse button (Qt::MouseButton), any keyboard modifiers (Qt::KeyboardModifiers), and the point where the click should be simulated (QPoint).

- A mouse movement by calling addMouseMove, passing the point to which the mouse cursor should move as a QPoint.

Each of these can optionally include a delay in milliseconds, or you can call addDelay to add a delay to the simulated event stream.

Listing 8–4 shows how you might append the text "Hello world" with some extraneous mouse movements to a QLineEdit in your unit test:

Listing 8–4. *Simulating events to a QLineEdit using QTestEventList*

```
QTestEventList events;
QLineEdit *lineEdit = new QLineEdit(this);
events.addKeyClicks("Hello world", 100);
events.addMouseMove(QPoint(qrand() % 256, qrand % 256), 25);
events.addMouseMove(QPoint(qrand() % 256, qrand % 256), 25);
events.addMouseMove(QPoint(qrand() % 256, qrand % 256), 25);
// simulate all the events
events.simulate(lineEdit);
```

The code creates first the events for the discrete key click events to type "Hello world," and then pauses for 100 milliseconds. Next, it creates three random mouse movement events to random coordinates bounded by the rectangle (left: 0, top: 0, right: 256, bottom: 256), pausing for 25 milliseconds between each move. Finally, it simulates these events on the line editor instance lineEdit.

If you need only simulate an event or two, it may be simpler to use the static QTest methods to do so. There's one corresponding to each of the kinds of events you can simulate using the QTestEventList class, namely:

- keyClick and keyClicks to simulate key clicks.

- keyEvent to simulate a specific key event.

- keyPress and keyRelease to simulate a single key press or release.

- mouseClick and mouseDClick to simulate a single- or double-click.

- mousePress and mouseRelease to simulate a single mouse button press or release.

- mouseMove to simulate a single mouse movement event.

Each of these takes the widget to which the event should be sent.

Finally, the QTest class has a few other static methods that can come in handy. Under the qSleep method, the process sleeps for the number of milliseconds you specify, blocking test execution and leaving events unprocessed (in other words, your test is non-responsive during this time). The qWait method waits for the number of milliseconds you specify, letting the test application still process events and handle network communication. The toHexRepresentation takes an array of bytes and returns a character string of space-separated hex characters to facilitate hex dumps, and the toString method returns a human-readable string representation of times, dates, byte arrays, points, sizes, rectangles, and other fundamental types that Qt defines.

Wrapping Up

We opened this chapter with the types of testing (dynamic vs. static, unit vs. integration) that you can perform to help flush out bugs in your application. Most important, we urged you to follow the best practices of test-driven development, including daily builds, buddy code reviews, treating compiler warnings as errors, and frequent execution on real devices.

Next, we gave you an in-depth look at Qt's test framework QTest, which provides a small self-contained library with a test harness and utilities ideal for unit testing and small integration or system-level tests. Using QTest, you can create small executables that run tests you write on a class (or a collection of classes). Defining the tests as private slots of a QObject subclass, you instrument your tests using helper macros such as QVERIFY and QCOMPARE to test for successful situations or test expected vs. actual results. Using the QSignalSpy class, you can also test your classes' emission of signals, ensuring that they emit the correct arguments and values for the situations you create for the object under test. You can even simulate sequences of common events like key strokes and mouse events, either as a collection using QTestEventList or singly with the static methods provided by the QTest class.

Chapter 9

Deploying Your Application

You've designed, written, and tested your application. Now it's time to bring it to market.

As we promised in the first chapter, it isn't hard. In this chapter, you learn precisely what you need to do. We begin by providing a deployment checklist before describing some final packaging steps that may be necessary for certain MeeGo and Symbian applications, and then discuss the important concept of *application signing* required by Symbian applications. Finally, we close the chapter by describing the publishing process through the Ovi Store.

Preparing a Deployment Checklist

While every application is different, there are some things common to deploying nearly all applications. Larger companies, especially those with clear development and release criteria, often provide some sort of deployment checklist or signoff—often called a release *gate*—that defines the criteria an application must meet before it reaches the customer. (Larger companies with mature development cycles may have a sequence of gates through which an application passes as it goes from inception through customer delivery.) Especially if you're just starting out, you should have a deployment checklist of things not to forget when you deliver your application. Your list should address things such as:

- Resources. Has your application been built with all production resources, or is it still using temporary artwork in places? Do you own the rights to distribute the resources (text, images, sounds, and music) with your application?

- Services. Does your application rely on back-end servers or services? Are they prepared to handle the load your application is expected to generate? What if they're not available when your application launches?

- Testing. How much testing is enough? On what platforms have you tested your application? Has your application been tested thoroughly? What defects remain? What *hasn't* been tested?

- Marketing. Is your marketing message ready? Where besides Ovi (your web site, other web sites, comarketing opportunities, and so forth) will you be marketing your application?

- Deployment. Do you have the necessary screenshots, icons, copy, and search terms for your submission to publish on Ovi Store? If your application needs to be signed (see "Signing Your Qt Application for Symbian Devices" in this chapter) have you done the necessary homework to obtain a digital certificate and left enough time in your schedule for the Symbian Signed process?

It's easy—especially when you're flying solo and doing it all yourself—to forget something you'll need later. Some, such as the search terms you'll provide to Ovi Store, are things to come up with on the spot. Others, like adequate testing, require planning and preparation; your deployment checklist can help you make sure you haven't forgotten anything.

Packaging Your Application

Although it's not immediately obvious when you're in the tight loop of coding, compiling, and testing on a device, the Nokia Qt SDK produces output to the device in a manner already roughly packaged for production. Symbian handsets require their applications to be packaged in a platform-specific format known as the Software Installation Script (SIS) file, a binary archive file that contains your application, application icon, and other files your application needs. As you learn in the section "Signing Your Application," later in the chapter, you need to cryptographically sign your application, yielding what's commonly called a *sisx* file because its extension is `.sisx`. MeeGo, on the other hand, uses the standard Debian software package format—called *deb* files—and does not support cryptographic signing.

Before we discuss signing—the last thing you can do to your file before publishing it— let's talk about a few last-minute details, such as including other files within your application and providing an application icon. We also touch on a minor platform-specific difference between Symbian and MeeGo, showing you how to get and use a unique id (UID) for your application on Symbian.

Including Other Files within Your Application on Symbian Devices

In Chapter 5, we showed you how to use Qt's support for data resources to include arbitrary text and binary resources in your application. Sometimes, there's a good reason to include this data as separate files—you're writing an image editing application, say, and you want to include some sample images. You could carry these as application resources and copy them to the appropriate place on the device, but then your application consumes twice as much space as it needs for data only necessary at installation time—a high premium for mobile devices. Instead, what you'd really like to do is include these sample files as files in the application's installer. You can do this by specifying the files to include in the installer in your application's PRO file.

Qt's PRO files, which you first encountered in Chapter 3, use variables that can contain lists of strings as the primary mechanism for its declarative power. For example, you include source files for compilation by adding them to the SOURCES variable. You can define your own variables, too.

When building your application, qmake also uses the contents of your application's PRO file to create the input scripts that the build system uses to generate your application's sisx and deb files. As it does so, it examines the DEPLOYMENT variable and copies the files you specify to the paths you specify. You do so by creating a variable that contains the list of files to install and the destination location, like this:

```
files.sources = photo1.jpg photo2.jpg photo3.jpg
files.path = /images
DEPLOYMENT += files
```

Note that we write += to add our variable's contents to the DEPLOYMENT variable so we append, rather than replace, any other files to be deployed.

Including Other Files within Your Application on MeeGo Devices

The principle for including additional files with MeeGo applications is similar, but instead of using the DEPLOYMENT variable, you use the INSTALLS variable, like this:

```
files.sources = photo1.jpg photo2.jpg photo3.jpg
files.path = /usr/local/share/photoeditor/samples
INSTALLS += files
```

Of course, this is best done in the context of PRO scopes, so you can support both platforms, like this:

```
files.sources += photo1.jpg photo2.jpg photo3.jpg
symbian {
    files.path = /images
    DEPLOYMENT += files
}
unix {
    files.path = /usr/local/share/photoeditor/samples
    INSTALLS += files
}
```

Here, the photo list remains the same for both platforms, but on Symbian, the installer is directed to copy the images to the root-level directory for images shared by all applications, while on MeeGo, the installer copies them to a separate directory. In addition, the appropriate PRO file uses the appropriate qmake variable in each case.

Including an Application Icon with Symbian Applications

For some time, Symbian has supported scalable vector graphics within both native applications and as resources for application icons; this makes it easier for applications to look polished across the variety of phone form factors and display technologies Symbian supports.

To include your application icon on Symbian, all you need to do is assign the path to the icon to the ICON variable in your PRO file, like this:

```
symbian {
    ICON = ./icon/icon.svg
}
```

Internally, qmake uses tools in the Symbian build chain to add the icon file to the registration file needed by Symbian's application framework, and ensures that it's part of the application installer script.

Including an Application Icon with MeeGo Applications

Including your application icon on MeeGo is a little trickier, as you provide several separate images of different sizes, so that the application manager can choose the appropriate image based on its needs. Each image is a separate Portable Network Graphic (PNG) or X Pixmap (XPM) image that your installer copies to a predetermined location. You name each image after the application name, but place the images in separate directories using the INSTALL variable as you see in Listing 9–1.

Listing 9–1. *Including application icons on MeeGo with your PRO file.*

```
unix {
    isEmpty(PREFIX) {
        PREFIX = /usr/local
    }
    BINDIR = $$PREFIX/bin
    DATADIR =$$PREFIX/share

    INSTALLS += iconxpm icon26 icon48 icon64

    iconxpm.path = $$DATADIR/pixmap
    iconxpm.files += ./icon/maemo/$${TARGET}.xpm
    icon26.path = $$DATADIR/icons/hicolor/26x26/apps
    icon26.files += ./icon/26x26/$${TARGET}.png
    icon48.path = $$DATADIR/icons/hicolor/48x48/apps
    icon48.files += ./icon/48x48/$${TARGET}.png
    icon64.path = $$DATADIR/icons/hicolor/64x64/apps
    icon64.files += ./icon/64x64/$${TARGET}.png
}
```

This example starts with a bit of magic, defining variables for the local installation directories for applications and their data (defaulting to /usr/local). Next, it adds the information for four icons to the INSTALLS list:

- The iconxpm image is a 16×16 image in XPM format.

- The icon26 image is a 26×26 image in PNG format.

- The icon48 image is a 48×48 image in PNG format.

- The icon64 image is a 64×64 image in PNG format.

Providing a UID for Qt Applications on Symbian

The Symbian platform requires all applications to have a unique id (UID)—a thirty-two bit integer—that identifies the applications. In native Symbian programming, UIDs are used in a number of places; in fact, your application actually has *three* UIDs, but the first two are the same across all Symbian applications, identifying your application as an executable binary.

During development, the UID usually doesn't matter, as long as it's unique. To facilitate application development, the Nokia Qt SDK randomly generates a UID from a subset of thirty-two bit values, letting you do your development without needing to stop and get a UID. However, before you can release your application, you need to obtain a unique ID. As we write this, there are two ways to do this.

First, if you plan on signing your own application with Symbian Signed (see the section "Signing Your Application") before submitting your application to the Ovi Store, you need to obtain your UID directly from Symbian Signed at `http://symbiansigned.com`. Before you begin, you must determine if you need to sign your application; see the section "Signing Your Application" to help you make that decision.

1. Log in to your Symbian Signed account.

2. Choose "UIDs" from the box on the left.

3. Choose "Request" from the box on the left

4. Follow the instructions and obtain UIDs from the protected range if you intend to sign your application, or the unprotected range if not.

Alternately, if you plan to submit your application through Nokia's Signing Symbian Applications Program, the process is similar, but Nokia will provide you with the UID.

Regardless, once you have the UID—a number such as 0xE1234567—you need to include the UID as a field in your PRO file's TARGET variable, like this:

```
symbian {
    TARGET.UID3 = 0xE1234567
}
```

Providing a Desktop File for MeeGo

The MeeGo application manager also requires a *desktop* file that includes information such as the path to your application. The format of this file matches a Windows initialization (INI) file, is named after your application with the suffix .desktop, and looks like this:

```
[Desktop Entry]
Encoding=UTF-8
Version=1.0
Type=Application
Name=Shake
Exec=/usr/local/bin/quake
Icon=quake
StartupWMClass=quake
X-Window-Icon=shake
X-HildonDesk-ShowInToolbar=true
X-Osso-Type=application/x-executable
Terminal=false
```

These fields are reasonably self-explanatory; the only catch is that you must ensure that the Exec field points to your application's binary—that is, the value of your TARGET variable in your PRO file. Like the icon files, you include this file in your INSTALLS variable, like this:

```
unix {
    INSTALLS += desktop

    desktop.path = $$DATADIR/applications/hildon
    desktop.files += $${TARGET}.desktop
}
```

The installer must place the desktop file in the /usr/local/share/applications/hildon directory in order for the application manager to see it and include your application in the application launcher screen.

Putting It All Together

Listing 9–2 shows the PRO file for the Shake application with scopes for both Symbian and MeeGo, including all we've discussed here.

Listing 9–2. *Including application icons, UIDs, and capabilities for a cross-platform application.*

```
symbian {
    TARGET.CAPABILITY = NetworkServices ReadUserData Location
    CONFIG += mobility
    MOBILITY += bearer
    TARGET.UID3 = 0xE1234567 # example UID
    ICON = ./icon/icon.svg
}
```

```
unix {
    isEmpty(PREFIX) {
        PREFIX = /usr/local
    }
    BINDIR = $$PREFIX/bin
    DATADIR =$$PREFIX/share

    INSTALLS += iconxpm icon26 icon48 icon64 desktop

    iconxpm.path = $$DATADIR/pixmap
    iconxpm.files += ./icon/maemo/$${TARGET}.xpm
    icon26.path = $$DATADIR/icons/hicolor/26x26/apps
    icon26.files += ./icon/26x26/$${TARGET}.png
    icon48.path = $$DATADIR/icons/hicolor/48x48/apps
    icon48.files += ./icon/48x48/$${TARGET}.png
    icon64.path = $$DATADIR/icons/hicolor/64x64/apps
    icon64.files += ./icon/64x64/$${TARGET}.png

    desktop.path = $$DATADIR/applications/hildon
    desktop.files += $${TARGET}.desktop
}
```

This example uses qmake's scopes to provide separate information to the Symbian and MeeGo install script generators, each with the code you've already seen for each platform.

Signing Your Qt Application for Symbian Devices

Your signature on a credit card transaction provides a way for a vendor to verify that you're the one who signed for a purchase—or for you to repudiate a fraudulent charge made by someone without your authorization. Similarly, application signing lets you prove that you are in fact connected to the application that you published—or not.

From the standpoint of identity, application signing uses a *trusted authority* and cryptography to prove your relation to your application. First, you must obtain a digital certificate from a trusted third party—a *certificate authority*. In the case of Symbian Signed, it's a firm such as TC TrustCenter. To obtain a digital certificate, you typically must contact the firm, start a request, and provide some sort of official documentation that you (or your firm) are who you claim to be. The company then responds by providing you with a file that contains your digital certificate. You then use this digital certificate to sign your application, and then provide it to a testing house to perform some basic application validation. The testing then ensures that the application is Symbian Signed—signed by a third party trusted by the Symbian Foundation, Nokia, and carriers—before you give it to Nokia to publish in the Ovi Store.

Fortunately, for a large percentage of today's applications, you no longer need to do this. Symbian applications may be *self-signed*, meaning that you can sign them yourself using a unique certificate that you generate (think of this as similar to the case where you go to a café and buy a coffee with your credit or debit card and you don't have to sign the receipt.) Self-signed applications prompt the user before using facilities that require the user's trust, such as determining the handset's location. Self-signed applications can use the following capabilities:

- Location, for determining the handset's position

- NetworkServices, for using the device's network connectivity

- UserEnvironment, for camera and audio recording and other sensors related to the device's immediate environment

- ReadUserData and WriteUserData for access to confidential user information such as the user's contacts.

Given the features of Qt Mobility and the relationship between those features and these capabilities, you can see that for a large number of applications, self-signing will suffice as long as your users can tolerate being asked to confirm the use of trusted services while the application runs. If that isn't appropriate, you can have your application Express Symbian Signed, in which you perform specific tests and submit your application to Symbian Signed for a potential audit.

If your application needs additional capabilities—say, reading device settings and parameters such as cell tower IDs—you need to obtain a certificate and make sure your application is Certificate Symbian Signed. A third-party testing house ensures that your application meets both functional and security requirements (the intent is not full functional testing, but to determine whether your application behaves appropriately, given the capabilities you gave it) before being signed. In that case, you can begin your development using a device certificate for testing (see `http://wiki.forum.nokia.com/index.php/Developer_certificate`), and when you are ready to submit your application, you sign it using the certificate that the certificate authority has given you.

If you determine that you need capabilities that require you to get your application Symbian Signed, you need to follow these steps through the Symbian Signed web site at `www.symbiansigned.com`:

1. Use a developer certificate while testing your application.

2. While you are finishing application development, obtain a certificate from a trusted certificate authority. This can take a few days to a week, so don't wait until the last minute thinking you can get your application signed and publish later the same day. Be prepared to spend money upfront for this service.

3. Finish developing your application. Once you have a third-party sign your application, you cannot make any changes to the installer!

4. Test your application to ensure that you'll pass the tests required to earn a signing for your application. You can find the tests at the Symbian.com website (currently they're at `http://wiki.forum.nokia.com/index.php/How_to_conform_with_Symbian_Signed_criteria`.)

5. Choose whether you want to sign your application through the Express Signed program or Symbian Signed. If you choose Certified Symbian Signed, select a testing house and follow its procedures to submit your application and any required documentation. The testing house may charge you a fee for this service.

6. When testing is complete, you will receive notification through Symbian Signed, You can download your Symbian Signed application from the Symbian Signed portal.

> **TIP:** Before you have your application Symbian Signed, check with Forum Nokia and look at the latest requirements for the Ovi Store. As we write this, Nokia is provides free signing for applications to be published to the Ovi Store.

Publishing with the Ovi Store

For publishers like yourself, the URL you need to remember isn't the one for Forum Nokia, but `http://publish.ovi.com`. There, you can register to become a publisher, submit new content for distribution, use the Ovi App Wizard to make RSS-based Web applications, and learn about Ovi Store distribution.

Registering with the Ovi Store

Before you can publish your first application, you must register with the Ovi Store. Registration entails giving Nokia the following information:

1. Contact information for you or your organization, including its location, URL, tax ID, and a single point of contact available via phone or email.

2. A public name, description, and icon or avatar that constitutes your organization's public presence on Ovi.

3. Contact information for an administrator for your relationship with Ovi (you can create additional accounts for other members of your organization later).

4. Your agreement to the Ovi Store's terms and conditions.

5. The payment of a one-time registration fee (currently €50), payable through a Visa or MasterCard. (Of course, the payment is due once the registration has successfully completed.)

Once you successfully register as a publisher, you can log in to your Ovi Publish account using the information it provides to your e-mail address. Like most online presences, your account has a profile, where you can change your password or request a temporary password if you lose it. Equally important, from your profile you can provide your bank details, so that the Ovi Store can pay you for your share of sales revenue for your content. When providing this information, you'll need:

- The payment type (for example, bank wire transfer).

- Your bank's name and bank code.

- Your bank account number.

- An e-mail to which Nokia will send information about payments to your account.

- Optionally (it's a good idea), your bank's street address and city.

Publishing Your Application

To publish your application, you should first assemble the following resources for registering your content on the Ovi Store:

- The application installer (sisx or deb) for your application.

- The internal and externally viewable names for your application (these may be the same).

- A short description of your application.

- The Ovi Store category—which you can determine by browsing the Ovi Store—for your application.

- The approximate price point.

- How you prefer your customers to be billed—usually via operator billing and credit card. Typically you'll want to opt for both, because operator billing is not available in all regions, and different regions have different expectations about the use of credit cards.

- A support e-mail address and web site where Nokia's customer care team can contact your organization for customer support.

- An icon and up to three small screen shots of your application.

- Search keywords for your application.

- For each file you want to distribute, a list of devices and languages that it supports and countries where it should be distributed.

As you plan your business strategy, you should be aware that the Ovi Store doesn't let you set precise pricing per locality. Instead, you enter an approximate price point for your application, one of:

- Free
- €1
- €2
- €3
- €5
- €7
- €10
- €15
- €20
- €25
- €30
- €40
- €50
- €60
- €80
- €100

The Ovi Store maps these amounts to similar amounts in local currency, such as dollars in the United States, pounds in Great Britain, and so forth.

Your customers can remit payment for your application through operator billing (where the charge for your application shows directly on their mobile service bill) and credit card, or only by credit card if you want to omit operator billing. You may choose which applies, but be aware that, in some areas, only credit card billing is permitted due to relationships between Nokia and local operators. Of course, it's probably best to support both, so that it's as convenient as possible for prospective users to pay. In either case, you are not directly involved with the billing transaction; the Ovi Store handles this for you.

Plan to spend some careful time crafting an application description and coming up with good search keywords for your application. The Ovi Store supports searching by keyword, and it's likely that a good number of potential buyers will discover your application through targeted solutions for a specific problem (e.g., determining the weather or playing a role-playing game). The category where your application is placed, which you pick from a drop-down menu, is equally important so that it catches the eye of people who window-shop in the Ovi Store.

To enter this information and publish your application, you sign in to your Ovi account and click "New Item". When you do so, you see a form that prompts you for this information. Once you've provided it, you will be prompted with a list of Nokia devices by configuration, presented as a tree view, to indicate how well your application works on those configurations. For each, you can specify:

- Fully Tested: You have executed all test cases with the application for this configuration successfully.

- Briefly Tested: The application's main functionality has been briefly tested with this configuration.

- Assumed to Work: You assume that platform compatibility will guarantee that this file works with this configuration.

- Might Work: The file has not been tested, but might work with this configuration.

- Not Compatible: The file should not work with the configuration. Do not even try.

- Not Known: This should only show when a new configuration is added and compatibility is not yet defined.

As with configurations, you enter the countries and languages in which you want to market your applications using the same tree view; countries are divided into regions (e.g., "Asia-Pacific"), while languages have a single-category hierarchy of "All Languages" and then a list of languages to which you may have localized your application.

QA in the Ovi Store

Once you enter the information and upload your file, the Ovi Store's QA team must test your application. During this time, you cannot change the application and metadata, and they will not be available on the Ovi Store. The testing is not comprehensive, but does look to ensure that the basic functionality your application promises exists and that your application meets Nokia's Terms and Conditions for the Ovi Store. Thus, it's important that you fully test your application (the key topic of the previous chapter). These tests include:

- Your application must be Symbian Signed for it to be accepted for Symbian devices.

- You must submit your application as Fully Tested for at least one configuration.

- Only Nokia billing is accepted. You cannot externally bill customers or incrementally bill them within the application.

- Your application must provide help and developer attribution somewhere.

- The language within the application must be consistent and appropriate throughout.

- The application must meet the Ovi Store's content guidelines.

While Nokia is testing your submission, you can see its testing status within your Ovi account for the application. When testing is complete you will receive a testing report letting you know that your application has passed or failed and, if it has failed, what you must correct before you resubmit your application.

While your application is being tested, you can make changes, but only if you unlock the installer file, which interrupts the testing process. You might wish to do this if you find a defect in your application, for example, or if you need to update the application's metadata. When you finish, lock your application again so that testing can resume.

Marketing Your Application through the Ovi Store

Once your application passes QA, it's live on the Ovi Store! Every application in the Ovi store receives a unique URL, which you can use in your own promotional materials or deep-link in your web site.

Nokia staff at the Ovi Store may choose to promote your application through the handset, mobile web site, desktop web site, or some combination of these. To ensure that the staff can do this, you need to be sure you provide additional marketing assets, including:

- Teaser text for the mobile web site (up to 23 characters).
- Large and medium spotlight banners.
- Small desktop images in 4:3, 3:4, and 9:16 aspect ratios,
- High and low-resolution spotlight images of the application.

These are optional, but a good idea in case Nokia selects your application for promotion. See the Ovi Publisher Guide for the precise sizes and uses of these marketing assets.

You can also market your application directly, of course; the Ovi Store provides a promotional banner creator that includes your application icon, name, category, and price, with a variety of banners, as you see in Figure 9–1. You can use the resulting banners in your own web marketing campaigns.

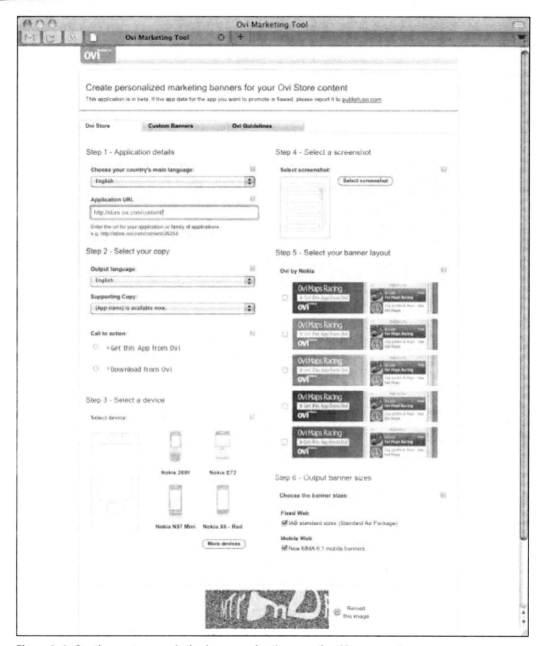

Figure 9–1. *Creating your own marketing banners using the promotional banner creator.*

From time to time Nokia may provide other comarketing or promotional opportunities, too. Keep an eye on the Ovi Publish web site at `http://publish.ovi.com` for details.

Wrapping Up

Publishing with the Ovi Store is about as simple as it can be, given that it provides wide reach, operator and credit-card billing, and multiple-country distribution.

Both Symbian and MeeGo applications require some work beyond simply coding your application: you must provide icons for consumers to recognize your application, and Symbian applications require a unique ID and signing as well. Obtaining a unique ID and signing requires that you work with Symbian Signed at symbiansigned.com, although in many cases Nokia may be willing to manage the unique ID allocation and signing on your behalf.

Publishing your application requires you to register as a publisher with the Ovi Store, a process that means gathering some information about your organization, including banking details, and entering them on the Ovi Publisher web site at http://publish.ovi.com. Once you've done this, Nokia will contact you with your login credentials, and you can publish your application.

To publish, you should be prepared to provide good metadata about your application, including engaging screen shots, an icon, and search metadata. Publishing entails entering this information, as well as indicating which configurations your application supports and waiting while Nokia conducts a brief test cycle of your application to determine its fitness for the store. Once the application passes, you can comarket your application with Nokia, on your own using the application's unique URL in the Ovi Store, or by creating banners with additional information about your application that link back to the Ovi Store.

Index

N

O

R

T

U

CPSIA information can be obtained at www.ICGtesting.com
Printed in the USA
LVOW050233140312

272996LV00003B/40/P